SEVEN CENTURIES OF SEA TRAVEL
FROM THE CRUSADERS TO THE CRUISES

SEVEN CENTURIES OF SEA TRAVEL

From the Crusaders to the Cruises

by Basil W. Bathe

PORTLAND HOUSE

New York

PHOTO CREDITS

Nederlandsch Historisch Scheepvaart Museum, Amsterdam: pp. 27, 36, 37, 66, 91 *(top)*, 107, 108, 111, 134 *(bottom)*, 154 *(bottom)*, 156, 157 *(top)*.
Museo de Bellas Artes de Cataluña, Barcelona: p. 28 *(right)* (Foto Mas).
Museo Maritimo-Reales, Barcelona: p. 17 *(top)*, (Foto Mas).
Foto Mas, Barcelona: pp. 74, 85.
Musée de la Reine-Mathilde, Bayeux: p. 10 (photo Giraudon).
Staatliche Museen Preussischer Kulturbesitz, Berlin: p. 24 *(left)*.
Chambre de Commerce de Boulogne-sur-Mer: p. 294.
Hôpital Jacques-Cœur, Bourges: p. 20 (photo Giraudon).
Focke-Museum, Bremen: pp. 116 *(top)*, 154 *(top)*, 155 *(top)*.
Hapag-Lloyd AG, Bremen: pp. 254, 255, 258, 259.
Cie des Chargeurs Réunis: p. 262 (photo Magnum).
Claret del Mar (Gerona), villa Sta. Clotilda: p. 39 (Foto Mas).
Compañia Costa: pp. 280 *(top)*, 284, 285.
National Maritime Museum, Greenwich: pp. 15, 23, 32, 37, 39, 46, 47, 51, 60, 62, 63, 67, 68, 69, 70-72, 76, 83, 84, 87, 89 *(top)*, 90, 92 *(top)*, 93-97, 102, 103, 113 *(bottom)*, 116, 135, 136, 139-141, 144, 146, 147, 151-153, 164 *(right)*, 170, 171 *(top)*, 174, 177, 186, 199, 201-204 *(bottom right)*, 205, 206, 208 *(top left)*, 213-217.
Museum für Hamburgische Geschichte: pp. 112, 114, 121 *(top)*, 149, 159 *(top)*, 165, 169, 180, 184 *(left)*.
Altonaer Museum, Hamburg: pp. 88, 89 *(bottom)*, 91 *(bottom)*, 92 *(bottom)*, 120 *(bottom)*, 142, 167 *(top)*, 171 *(bottom)*, 191, 200, 221, 222 *(bottom)*, 223, 225.
Deutsche Atlantik-Linie, Hamburg: pp. 253, 256, 257.
Hapag-Archiv, Hamburg: pp. 164 *(left)*, 167 *(bottom)*, 190, 207, 226.
L'Illustration: pp. 21, 131 *(top)*, 134 *(top and right)*.
British Museum, London: pp. 12, 13, 61.
The Science Museum, London: pp. 30, 38, 42 *(bottom)*, 44, 45, 54, 115, 118 *(bottom)*, 246 *(right)*, 269.
Victoria & Albert Museum, London: p. 77.
Cunard Line, London: pp. 113 *(top)*, 117, 118, 197, 246 *(left)*, (photos Stewart Basle), 247, 248 (photo Elsam, Mann & Cooper Ltd.), 248, 249 to 251, 268 *(bottom)*, 274.
P & O Orient Lines, London: pp. 110, 133, 163 *(right)*, 173 *(bottom)*, 182 *(left and centre)*, 183, 196, 198, 229, 266, 267 *(left)*, 268 *(top)*, 270-273.
Bibliothèque nationale, Paris: pp. 9, 14, 16, 17 *(bottom)*, 18, 19, 35, 58, 59, 193, 195.
Musée de la Marine, Paris: pp. 22, 28 *(left)*, 29, 99, 137.
Compagnie Transport et Voyage, Paris: pp. 276, 277, 292, 295.
Compagnie Générale Transatlantique, Paris: pp. 109, 122-127, 138 *(top)*, 160-162 *(right)*, 192, 209, 235-245, 261, 265.
Messageries Maritimes, Paris: pp. 138 *(bottom)*, 168, 181, 194 *(top)*, (photo A. Sylvain), 219, 220, 260, 263 (Reportage René Simon).
Gordon Moore — *Réalités*, Paris: p. 264.
Michel Desjardins — *Réalités*, Paris: pp. 275, 278.
Maritien Museum 'Prins Hendrik,' Rotterdam: p. 25.
Museum of the City of New York: pp. 172, 173 *(top)*, 175 *(top)*, 188.
The New York Historical Society Museum: pp. 100, 101.
Steamship Historical Society of America, Inc., New York: pp. 208 *(right and bottom left)*, 210.

The Mariners Museum, Newport News (Virginia): pp. 33, 42 *(top)*, 43, 50, 52, 53, 65, 73, 78, 79, 80, 105, 106, 119, 120 *(top)*, 129, 130 *(right)*, 131 *(top)*, 140, 145, 148, 156 *(bottom)*, 157 *(bottom)*, 158, 159 *(bottom)*, 162 *(left)*, 163 *(left)*, 175 *(bottom)*, 177, 179, 184 *(right)*, 187, 189, 194 *(bottom)*, 211, 212, 252, 289, 290.
Norwegian America Line, Oslo: pp. 288, 293.
The Peabody Museum of Salem (Massachusetts): pp. 56, 57, 64, 81, 130 *(left)*, 132 *(left and bottom)*, 166.
Mystic Seaport, Marine Historical Association: p. 132 *(top)*.
Società di Navigazione 'Italia': pp. 279, 280 *(bottom and right)*, 281, 283, 286.
Maritime Museum and the warship 'Wasa,' Stockholm: p. 38.
Lloyd Triestino, Trieste: pp. 121 *(bottom)*, 155 *(bottom)*, 182 *(far left)*, 221, 222 *(top)*, 224 *(bottom)*, 227, 231, 282.
Union Castle Line: p. 224 *(centre)*.
Museo Storico Navale, Venezia: pp. 40, 228, 230, 231, 232, 233.
Fonds Albertina aus der österreichischen Nationalbibliothek, Wien: p. 24 *(right)*.

The photo research department of the Office du Livre would like to thank the museum curators as well as the steamship companies who helped them bring together the illustrative material for this book, much of it never before published.

We are particularly grateful to: Dr. G. B. Rubin de Cervino of the Museo Storico Navale, Venice; Commandant Vichot, of the Musée de la Marine, Paris; Dr. J. Meyer, of the Altonaer Museum, Hamburg; Dr. Ulrich Bauche, of the Museum für Hamburgische Geschichte; Dr. Rosemarie Pohl-Weber, of the Focke-Museum, Bremen.

We should also like to thank: M. Gobert, of the Messageries Maritimes; M. Bouvard of the Compagnie Générale Transatlantique; Laurence E. Kimpton, of the P & O Co., London; Dante B. Pagnacco, of the Lloyd Triestino Co.; Dr. Huffmann, of the Hamburg-Amerika Linie; The Mas Agency, Barcelona. The photo research department further wishes to extend its thanks to Mr. and Mrs. Tucker, of the Greenwich National Maritime Museum for their advice and assistance.

Mme Marianne Pini found precious help whenever she turned to the maritime museums in the United States, notably: The Peabody Museum of Salem; The Mariners Museum, Newport News; The New York Historical Society Museum; The Mystic Seaport, Maritime Historical Association; The Steamship Historical Society of America, Staten Island. She would like here to express her appreciation of their help.

Photoresearch by Denise Blum

Reprinted with permission by William S. Konecky Associates, Inc.

This 1990 edition published by Portland House, a division of dilithium Press, Ltd.
distributed by Crown Publishers, Inc., 225 Park Avenue South, New York, New York 10003

Printed and bound in Hong Kong

ISBN 0-517-01754-7

h g f e d c b a

Summary

INTRODUCTION

From the very earliest times men have used rafts, boats and ships for fishing, fighting and transport on the rivers, lakes, seas and oceans of the world. This book is an attempt to provide a general summary of the history of ships and sea travel during the past seven or eight centuries. A brief account of the developments in the design and construction of ships also shows how these developments improved conditions for the passenger. For the first part of this period, with the absence of contemporary plans and pictures, any reconstruction of the interior arrangements of a ship must be regarded as conjectural. The accounts of travellers provide a vivid picture of life at sea, but do not contain very much information about practical matters like cooking and sanitary arrangements. After 1600 more precise information becomes available. The salvage of the Swedish warship *Wasa*, which sunk in 1628, has made a tremendous contribution to the knowledge of early 17th-century ship construction, equipment and domestic economy. For the 18th century, accurate draughts of various types of ships are extant, and many very detailed contemporary ship models have been preserved. During the latter part of the 18th century and for the first half of the 19th century, artists of the period provide fine illustrations of passenger accommodation, and the introduction of the camera has produced a very complete photographic record of the cabins and public rooms in passenger ships.

This book also describes some of the perils and hardships of sea travel. During the long voyages of the sailing ships sickness and disease took a terrible toll of crew and passengers. Piracy and the almost continuous wars of the 17th and 18th centuries forced merchant vessels to carry artillery and passengers were expected to assist in the defence of their ship.

Scientific and technological advances led to the adoption of steam propulsion and with the use of iron and later steel for ship construction the size of passenger ships was gradually increased. The race for speed on the North Atlantic routes became a matter of national prestige and the huge superliners of the early years of the 20th century provided a standard of comfort for the passengers which was not excelled by hotels on shore.

Now that the aeroplane has taken the place of the ship for the transportation of the passenger across the sea, a new type of ship is emerging, vessels specially designed as cruise ships.

In the book the size of a ship usually denoted by a length and breadth measurement and by the tonnage of the vessel. The methods used to calculate the tonnage of a vessel are complicated and have been subject to many alterations during the long period under review. The tonnage figures stated for the later steamships are the gross register tonnages.

Although generally the text and illustrations are arranged in chronological order there are instances in which, for various reasons, it has been necessary or desirable to depart from this rule.

It is not possible to write a general survey of the development of sea travel, from the 12th century until the present time, without consulting books which deal in detail with the ships and travellers of a particular period. The author acknowledges with gratitude the works of historians who have devoted much time, study and thought to various aspects and problems relating to the ship and sea travel. Some of the more important works consulted are listed in the bibliography at the end of the book.

To Mr. A. L. Tucker, who wrote the captions for the illustrations, and to Mrs. Anita McConnell, who helped in the preparation of this book, particular thanks are due. I am also most grateful to my friends in the Science Museum and the Science Museum Library for their help and advice.

I THE MIDDLE AGES – FROM KNORR TO GALLEON

A scene from the story of Tristan in a fourteenth-century French manuscript.

The first sea voyagers have left us no direct records, though archaeological investigations have shown that quite long sea crossings were being made by the fourth millennium B.C. and perhaps even earlier. The colonization of islands which began after the last Ice Age saw men reaching Australia, the Mediterranean islands, the Canaries, the Pacific islands, and many others around the globe. This movement continued into historic times with the Viking migrations and the expansion of Polynesian tribes across the Pacific.

In Britain, which was part of the mainland of Europe until the sixth millennium B.C., there was an indigenous population of hunters, but these were joined around 4000 B.C. by neolithic farmers who crossed the channel with their families and their livestock and crop seeds. The only records of the type of boats they may have used are rock carvings discovered in Scandinavia. The carvings show boats which were probably constructed of animal skins on a wood framework. Such boats, weighing little and having great flexibility in rough seas, continued to be used until the present day in the form of Eskimoan kayaks and umiaks, and the Irish curragh. The construction of the Eskimoan boats is probably closest to that of the neolithic colonizers, as the present day Irish curraghs owe quite a lot to the technology of plank-built boats, an Iron Age development. In a skin-covered boat, built in the same way as a forty-foot-long umiak, neolithic farmers would have been able to carry two or three cattle, or about ten pigs, sheep or goats. The legs of the animals would have been tied and they would have been laid on litter or brushwood in the bottom of the boat. The length of the journey must have been limited by the length of time that livestock could be kept alive without being fed or watered, as well as by the endurance of the rowers or paddlers.

During the succeeding Bronze Age there is evidence of considerable trading across the North Sea as a regular occurrence, and during the Iron Age, there were further migrations from Belgium and France. In the Mediterranean, colonization of Crete, Cyprus and the other islands by farmers bringing livestock was slightly earlier, and by the third milennium B.C. big rowing boats of up to thirty oars were in use.

With the penetration of Roman armies into north-western Europe the written record supplements the archaeological

Part of the Bayeux tapestry showing the Norman invasion fleet off Pevensey in 1066. The ships are similar to those of the Vikings and are steered by a large paddle fastened to the starboard gunwale. They have a single square sail set on a mast which can be unstepped. Both bow and stern posts are raised and the majority are decorated with dragon heads. Those ships transporting warriors show shields carried on the gunwales, as in the Viking ship from Gokstad.

evidence. Julius Caesar, commenting on the Veneti, a Gaulish tribe of the Brittany coast, notes:

'These Veneti exercise by far the most extensive authority over the sea coast in those districts, for they have numerous ships in which it is their custom to sail to Britain, and they excel the rest in the theory and practice of navigation.'

Sailing to Britain, even by the shorter sea crossings, could be a lengthy business; Caesar himself was becalmed during his crossing, which took twenty-four hours. He describes the fleet of the Veneti and compares it to the Roman ships:

'The ships of the Gauls were built and equipped in the following fashion. Their keels were considerably more flat than those of our ships, that they might more easily weather shoal and ebb tide. Their prows were very lofty and their sterns were similarly adapted to meet the force of waves and storms. The ships were made entirely of oak to endure any buffetting. The cross-pieces were beams a foot thick fastened with iron nails as thick as a thumb. The anchors were attached by iron chains instead of cables. Skins and pieces of leather finely finished were used instead of sails either because the natives had no knowledge or supply of flax, or because it enabled the ships better to ride out storms.'

Curraghs were also in use in Roman times; a writer of the 3rd century A.D. described how small boats formed of pliant twigs, covered with the skins of oxen, crossed the rough and stormy sea between Ireland and Britain.

The Norse tradition of seafaring began in prehistoric times using the skin-covered boat, but with the introduction of metal tools the production of planked craft became feasible, and it was in boats of this type that the Vikings carried

out their coastal raiding and, later, their exploration and colonization of the Arctic and subarctic coasts and islands. Various planked boats have been uncovered by archaeologists; of these, the earliest is the Danish Hjortspring boat, an open rowing boat with twenty paddle-oars but without oarholes or rowlocks. There is no mast fitting. It was apparently a warship, but its frail construction made it unsuitable for the open sea. The great step forward was probably taken around the 6th century; a boat discovered at Kvalsund in Norway dates from about 600 A.D. and represents the first phrase of northern sea-going sailing-ship construction. This boat had twenty oars and could also have carried a mast and sail. In the following centuries ships like this made the first voyages from Scandinavia across the ocean to the islands of the western Atlantic. A sculptured stone from Gotland shows a fully equipped ship of the 8th century with a stayed mast amidships carrying a square sail with reefing lines.

By about the middle of the 9th century, the keel and mast were sufficiently strong to allow sailing at sea in all weathers. The Viking ship burials sometimes reveal details of the equipment carried by these sea-going ships. The Viking longships discovered at Gokstad and Oseberg in Norway were particularly well preserved. The Gokstad ship, of about 900 A.D., was nearly 80 feet long and rowed by sixteen oars a side, with a single mast and square sail. In the vessel a number of kitchen utensils were found, including a large bronze cauldron which may have been used to cook food for the crew, a large pot-hook, several cutting boards, plates, a number of knifes, wooden cups and trays, and two candle-

11

Richard II returning from Ireland in 1399. From an English fifteenth-century manuscript. As was common in Northern Europe, the ships are clinker-built. They have tapering forecastles but no bowsprits. This is an early representation of reef points used for shortening sail. The soldiers wear hounskull or pig-faced helmets and chain-mail.

sticks. The remains of a number of beds were also found, all made so that they could easily be taken apart. The Oseberg ship, of about 800 A.D., also carried kitchen utensils. During the Viking and Saga periods the longships were quite open and had no accommodation below deck.

On the bigger vessels a tent was stretched over the ship at night, as frequently mentioned in the sagas, but we also hear of tents being pitched ashore after the ship had been made fast for the night. The provision of tents perhaps explains why beds were carried on board together with quilts

and blankets; these may have been for sleeping ashore. During long sea crossings the protection for the crew while they were sleeping must have been minimal.

Some of the longships of the 11th century were much larger and a little of their history is related in the Norse sagas. One vessel, believed to have been about 150 feet long and known as the *Long Serpent*, is said to have been the finest warship of the period. These longships known as 'drakkers' were warships and probably rarely carried passengers. When the Vikings with their families and cattle

A scene from a fourteenth-century French manuscript showing the raising of a siege. The prince and his army are embarking in a ship which is clinker-built and has a permanent raised deck aft, with the entrance to a cabin visible in the bulk-head. The forecastle appears to be a temporary structure.

comptetons autres choses.

An illustration from a fifteenth-century French manuscript depicting Marco Polo's voyage. The ship, which is carvel-built in Mediterranean fashion, has been beached stern first. The staggered joints of the planking are clearly shown, and the single sail is set on a yard abaft the mast.

crossed the sea to Iceland and Greenland they probably travelled in merchant vessels known as 'knorrs'. These vessels were wider and deeper than longships and perhaps some more permanent form of shelter was provided, at least at the bow and stern, for the passengers.

The ships employed by William the Conqueror to transport the Norman army, with its horses and supplies, across the Channel in 1066, are depicted on the famous Bayeux Tapestry (Ill. pp. 10, 11). The ships differ only slightly from the earlier Viking ships discovered in Norway. The vessels shown are clinker-built with high carved stems and sternposts, with a steering paddle on the starboard quarter, and rigged with a one-square sail on the single mast. Further evidence of the development of the northern ships is provided by the contemporary seals (Ill. p. 15) of towns and offices concerned with maritime affairs. Although in many cases

14

the artist has distorted the shape of the vessel to fit the confined space on the seal, it is quite evident that ships of the Viking type were used during the 13th and 14th centuries throughout the northern seas.

During the medieval period in Europe there was a considerable diversity of types of ship in use. When interpreting the literature it is difficult to decide what the different names of ship mean. Contemporary pictures are often inaccurate, the etymology of the names is unclear, and on occasion the same name is applied to vessels of very different appearance. Contemporary technical descriptions and records of the dimensions of vessels known as 'nefs', 'busses', 'cogs', 'esneccas' and 'dromons' are not extant but there was a fundamental division between the ships which were rowed and those which relied on sail. Oared vessels had of necessity to be narrow-beamed, whereas sailing ships became more rounded in form. Typical of northern waters was the 'esnecca' or 'snekkjur', a vessel of the galley type propelled by sail and oars, probably derived from the northern longship, but with some features of the Mediterranean galley. Rowed ships were particularly suitable for the Mediterranean, and galleys used as warships also served as traders. In the 6th century A.D., the 'dromon' was a light, fast Byzantine galley but later there were different classes of dromons including large vessels with the oars arranged on two levels, fitted with three masts and with a complement of more than a thousand men. Despite all the irritations and perils of the voyage, the fact remains that from the point of view of practical navigation, the Mediterranean was almost as well known in the 13th century as it is today, and the traveller who took ship at Marseilles or Venice could count on reaching Jaffa in safety more surely than if he had undertaken the long land journey.

During the 14th and 15th centuries Venice employed numbers of large galleys for war and merchant purposes. The very large Venetian merchant galleys were about 160 feet long with an overall breadth of 33 feet and were capable of long voyages. These huge merchant galleys, owned by the state of Venice, were in use from the 14th century until they were replaced as cargo-carriers by the much improved

Common seal of the town of Hythe.

The fourteenth-century seal of the town of Winchelsea depicts a vessel of the Viking type, clinker-built with high prow and stern. The steering oar appears to be a permanent fixture.

Chronicle of Jehan de Wavrin, a fifteenth-century French manuscript. The vessels appear to have ladders in lieu of forestays, but no shrouds.

cargoes were brought by sea principally to Venice. Venetian galleys and carracks then carried the goods as far as England and Flanders. In 1509, Venetian galleys are said to have sailed from Southampton to Otranto, a distance of about 2,500 miles, in thirty-one days. The state galleys did not normally carry many passengers and pilgrims travelled in smaller privately owned galleys. These galleys were preferred as passenger ships because they sailed along the coasts and put into port at night whenever possible, so enabling fresh water and food to be obtained. Pilgrims travelling on 'round' ships were charged less for the passage but the vessels usually sailed long distances between ports of call, and relying on sail alone, could be becalmed for varying periods; consequently more hardships had to be endured by the passengers. The improvement in the design, armament and sail plan of the 'round' ship in the early years of the 16th century made the merchant and pilgrim galleys, with their limited load capacity and large crews, uneconomic and after about 1540 they were no longer employed for these services.

The nef, the buss and the cog were all 'round' ships for which sails were the principal means of propulsion.

Busses of variable size were used as transports, and contemporary records show that in the Mediterranean the buss *St Leonard* transported two hundred pilgrims, who were carried on the three decks. The 'paradise' and castle at the stern were reserved for the wealthier pilgrims and the hold for cargo. During the Crusades the transport of horses was a recognized business, with the spaces between the decks divided into temporary stalls by means of hurdles. The horses entered the ship through a door cut in the ship's side (Ill. p. 21).

The early cogs were apparently smaller than busses—an account of 1300 shows that the cargo of a certain cog was 104 tuns of wine. Cogs were used by the merchants of the Hanseatic League—a federation of German towns—and the vessels shown on the seals of the towns are thought to represent cogs. Used also as warships, the cog increased in size during the 14th century and perhaps developed into the carrack (Ill. pp. 17, 24, 25, 28) of the 15th and 16th centuries.

The 12th to 15th centuries saw the rise of militant Christianity in Europe. The Crusades were organized as expeditions to fight against the Muslims in the Iberian peninsula, North Africa and the Levant. Large numbers of fighting men with their horses and supplies, as well as a great many pilgrims, were carried across the Mediterranean from French and Italian ports. This great increase in traffic caused the port authorities to lay down conditions for intended passengers. These regulations for life on board, together with the

'round' ship at the beginning of the 16th century. For two hundred years, the great galleys of Venice, rigged with two or three masts and lateen sails, and with a hundred and fifty or more oarsmen, formed the most efficient merchant service of the period. Although their cargo capacity was very limited, the combination of sail and oar made the galleys fast, reliable and reasonably secure from enemy attacks.

During most of the 15th century the precious merchandise of India—spices and silks—continued to be brought by overland routes to the Levant. Then from Acre and Jaffa the

Scene from an altar-piece to St. Ursula. Two carracks have wooden superstructures to hold awnings over the after deck and forecastle.

Detail from a fifteenth-century manuscript. The ship has an animal figurehead and the shields are decorated with a double eagle device.

tales of the travellers themselves, provide a clear account of what conditions on board were like during this period.

Philippe de Mézières (1327–1405) made several voyages as a pilgrim and wrote a story in which he described a typical pilgrim ship.

'*La Gracieuse* has three long and wide decks, one above another. The poop is protected by fortified towers. At the bow there is a great castle, well equipped for offence and defence. Amidships there is a tall mast of "cypress" wood and high up on this a long cross-piece or yard from which hangs a great square sail. At the top of the mast there is a small castle called the "hune" and above this flies a banner or standard bearing the arms of the lord of the ship.'

After describing the rudders and anchors he continues:

'Above the compass box there is a great lantern made of shining crystal and in this lantern a lamp which gives light to the whole ship's company. In the 'tween decks are stored all sorts of provisions and there is a special store for sweet-smelling herbs. At the front of the mast are machines, pulleys and other gear, by which the yard and sail can be hoisted, no easy thing . . . At the bow and stern of our ship there is a great gate through which one can enter the three decks. We must not in our pride forget the bilge; that is the lowest part which runs along the whole length of the vessel. Here collects all the filth and refuse of the ship and if it is not frequently cleaned out there will be few people aboard who will escape the foul smell arising from it.'

The port of Marseilles laid down the exact number of passengers to be carried in ships of a certain tonnage.

Venice legislated for something like the Plimsoll line, all Venetian ships having to have iron crosses placed on their hulls. During the first seven years of her life the ship could be laden to 2½ feet above the cross lowest in the water. Thereafter she could only be laden to 2 feet above it.

On arrival at the quays of Marseilles, Genoa or Venice the prospective passengers made a contract, either singly or in groups, with the ship's master. On embarking, the pilgrim's name was entered by the escrivain in his manifest, together with the person who was responsible for feeding him. This list was made out in duplicate, one copy remaining with the shipmaster, the other being handed to the court of the commune from which he sailed and an extract was given to the pilgrim. During the 13th century the escrivain was an important member of the crew of Mediterranean ships and probably of northern ones also. He was equivalent to the modern purser, and prepared cargo lists, passenger lists and any other writing needed. The wealthier passengers were able to secure accommodation in the more

A fleet at anchor, from a fourteenth-century French manuscript. The ships have median rudders and their hulls are protected with strong rubbing strakes.

◄ An episode from the life of St. Catherine from a fifteenth-century French manuscript. The vessel in the centre is propelled by oars and sail.

A stained-glass window made by order of Jacques Cœur, wealthy French merchant banker and grand treasurer to the king, between 1443 and 1453. An interesting feature of the vessel is the rigging of the lifts on the yard.

comfortable and less crowded aftercastle, but the ordinary pilgrim was allocated a space about 6 feet by 2 feet on the lower deck.

In the early days of the Crusades the passengers appear to have been paired in berths, sleeping side by side with the feet of one against the head of the other, but during the greater part of the Middle Ages the pilgrims slept with their heads to the sides of the ship, and their feet to the middle, leaving a gangway down the centre of the ship which was generally obstructed by the chests and bundles containing the pilgrims' belongings.

Trading was carried on not only by the ships' owners but by the crew and passengers also and this led to so much overcrowding of deck and cabin space that, in the 13th century, Venice found it necessary to limit merchants, sailors and knights to one chest each and forbid any servant to have one.

A contemporary record gives an account of the contract made by one pilgrim, Felix Faber, a Dominican father of Ulm, who made two voyages from Venice to the Holy Land between 1480 and 1483.

The company of about a dozen Germans, with whom Faber travelled, drew up a schedule of twenty clauses with Pedro Lando, the master of the galley in which they wished to sail. The master was not to call at any other ports than those usually touched at by the ships making the passage to the Holy Land, and in particular was to avoid Cyprus, the air of which island was said to be dangerous to Germans. Every day each pilgrim was to receive two meals, and in the morning a small glass of Malvoisie. The two meals were to be of good food and drink, and any pilgrim was to have his food even if he did not come for it. The master was to protect the pilgrims from the crew, and to allow them space to keep hens in, and to give their cook the use of the ship's galley. Sick pilgrims who were unable to bear the terrible stench of the lower deck were to be allowed places in the forecastle, poop or on deck amongst the rowers' benches. On reaching the Holy Land the master was to pay landing dues, tolls and charges for the hire of asses and the more heavy costs, the smaller charges being met by the pilgrims.

The allocation of space on a Venetian ship was also described by Faber: the chambers at the prow and poop were reserved, the first for spare sails and ropes, while the stern castle, higher than the prow, contained three storeys. In the top one was the helm, where the steersman kept his compass and other nautical instruments. Below this was the room in which the patron and his companions lived, whilst the bottom storey, presumably on a level with the lower deck, was

Crusaders embarking with their horses. The ship has a loading port in the port side of the hull which gives access to the lower deck. On the left of the picture is a vessel with two large lateen yards.

assigned to any noblewoman who might be making the passage. It was lighted by a sort of skylight. Access to the lower deck, where the ordinary pilgrims slept, was by ladder through a hatchway. On the same deck but nearer to the stern was a cooking place and a 'stable' for animals. At this date the crew and passengers slept on mattresses stuffed with straw, laid on the deck. During the day the bedding was rolled into a bundle and hung from a hook in the ship's side.

Each morning the passengers had a draught of Malvoisie, a wine which was considered an antidote to sea sickness. Two meals, announced by a trumpet call, were served each day. The privileged ate in their own cabins or at a table by the mainmast. Any women aboard were often served separately while the ordinary passengers ate from tables in the

after part of the vessel. The food supplied was extremely bad. Bread only lasted a few days, after which hard biscuits were served. Salted meat had to suffice, unless the cooks had killed off sick animals from the 'stable', washed down with musty drinking water or sour wine. Passengers sometimes took with them their own hens, wine and cooking utensils.

No regard was paid to hygiene and the death rate rose quickly within a few days of the vessel leaving harbour. Faber remarked that he had seen few men perish in storms, but many in calms. Fever and disease claimed more victims than wind and storms in the pilgrim ships. In the eastern Mediterranean, in the crowded ships of the period, a flat calm was perhaps worse to endure than a storm. With the hot sun beating down on to the ship, the drinking water became fetid, the food, never good as we have seen, became worse, and the inaction caused arguments and quarrels among the passengers and crew.

On a pilgrim ship three religious services were held every day. The first was at daybreak, when the pilgrims rose. The servants of the padrone elevated a picture of the Virgin and everybody said an *Ave Maria*. The second service was at 8 o'clock in the morning and the last service in the evening. The morning Mass was held at the mainmast where a space, called the forum, was reserved for assembling all hands. The evening service was held at the poop, where it began with a *Salve Regina;* then the chamberlain of the padrone, on his master's behalf, wished everyone a good night and raised the picture of the Virgin. Everyone said three *Aves,* after which the pilgrims went below, the crew remaining on deck while the escrivain said a prayer in their native language. Even on Sundays this routine was little altered; a sermon might be added at morning Mass but this was liable to constant interruption from crew or passengers.

The pilgrims passed the time as best they could, reading or playing dice and cards, or in talking and argument. In the 13th century dicing was forbidden to all except the barons, and even to them during the Crusade of 1248, but by the 15th century it had become the usual way of passing the time, and it was by no means uncommon for men who had left adequately provided with money to arrive in Jaffa penniless and never see the Holy Places. The Church fulminated against the practice but was unable to stop it.

A dreaded peril was fire, to which the wooden ships of the period were very vulnerable. The large number of lanterns carried in ships must have caused the loss of many vessels.

Lights were supposed to be extinguished after the evening service, but apparently this instruction was often ignored. Also if the private cooks of pilgrims had the right to use the ship's galley, this could easily lead to an outbreak of fire. A later French instruction, dating from 1542, requires captains of vessels to 'put out all the lights in your ship except in the cabins of the gentlemen who may have lamps trimmed with water covered with oil, but neither candles nor any other kind of light by reason of the danger that may come from them.'

Medieval ships were usually ballasted with sand or gravel, and in passenger galleys the pilgrims buried in this eggs, wine or anything that they wanted to preserve.

The voyage to the Holy Land was usually made in the spring or late summer and the pilgrim ship normally called at Corfu, Modon on the south-west coast of Greece, Rhodes, and Cyprus, finally landing the pilgrims at Jaffa or Acre. The fare in the late 15th century is said to have varied from twenty ducats to fifty-five ducats.

The relationship of sailors to masters was usually closely defined by contracts which differed somewhat in different countries and at different times. These laid down the conditions under which a sailor might be dismissed, and the occasions when the sailor was entitled to leave the ship as a result of the master breaking his side of the bargain. Contracts specify the amount of food and wine that sailors must be given, the clothes with which they are to be kitted out, and the amount of personal belongings that they were entitled to take on board ship. The food of the galley-slaves seems to have been generally pease pudding or lentils, biscuits and wine vinegar, while the sailors' diet included salt meat and fish. The clothing of the sailors generally consisted of a coarse woollen coat and hood, sailcloth trousers and shoes. Galley-slaves were issued with two shirts, a vest and two pairs of trousers a year. While the galley-slave slept on his bench with nothing to protect him from the night frosts but a long robe, the sailor also possessed a mattress and a coverlet of coarse cloth. He was entitled to one chest in which to keep his belongings, which, as we have seen, often included trade goods.

In the Mediterranean, fore and aft, lateen-rigged, two and three-masted vessels were in use before 1400 but the north-

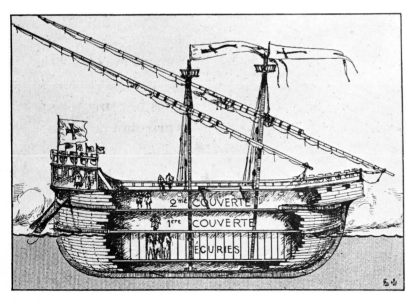

Reconstruction of a section of a Crusaders' ship as described in *Contractus navigii.* The vessel is lateen-rigged and has two steering oars.

An etching by Atkinson published in 1812, showing a representation of a thirteenth-century Crusaders' transport with a port in the stern of the ship for embarking horses.

ern seamen managed with a single mast and square sail for his ship. As northern and Mediterranean 'round' ships increased in size an additional mast and sail was added to the rig. This two-masted square sail rig was not efficient for the size and type of hull in use, and by about the middle of the 15th century, a three-masted rig had been adopted for the larger ships. Thus the transformation, from the simple sail plan of single mast and sail of the early cog and buss to the three-masted carrack completely square-rigged except for a lateen mizen sail, took place in the hundred years from 1400 to 1500. In the first half of the 15th century, small lateen-rigged Portuguese vessels were making voyages exploring the coast of Africa but it was the three-masted rig, with square driving sails on the main- and foremasts, a lateen sail on the mizen and a square sail (known as a spritsail) set forward beneath the bowsprit to act as a headsail, that helped

Contemporary engravings of small Flemish merchantmen by the artist W.A., *c.* 1470. Both vessels have three masts and a bowsprit. The one on the left has an animal figurehead and the lateen yard rests in a crutch. A bonnet is attached to the foot of the mainsail.

to make possible Bartholomew Diaz's voyage round the Cape of Good Hope in 1488, Christopher Columbus's exploratory voyages to the New World in 1492 and 1493, and Vasco da Gama's voyage to India via the Cape of Good Hope in 1497. Contemporary scale draughts of the 'round' ships of the late 15th and early 16th centuries are not extant, and pictures of the numerous votive models which once hung in the churches of Europe are usually very poor representations of the actual vessels. However, one votive model (Ill. p. 25), dating from about 1450, still exists and is the only contemporary model known of a ship of the period. The model, to a scale of about 1:24, shows a small Spanish carrack about 80 feet long with a beam of about

33 feet. The vessel was carvel-built and strengthened with heavy external longitudinal timbers, known as wales. Small raised platforms at the bow and stern are the precursors of the towering forecastles and aftercastles of the later carracks.

The model is believed to show a ship very similar to the *Santa Maria*, the flagship of the squadron of three vessels commanded by Christopher Columbus during his famous voyage of 1492 which led to the discovery of America. Contemporary pictures or drawings of the *Santa Maria* are not known. Columbus's diary of the voyage states that the *Santa Maria* had five sails—mizen sail, mainsail, main topsail, foresail and spritsail—and it is known that the vessel carried one cannon and one boat, and had a crew of about forty men. The *Santa Maria* with two smaller vessels–caravels–the *Pinta* and *Niña* sailed from Palos, near Cadiz, on August 3rd 1492, and on October 12th, land was sighted (probably the present Watling Island in the Bahamas). After service in exploring other islands in the West Indies, the *Santa Maria* ran aground on a sandbank off the island now known as Haiti on December 25th 1492 and was finally abandoned.

A contemporary model of a carrack from Mataro near Barcelona, *c.* 1450. This is the only known model of the period.

Columbus then returned to Spain in the *Niña*. In 1493, he sailed with more ships and discovered the island of Dominica, returning to Spain again in 1496. Columbus's later voyages brought him to the mainland of South America and to the exploration of the Gulf of Mexico. He died in Spain in 1506.

In the absence of contemporary models and draughts it is fortunate that paintings and drawings by late fifteenth-century artists provide reasonably accurate and very detailed pictures of the great carracks of the period. Pictures of different types of vessels by the Flemish artist, only known from his initials as W.A., have survived. This artist was working in the 1470's and his drawing of a carrack (Ill. p. 28) is particularly detailed. The hull of the carrack is carvel-built and is strengthened and protected by four wales on each side. Additional protection amidships is provided by five vertical skids. The bow shows the high two-decked, overhanging forecastle so typical of the carrack. The round stern is surmounted by a lower superstructure, to the after end of which a small open gallery is fitted. The small compartments at each end of this gallery are probably privy closets for the use of senior officers and important passengers. Supports for awnings, which would provide protection from sun and rain, are shown over the uppermost decks of the forecastle and aftercastle or poop. An armament of ten guns, carried on the deck aft of the mizenmast would have been a powerful deterrent to attacks from enemy galleys and the topcastles at the fore and main mastheads were supplied with darts and javelins, and with cranes for hoisting stones and other missiles which could be thrown down on the enemy. In addition, a small swivel gun is fitted to the mizen top. The large cargo-port in the side of the carrack, near the stern, is reminiscent of the loading ports in the ships of the Crusaders. The rig of W.A.'s carrack is typical of the very early three-masted ship, prior to the introduction of the main topsail and before a spritsail was set under the bowsprit. The foremast is very short and it would seem likely that the tiny foresail served principally as a headsail, but on the even shorter mizenmast the long lateen yard supported a larger sail. Although drawn by a Flemish artist, it is probable that this carrack was of Mediterranean origin.

Following Vasco da Gama's historic voyage to India by way of the Cape of Good Hope in 1497–9, the Portuguese attempted to keep a complete monopoly of trade with the East. However, although the Portuguese guarded the secrets of their route with great care and maintained warships in the Indian Ocean to deal with interlopers, the ever-increasing desire of other nations to share in this lucrative trade could not be halted. During the latter half of the 16th century and in the 17th century, overseas trading Companies were established by several European countries. The Companies were granted State charters to trade to a particular region and often held a monopoly for this trade, opposing most strenuously the activities of other commercial interests in their areas. From time to time the Companies were responsible for the organization of voyages of discovery and exploration, and for the establishment of colonies. In England, as early as in 1553, Sebastian Cabot, Governor of the Mystery and Company of the Merchant Adventurers — afterwards known as the Muscovy Company — was granted a licence by King Edward VI to 'find out a passage by the North to the East Indies.' Three ships were prepared for the voyage and sailed under the command of Sir Hugh Willoughby in May 1553. A gale separated the vessels off the coast of northern Norway and Willoughby with the crews of two vessels perished while trying to winter in a harbour in the Kola peninsula. The third vessel rounded Cape North and reach Archangel. Thus this early attempt to find a shorter route to the East failed. However, the following extracts from the Instructions and Ordinances compiled by Cabot for the direction of the voyage provide a vivid insight into life aboard a merchant ship at the middle of the 16th century:

'3. Item, where furthermore every Mariner or Passenger in his Ship, that given like Oath to be obedient to the Captain-general, and to every Captain and Master of his Ship, for the Observation of these present Orders contained in this Book, and all other which hereafter shall be made by the twelve Counsellors in this present Book named, or the most Part of them, for the better Conduction, and Preservation of the Fleet, and atchieving of the Voyage, and to be prompt, ready and obedient in all Acts and Feats of Honesty, Reason, and Duty to be ministred, shewed and executed, in Advancement and Preferment of the Voyage and Exploit: Therefore it is convenient that this present Book shall once every Week (by the Discretion of the Captain) be read to the said Company, to the Intent that every Man may the better remember his Oath, Conscience, Duty and Charge.'

'5. Item, all Courses in Navigation to be set and kept, by the Advice of the Captain, Pilot-major, Masters, and Masters-mates, with the Assents of the Counsellors, and the most Number of them, and in Voices uniformly agreeing in one to prevail and take place, so that the Captain-general shall in all Councils and Assemblies have a double Voice.'

'6. Item, that the Fleet shall keep together, and not separate themselves asunder, as much as by Wind and Weather may be done or permitted; and that the Captains, Pilots and Masters shall speedily come aboard the Admiral, when and as often as he shall seem to have just Cause to assemble them for Counsel or Consultation to be had concerning the Affairs of the Fleet and Voyage.'

'7. Item, that the Merchants, and other skillful Persons in Writing, shall daily write, describe, and put in Memory the Navigation of every Day and Night, with the Points and Observation of the Lands, Tides, Elements, Altitude of the Sun, Course of the Moon and Stars; and the same so noted by the Order of the Master and Pilot of every Ship to be put in Writing, the Captain-general assembling the Masters together once every Week (if Wind and Weather shall serve) to confer all the Observations and Notes of the said Ships, to the Intent it may appear wherein the Notes do agree, and wherein they dissent; and upon good Debatement, Deliberation, and Conclusion determined, to put the same into a common Leger, to remain of Record for the Company: the like Order to be kept in proportioning of the Cards, Astrolabes, and other Instruments prepared for the Voyage, at the Charge of the Company.'

'12. Item, that no blaspheming of God, or detestable Swearing be used in any Ship, nor Communication of Ribaldry, filthy Tales, or ungodly Talk to be suffered in the Company of any Ship, neither Dicing, Carding, Tabling, nor other devilish Games to be frequented, whereby ensueth not only Poverty to the Players, but also Strife, Variance, Brawling, Fighting, and often-times Murder, to the utter Destruction of the Parties, and provoking of God's most just Wrath, and Sword of Vengeance. These, and all such like Pestilences, and Contagions of Vices, and Sins to be eschewed, and the Offenders once monished, and not reforming, to be punished at the Discretion of the Captain and Master, as appertaineth.'

'13. Item, that morning and evening prayer, with other common Services appointed by the King's Majesty, and Laws of this Realm, to be read and said in every Ship daily by the Minister in the Admiral, and the Merchant, or some other Person learned in other Ships, and the Bible or Paraphrases to be read devoutly and Christianly to God's Honour, and for his Grace to be obtained and had by humble and hearty Prayer of the Navigants accordingly.'

'14. Item, that every Officer is to be charged by Inventory with the Particulars of his Charge, and to render a perfect Account of the diffraying of the same, together with modest and temperate dispending of Powder, Shot, and Use of all kind of Artillery, which is not to be misused, but

A contemporary print by Galle after Stradanus showing Petrus Plancius using an astrolabe on the quarterdeck of a three-masted ship which is lateen-rigged on the main and mizen, has a square sail on the foremast and a spritsail under the bowsprit. In 1592 Petrus Plancius published a map of the world.

diligently to be preserved for the necessary Defence of the Fleet and Voyage, together with due keeping of all Instruments of your Navigation, and other Requisites.'

'15. Item, no Liquor to be spilt on the Ballast, nor Filthiness to be left within Board; the Cook-room, and all other Places to be kept clean for the better Health of the Company; the Gromals and Pages to be brought up according to the laudable Order and Use of the Sea, as well in learning of Navigation, as in exercising of that which to them appertaineth.'

'16. Item, the Liveries in Apparel given to the Mariners to be kept by the Merchants, and not to be worn but by the Order of the Captain, when he shall see cause to muster or shew them in good Array, for the Advancement and Honour of the Voyage, and the Liveries to be re-delivered to the keeping of the Merchants, until it shall be thought convenient for every Person to have the full Use of his Garment.'

'17. Item, when any Mariner or any other Passenger shall have need of any necessary Furniture of Apparel for his Body, and Conservation of his Health, the same shall be

Contemporary engraving of a carrack of about 1480 by the artist W. A. The fore and mainmasts have square sails and the mizen has a lateen. The shrouds are turned in to heart-shaped three-holed deadeyes. Cranes to hoist up missiles are on the main and fore tops and a hand-gun is shown on the mizen top.

In 1522 the island of Rhodes was besieged by the Turks under Emperor Solyman II. This picture shows part of a sixteenth-century tapestry from Barcelona. The heavily armed Turkish ships have high forecastle and poop decks, similar to the Spanish galleons. Turkish flags are prominent.

delivered him by the Merchant, at the Assignment of the Captain and Master of that Ship wherein such needy Person shall be, at such reasonable Price as the same cost, without any Gain to be exacted by the Merchants, the Value thereof to be entred by the Merchant in his Book, and the same to be discounted off the Party's Wages, that so shall receive, and wear the same.'

'18. Item, the sick, diseased, weak, and visited Person within board, to be tendred, relieved, comforted, and helpen

in the Time of his Infirmity; and every manner of Person, without respect, to bear another's Burden, and no Man to refuse such Labour as shall be put to him, for the most Benefit, and publick Wealth of the Voyage, and Enterprise, to be atchieved exactly.'

'19. Item, if any Person shall fortune to die, or miscarry in the Voyage, such Apparel, and other Goods, as he shall have at the Time of his Death, is to be kept by the Order of the Captain and Master of the Ship, and an Inventory to be

Detail from an engraving by Bruegel, *c.* 1565. This picture of two four-masted ships in a storm shows an enormous amount of detail, especially in the rigging. Both ships have ram-like projections at the bows.

made of it, and conserved to the Use of his Wife, and Children, or otherwise according to his Mind and Will, and the Day of his Death to be entred in the Merchants and Stewards Books; to the Intent it may be known what Wages he shall have deserved to his Death, and what shall rest due to him.'

'20. Item, that the Merchants appointed for this present Voyage, shall not make any Shew or Sale of any kind of Merchandises, or open their Commodities to any foreign Princes, or any of their Subjects, without the Consent, Privity, or Agreement of the Captains, the Cape-merchants and the Assistants, or four of them, whereof the Captain-general, the Pilot-major, and Cape-merchant to be three, and every of the petty Merchants to shew his Reckoning to the Cape-merchant, when they, or any of them shall be required; and no Commutation or Truck to be made by any of the petty Merchants, without the Assent abovesaid; and all Wares and Commodities trucked, bought, or given to the

Company, by way of Merchandise, Truck, or any other Respect, to be booked by the Merchants, and to be well ordered, packed, and conserved in one Mass entirely, and not to be broken, or altered, until the Ships shall return to the right Discharges, and Inventory of all Goods, Wares, and Merchandises so trucked, bought, or otherwise dispended, to be presented to the Governor, Consuls, and Assistants in London, in good Order, to the Intent the King's Majesty may be truly answered of that which to his Grace by his Grant of Corporation is limitted, according to our most bounden Duties; and the whole Company also to have that which by Right unto them appertaineth, and no Embezelment shall be used, but the Truth of the whole Voyage to be opened to the Commonwealth and Benefit of the whole Company and Mystery, as appertaineth, without Guile, Fraud, or Male-engine.'

This abortive attempt to find a North-East Passage was not a complete loss. As a result of negotiations by the commander of the vessel that reached Archangel, trade between England and Russia was encouraged and the Muscovy Company was soon organizing regular trading voyages to Russia.

The Muscovy Company and the Levant Company, which was granted a charter in 1581 to trade to ports in the eastern Mediterranean, were corporations in which each member traded on his own capital, subject to the common rules of the Company. However, the Company of Merchants of London Trading unto the East Indies, founded in 1600, was a joint stock Company in which trade was conducted by the Corporation and the profits and losses were divided among the shareholders. This Company, later known as the Honourable East India Company, dominated British commerce with the East for more than two hundred years. The newly established East India Company soon prepared its first expedition, and a fleet of four vessels, with a victualler, under the command of Sir James Lancaster, left England in 1601, sailed to Sumatra and Java, returning to England in 1603 with valuable cargoes of spices, particularly pepper. The stockholders were allowed to take 5,339 pounds of pepper for each £230 share held and made a profit of nearly 100 per cent. The rich rewards from trade with the East was apparent to other nations and, five years before the foundation of the English East India Company, a Dutch expedition of four vessels under the command of Cornelis Houtman had rounded the Cape of Good Hope and reached the East Indies. In 1602 all the Dutch interests trading with the East were combined into a corporation which was granted a charter to enable it to start colonies, build forts and

maintain armed forces, with full administrative and judicial authority between the Cape of Good Hope and the Strait of Magellan. In France, King Henri IV arranged in 1604 for the formation of the Compagnie Française des Indes; while Danish trade with the East began in 1616 with the foundation of an East India Company, and the acquisition in 1620 of the colony of Tranquebar on the east coast of India.

By the second decade of the 17th century the Portuguese monopoly in the Indian Ocean had been broken, the Dutch had gained control of trade in the East Indies and ships of the English East India Company were forced further west to the mainland of India where forts and trading centres were established. During the first twenty years of its existence this Company had dispatched more than eighty ships eastward; eleven of these vessels had been seized by the Dutch and fourteen wrecked or worn out.

At the same time European nations were also probing northward and westward. In 1607 the Muscovy Company commissioned Henry Hudson to try and find a way to China by a northern route. Hudson in a small vessel manned by ten seamen sailed up the east coast of Greenland until he reached the ice barrier, then turned eastward to Spitsbergen and eventually reached 80° N latitude. The following year Hudson was sent to search for a North-East Passage but after sailing the Barents Sea between Spitsbergen and Novaya Zemlya, he failed to find an opening and returned to England. Hudson's most famous voyage in 1609 was made in the service of the Dutch East India Company. This Company sent Hudson in a vessel of 80 tons named the *Half Moon* (Ill. p. 33) on yet another attempt to find a North-East Passage. However, after sailing north to the Barents Sea, Hudson turned west, to pass the Faroe Islands, Newfoundland, and Nova Scotia until he reached New York Bay. Exploring the river which now bears his name, Hudson landed at a place where a few years later, the first Dutch settlers were to found New Amsterdam — later New York.

Throughout the 16th century, the Spanish, Portuguese and French sent expeditions to North America, exploring the eastern seaboard and establishing settlements. For nearly a century after John Cabot's historic voyages of 1497–8, the English paid no further attention to the mainland of North America. From 1583 temporary settlements were founded in Virginia, but it was not until 1606 that the first permanent colony was established. During the next fifty years organizations like the Virginia Company and the Massachusetts Bay Company financed and arranged emigration across the Atlantic, and more than twenty-five thousand

Henri-Grâce-à-Dieu, 1540. This warship, which was popularly known as the *Great Harry,* was built at Woolwich in 1512–4. The model shown above was based on a contemporary drawing in Anthony Anthony's *Roll of the Navy,* 1546.

men, women and children were sent to New England, Virginia and other colonies.

Unfortunately there is little contemporary evidence extant as to the exact size, form and internal arrangements of the ships used for the voyages to the East and to America. Documents of the period usually state only the tonnage and armament of the various vessels so that even the precise dimensions of the ships are not known. However, contemporary paintings (Ill. pp. 36, 37), and particularly of Dutch

ships, provide excellent representations of the outward appearance of the merchant ships. It is evident that these vessels were not the towering and clumsy carracks and galleons of the Spanish and Portuguese merchant fleets. It would seem that the changes and improvements in the design of warships that took place towards the end of the 16th century also occurred in merchant ships.

The surviving draughts of ships made by an English master-shipwright Matthew Baker in about 1585, show that

King Henry VIII embarking at Dover on May 31st 1520 on his way to meet Francis I of France at the Field of the Cloth of Gold. Tudor ships were gaily decorated in bright colours. This line engraving by J. Basire after S. H. Grimm from an original painting in Windsor Castle, was published in 1781.

warships were then designed with fairly good underwater lines. Merchant ships, although still very similar in general outward appearance to the smaller warship, were, by this date, beginning to differ a little in hull form. A late sixteenth-century authority, comparing the proportions of warships and merchant ships, states that a merchant ship 'for the most profit' should have the length by the keel double the breadth amidships and the depth in the hold half that breadth; while ships of war 'made for the best advantage of sailing' should have the keel three times that of the breadth and the depth in the hold two-fifths of the breadth. It should be remembered that, because of the large overhangs at the bows and sterns of the vessels, the overall length to breadth proportion was considerably greater. Most merchant ships in the 17th and 18th centuries were rigged with three masts. A four-masted rig was used for some of the larger vessels, particularly warships, during the period 1580–1640, but with the introduction of square topsails in place of lateen topsails in about 1611 for the mizenmast, it was soon found

that more effective sail power aft could be obtained by increasing the size of the mast, rather than by fitting a second mizenmast, and the use of four masts was discontinued until the 19th century when the increased size of sailing ships made possible the fitting of four or more masts. The simple arrangement of six sails — courses and topsails on fore and mainmasts, lateen sail on the mizenmast and a spritsail under the bowsprit — at first fitted to the three masts was gradually improved with the introduction of topgallant sails, royals, jibs, stay sails, studding sails and the substitution of a gaff sail for the lateen sail, until, by the end of the 18th century, thirty-seven sails formed the sail plan of even a small merchant ship.

Until well into the 18th century even the small ocean-going merchant ships were usually rigged with three masts. However, two-masted vessels — brigs, snows, schooners and ketches — gradually increased in popularity and by the beginning of the 19th century the three-masted square-sail rig was seldom used for vessels of less than 300 tons.

32

II PASSENGERS, PIRATES AND PRIVATEERS

A modern painting by Gordon Grant of the *Half Moon*. The ship belonged to the Dutch East India Company and Henry Hudson sailed in her to America in 1609, while in search of the North-East Passage. The river on which New York stands is named after this great explorer. The ship was burned in 1618.

Throughout the 17th and 18th centuries the crews of merchant ships had to be prepared to defend themselves against the attacks of privateers and pirates. Most merchant ships carried guns and indeed the larger vessels were usually heavily armed. The *Red Dragon*, of 600 tons burden, the leading ship in the fleet sent by the English East India Company to the East Indies in 1600, carried thirty-six guns, including sixteen culverins, each weighing two tons and firing a projectile weighing almost 18 pounds. Male passengers were expected to take part in the defence of the ship. Advertisements appearing in newspapers of a later period make it clear that, even for coastal voyages, in time of war, defensive measures were necessary. An advertisement of the sailing on February 5th 1782 of the Carron Shipping Company's vessel the *Paisley* from Carron, in Scotland, to London states that the ship had twenty 18-pounder guns. 'The Carron vessels,' it continues, 'are fitted out in the most complete manner for defence, at a very considerable expense, and are well provided with small arms. Able-bodied landmen, who are desirous to serve on board those vessels for three years certain, will meet with the best encouragement, and be protected; and all Mariners, Recruiting Parties, Soldiers upon Furlough, and all other steerage passengers who have been accustomed to the use of fire arms, and will engage to assist in defending themselves, shall be accommodated with their passage to or from London, upon satisfying the Master for their provisions, which in no instance shall exceed Ten Shillings and Sixpence Sterling.

'The Carron vessels sail regularly, as usual, without waiting for convoy.'

As already stated, little contemporary information—either documentary or in the form of plans—is available about the accommodation arrangements in merchant ships before the 18th century, and all modern representation of these arrangements must therefore be regarded as somewhat conjectural. However, modern drawings of the very famous *Mayflower* (Ill. p. 43) produced after careful research provide a very reasonable reconstruction of a small merchantman of about 1620. The *Mayflower* in which a group of English Protestants, known as the Pilgrim Fathers, sailed

33

from Plymouth to New England in 1620 is believed to have been built in 1588 and had previously been employed in voyages to ports in Western Europe, principally La Rochelle and Bordeaux. It is also known that the vessel was of 180 tons burden. Beyond this no details have survived but from the extant evidence of the dimensions of another vessel of the same type, date and tonnage, it has been calculated that the *Mayflower* was about 90 feet long with a beam of about 22 feet. In this tiny vessel one hundred and two emigrants, comprising fifty men, twenty women and thirty-two children, with a crew of about twenty men, had to endure the privations of a voyage lasting three months. With the exception of four families who occupied cabins under the poop, all the passengers were accommodated on the lower and orlop decks, with canvas screens providing a little privacy.

A unique and most important contribution to our knowledge of life on board a ship in the early years of the 17th century has been provided by the salvage and preservation of the Swedish warship *Wasa*. This 64-gun ship had been built to the order of King Gustavus Adolphus in the dockyard at Stockholm. Sailing on her maiden voyage on a Sunday afternoon, August 10th 1628, she had only reached the middle of the harbour when she was caught by a sudden gust of wind, heeled over and sank. In 1961 the almost perfectly preserved wooden hull was brought to the surface from a depth of 110 feet. Over twenty thousand objects including carvings, textiles, leather, coins, equipment and skeletons of the unfortunate seamen were recovered.

Although the *Wasa* was a warship, much of her equipment and domestic economy would have been similar to that of a merchantman. From the finds it is evident that nearly all the food served would have been either dried or salted. The basic provisions were grain and flour for bread, dried or salted beef, salted pork, dried or salted fish and butter. Fishing gear was carried so that fresh fish could be caught when the opportunities arose. Earthenware bowls and wooden dishes were most commonly used for cooking, storing and serving food, with pewter utensils for the use of officers. The table from the captain's cabin (Ill. p. 38) is shown laid with salvaged items, including a brass candlestick, pewter can and tankard, and a Dutch delftware dish.

The *Wasa*'s galley or cookhouse (Ill. p. 38) was located on the ballast in the hold just before the mainmast. It was constructed of bricks with an open hearth over which a 45-gallon cauldron was suspended. In most other ships of the period the galley was probably placed in the same position despite the obvious dangers of fire and other disadvantages. In Eng-

land recommendations were made, as early as 1578, that the galley be moved from the hold to a position under the forecastle but it would seem that this improvement did not become general until the middle of the 17th century.

In the 17th century uniforms were not worn by seamen serving in warships or merchant ships; and the clothing from a skeleton of a man of about 30 to 35 years of age found in the lower gundeck of the *Wasa* is probably typical of the costume worn at sea by seamen and ordinary passengers. A linen shirt was worn with plain woven woolen trousers, linen stockings and buckle shoes. Over this was worn a skirted jacket with short sleeves. A sheath knife and money pouch was carried at the waist.

In the 17th century it was the custom for some seafarers to write an account of their experiences in the form of a journal. A few of these journals have survived and have been published. One such journal is that of Edward Barlow in which he describes his life at sea in King's ships, East and West Indiamen and other merchantmen, from 1659 to 1703.

Barlow's third East India voyage was in the *Delight*. He joined the vessel in November 1682 as chief mate at six pounds five shillings per month. The *Delight* sailed from Gravesend on January 4th 1683 with three passengers and a cargo including 400 small pigs of lead, 150 barrels of gunpowder, 50 large bags of black pepper, 32 bales of broad-cloth, 30 barrels of tar, 10 barrels of pitch, 37 chests of East India 'olilinum', 16 bales of East India calicoes, 13 'sorn' anchors, 10 bales of 'purpetanos', 30 small brass guns, between 2 and 3 hundredweight apiece, 8 barrels of nails, 1 chest of sword blades, 7 bales of broad cloth fine, 5 chests of muskets, 2 cases of glasses, 1 bundle of saws and 2 small chests of treasure in money and plate. The *Delight* was bound for China and the Macao Islands, but Barlow did not complete the voyage, as he quarrelled with the Captain and was 'turned out of the ship and put ashore' at Achin on Sumatra.

The practice of carrying livestock and poultry in sailing ships, to provide fresh meat, milk and eggs, a practice which continued until the 19th century, was firmly established in the 17th century. Barlow relates that when the East Indiaman *Wentworth* left the Downs on November 22nd 1699, 'We provided ourselves with fresh provisions, as fowls, hogs and sheep, geese and turkeys, and a couple of live bulls.' However, in this instance bad weather in the English Channel 'drowned a hundred fowls, hens, cocks, turkeys and geese, and several pigs and hogs, and some sheep and bruising much the live bullocks we had aboard, spoiling their flesh very much.'

An engraving of a Dutch warship by C.I. Visscher, dated 1594. The vessel has four masts and carries topgallant yards on the fore and main and a lateen topsail on the mizen-mast. The rigging, shown in great detail, has an enormous number of 'crows feet' to spread the strain on the spars and stays.

The Indiamen were built for cargo-carrying and were not designed for speed. The ships bound for Ceylon, India and China could be expected back in their home ports in about eighteen months from the date of sailing. The victuals stored in the holds of the vessels deteriorated during the long periods between landfalls. The meat, kept in casks,

'as none could be had but at excessive rates; neither did the Governor care to spare us anything nor was very willing we should have anything, for indeed the Dutch do not much care for the English'.

Detailed accounts of the experiences of passengers do not often occur in these seventeenth-century journals but Barlow

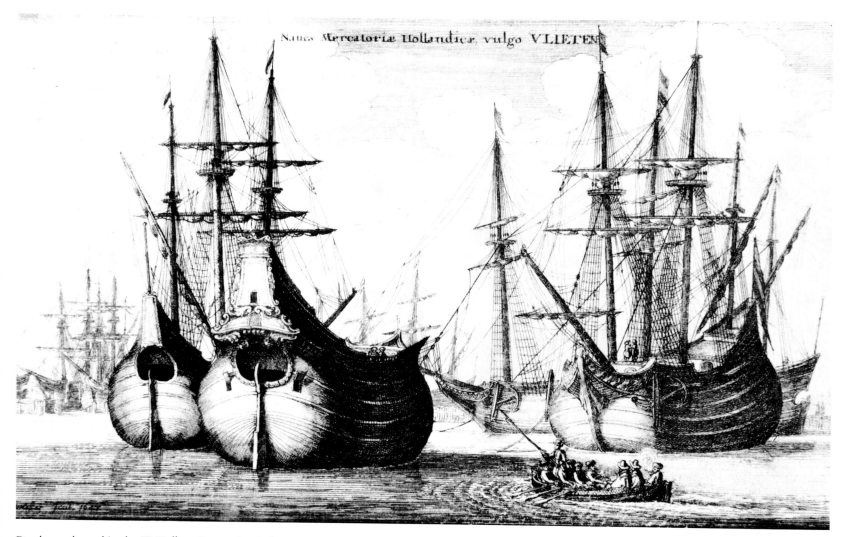

Dutch merchant ships by W. Hollar. Due to the shallow seas around the coast of Holland it was necessary to build shallow draught ships. Early in the 17th century the Dutch had an enormous fleet of merchant ships consisting mostly of fluyts and pinnaces.

suffered from the ravages of the cacara — 'a most devouring worm'. The Indiamen were not always allowed provisions when they called at places on their voyage. Barlow states that when the *Delight* stopped at Capetown a boat was sent ashore for fresh provisions but it returned without purchases

relates an incident during the voyage of the *Cadiz Merchant* from Jamaica to England when 'a great sea broke into our great cabin windows and broke them all to pieces, and filled the great cabin so with water that it beat down the nurse and little child, so that the little infant was almost drownded and a great deal of water going down between decks and into the steerage, did a great deal of harm.'

There is an amusing account of the treatment some passengers received in another surviving journal. The author of the journal, Edward Coxere, describes a voyage from Dover to Cadiz in 1650, when he served as cabin boy. Coxere

that cabin and would be often ringing of the bell for me to rise a-nights. I perceived the master did not like it that I should give her so much tendance. I got some oakum and tied it about the clapper of the bell, so that the bell would not sound. By that means I lay quiet a-nights and slept.'

One wonders how often the hard-pressed steward on an

The return of the Dutch East India fleet to Amsterdam on May 1st 1599; painting by Andries van Ertvelt. The third ship from the right is flying the Portuguese merchant flag, possibly because Prince Manuel of Portugal, who was then living in exile in Holland, was one of the Dutch East India Company's patrons.

continues: 'After we had been at Cadiz some time we took a voyage to San Sebastian in Biscay. We carried with us a Dutch woman, a passenger, called Yuffrow Doctoers, and her son and a negro maid, her servant. This woman was counted to be a whore to the merchants in Spain. She lay in

Atlantic liner of the 1930's would have liked to take the same action!

Pleasure Craft
State barges and similar ceremonial and pleasure vessels

The captain's table from the *Wasa*, laid with utensils found in the ship.

The galley of the Swedish warship *Wasa* with its huge cauldron.

are of the greatest antiquity. The Egyptians used ceremonial craft on the River Nile 4,000 years before the birth of Christ. The Roman Emperors had pleasure barges on Lake Nemi and elaborately decorated vessels as the *Bucentaur* (Ill. p. 40) served on religious and state occasions in the Middle Ages. It would seem that the name 'jacht', originally meaning 'hunting' and later introduced into the English language in the form of 'yacht', was first applied to vessels in Holland at the end of the 16th century. During the first half of the 17th century the fore and aft rigged 'jacht' was used extensively, in Holland, for conveying persons of importance, as a dispatch boat and as a pleasure boat. Many pictures of the period showing regattas, galas and aquatic ceremonies include representations of jachts of various types and sizes (Ill. pp. 46, 48).

King Charles II of England became familiar with these pleasure craft while in exile in Holland, and soon after the Restoration he was presented with two yachts by the Dutch East India Company. So great was the King's interest in these vessels that he instructed some of the leading English shipwrights to design and build other yachts which might exceed the Dutch yachts in speed. Besides using these yachts for occasions of pleasure and state, both the King and his brother, the Duke of York, encouraged sailing contests between vessels and so laid the foundation of yacht racing in England.

The Stuart Royal yachts ranged in size from about 30 tons to 200 tons burden. In a typical yacht the King had three luxurious cabins. A decorated staircase led down from the quarter-deck to a lobby which extended across the breadth of the vessel. Aft of this lobby was the King's sleeping apartment and the great cabin, with light and air from the row of windows across the stern. Forward of the lobby a large dining cabin was lit by a deck light. The officers' quarters and those of the crew and the King's staff were forward. The cooking galley was also well forward in the vessel with a chimney let up through the deck. A good description of the ornate decorations of this type of vessel is supplied by a contemporary account of work carried out in 1706 on the apartments of the *Peregrine*, a vessel of 197 tons, which had been built in 1700 and was renamed *Caroline* and made into a yacht in 1716. The account reads: 'Decorations to the Lodging Room of the Peregrine galley: The necessary House new japanned with Gold. A table new japanned with Gold. 4 port holes new japanned with scarlet and gold. 4 panels abaft with the topsides and back of ye seat or Locker new drawn with gold. The Base round the room new japanned. The rest of the Room both sides and ceiling refreshed and

Painting from Gerona, Spain, by an unidentified artist, probably 17th century. The small boat with the single sail is fitted with leeboards after the Dutch fashion.

also mended where the Gold and Japan was off. The Looking Glass frames mended with Blew Glass and a fire shovel and tongs japanned.'

The first yacht club was in Ireland: the Cork Harbour Water Club, later known as the Royal Cork Yacht Club, which was established in 1720. During the 18th century yachting developed slowly. Sailing races were held at Cowes as early as 1780 but the famous Royal Yacht Squadron, later the Royal Yacht Club, was not founded until 1812.

Eighteenth-Century Merchant Ships

As merchantmen were usually armed, throughout the 18th century their appearance did not differ greatly from that of warships of the same size. The merchantman carried fewer guns than a warship of the same size, but at sea immediate identification was difficult and on occasions the larger East Indiamen, carrying about thirty guns, with a line of dummy gun-ports painted at the lower deck level, were mistaken for 64-gun warships.

The last of the *Bucentaurs,* launched in 1728. Symbolic of her maritime power, the marriage between Venice and the Adriatic Sea was celebrated annually on the feast of Ascension, when the Doge was rowed in the *Bucentaur* to the mouth of the Lido and there dropped a consecrated ring into the sea.

Most of the vessels trading to the East were still quite small, the majority of between 400 and 500 tons. Even smaller vessels were used in the trade. A merchant ship named the *Mary Galley* built at Rotherhithe on the River Thames in 1704 made a voyage to Batavia and back. The *Mary Galley* was of about 170 tons with a length overall of about 80 feet and a beam of 21½ feet. She was flush-decked and, in addition to the usual masts and sails, was provided with eight oars, which at the beginning of her outward voyage assisted her to escape from French privateers in the English Channel. The *Mary Galley* was an 'interloper', trading without licence from the East India Company.

Elector Palatine and his bride Princess Elizabeth Stuart in the *Prince Royal* painted by Adam Willaerts. The *Prince Royal* was built by Phineas Pett in 1610 and was the only ship of importance built during the reign of James I.

The normal size of vessels employed by the East India Company had increased to about 800 tons by 1775, and to over 1,000 tons before the end of the century. East Indiamen were built and owned by private individuals and were chartered by the Company for a voyage to the East and home again. Some vessels were chartered successively for six voyages. The ships bound for the East took aboard their cargoes at Blackwall or Deptford on the Thames and after sailing down the river, anchored at Gravesend to take on passengers, additional cargo, water and livestock. They then proceeded to the Downs off Deal on the south coast of England, where the mails and last passengers came aboard. If Great Britain was at war, the Indiamen made a further call at Portsmouth where the warships which were to guard the convoy were assembled. Convoys sailed at intervals throughout the year and as the Indiamen were built for cargo-carrying and were not designed for speed, fast passages were not to be expected, the round voyage from England to China and back to England still taking more than a year. The outward-bound Indiamen for Madras, Bengal and Bombay carried numerous passengers, principally officials of the East India Company and Government troops,

41

were temporary constructions of wood or canvas on wooden framing. The best cabins were right aft, with the advantage of the quarter and stern windows. The great cabin, on the main deck at the stern, was often also divided by temporary partitions to form extra cabins. The apartment, known as the cuddy, in which the ship's officers and the passengers dined, was situated under the poop deck, with windows in the forward bulkhead giving a view onto the quarter-deck.

Fares for the ordinary passengers from England to India or for a homeward passage, which were fixed by and paid to the commander of the ship, could be as much as £1,000 according to the size and position of the accommodation. Officials of the East India Company were carried at fixed rates which varied according to rank from £95 for a cadet to £250 for a general.

Normally the passengers had a breakfast of tea and biscuits at 8.0 a.m. Dinner, a more lavish meal, was served in the cuddy at 2 p.m. Tea was served at 6.0 p.m. and the last meal of the day, a light supper, at 9 p.m. The adult passengers with the officers—the captain, chief and second officers, surgeon and purser—usually occupied the same position at the table throughout the voyage. Accounts of life aboard an East Indiaman at the end of the 18th century and early 19th century written by passengers and officials travelling to and from India have been published. The following extracts from the memoirs of William Hickey describe events when Hickey returned to England from India in 1808 on the East Indiaman *Castle Eden*. The *Castle Eden* sailed on February 19th, in company with other merchants, es-

One of the ships owned by the Dutch East India Company and sailed by Henry Hudson the explorer. From *The Memorial History of the City of New York*.

Galley stove from a contemporary model of a 20-gun ship of 1745. This type of stove replaced the open hearth used in the 17th century.

with a crew of about a hundred men. The cargo included manufactured goods, woollen goods and iron. On the homeward voyage, the ships, unless specially chartered as troopships, carried fewer passengers but were heavily laden with a cargo of silk, cotton goods, spices, rice and sugar, and more exotic commodities such as ebony, amber beads, sandalwood, ivory and leopard skins.

The cabin passengers, up to about thirty in number, were accommodated in the after part of the Indiaman, in the poop and on the main deck (Ill. p. 51). Most of the compartments

Reconstruction of the *Mayflower* in which the Pilgrim Fathers sailed for America in 1620. It is believed to have been built in 1588, and to have been about 180 tons, 90 feet long and about 25 feet wide. The drawing of the profile (top left) gives an idea of the passenger accommodation and stowage of provisions and goods.

corted by two warships. Hickey relates that on the first evening the commander of the Indiaman, Captain Collnett, took his place at the middle of the dining table, facing the windows that looked on to the quarter-deck. Hickey with eleven other passengers and four of the ship's officers then took their seats. On February 29th, 'the Quarter Bill was made out, when every person in the ship was stationed either at a great gun or small arms, except those appointed to work the sails, steer, etc. so that in the case of the appearance of the enemy each knew his place. We had a strange

motley crew, consisting of natives of almost every nation of Europe, besides nine Americans and eighteen Chinese. Certainly we had not more than ten English seamen on board.'

At the beginning of April bad weather was encountered in the Indian Ocean and Hickey states that 'the dead lights being obliged to be fixed in, reduced me to the necessity of constantly burning candles in my cabin. I had the mortification to find that the ship's upper works were in a dreadful leaky state, the sea pouring in through her side and stern at each particular seam, literally in torrents, which kept my

43

cabin absolutely deluged.' On April 13th, the crew were in trouble. 'In the evening our ship was in the utmost confusion owing to many of the crew being in a state of intoxication. An enquiry took place thereupon, in which it was discovered that the sail-maker, aided by one of the foremast men, had contrived to break open the door of the Lazaretto where the liquor was kept, from whence they supplied themselves and friends with a sufficient quantity of rum to make them excessively drunk, there were altogether twenty-one persons evidently inebriated. After an examination into the particulars, the two principal culprits, being the sail-maker and a foremast man, were immediately tied up to the main shrouds and severely flogged: four others were put into irons, the rest, expressing much contrition for the offence they had committed, were pardoned and order was restored.'

Early in May the bad weather prevented Hickey from sleeping and the captain suggested that he changed his fixed bed for a swinging cot: 'I therefore on the 4th (May) caused one to be rigged, constructed upon the best principles for counteracting the effect of violent motion and had it hung up in my cabin. The first night I used it I had several hours comfortable sleep which greatly recruited my strength that had been rapidly declining.' The bad weather continued

Model of the *Zeven Proven*, one of the large ships built for the Dutch East India Company between 1720 and 1730.

Rigging plan of a merchant ship engraved by J. Baily for William Falconer's poem ▶ *Shipwreck* published in 1762 (see p. 75).

and the *Castle Eden*'s supply of fresh water ran low. However, Hickey had taken precautions and on May 27th wrote: 'Now it was that the stock I had laid in previous to leaving Bengal, and in bottles, proved of the utmost importance, enabling me to assist Mrs. Todd and other of my fellow-passengers with an ample supply during the scarcity, every person on the ship without distinction, having been put to an allowance of one pint a day.'

William Hickey finally left the *Castle Eden* at Deal on August 15th 1808 and writes: 'The small part of the crew that remained on board did me the honour of giving three cheers upon my leaving her side, which we in the pilot boat very heartily returned.'

Throughout the 17th and 18th centuries, and indeed into the 19th century, the crews and passengers of a sailing ship, in addition to the usual perils of sea and wind, had to con-

most common at sea were scurvy, dysentery and fever. Scurvy, a diseased state of the blood, with swollen gums, livid spots and prostration, caused by the lack of Vitamin C in a diet which did not include fresh vegetables, was perhaps the most dreaded sickness at sea. Although in the 16th century, during the early voyages to the East, it had been found that lemon and lime juice would prevent or cure scurvy, and despite later knowledge of other preventatives, the disease continued almost unchecked until the end of the 18th century when regulations enforcing the issue of anti-scorbutic were applied.

On some voyages the suffering and deaths from scurvy were appalling. During a voyage round the world in 1740–4 the ships of Commodore Anson's squadron lost more than six hundred men out of a total complement of nine hundred and sixty-one.

Longitudinal section of a seventeenth-century yacht, from *Gli Argonauti* by Coronelli, *c.* 1790. The large dining cabin is lit by a deck light. The sleeping cabin is right aft, while the galley and stores are forward of the mast. The yacht is elaborately furnished and deck levels are arranged to give maximum headroom.

tend with two other great dangers—disease and attacks by privateer and pirate ships. Sickness at sea was a grave problem. Conditions on board ship were usually overcrowded and ventilation below decks was very poor. The latrines were inadequate and water in the bilges became contaminated. On a long passage provisions decayed and deteriorated, while the drinking water was often foul. The diseases

Unlike most other merchant ships of the period, the East India Company's vessels carried surgeons, who could on some occasions alleviate the effects of sickness. The surgeon of the Indiaman *Europe* on a voyage from England to Madras in 1792, related that soon after the voyage began there was an outbreak of 'an infectious fever' and although three hundred and fifty out of a total of three hundred and

A contemporary print by an unknown artist entitled *Society at Sea* shows officers and passengers taking the air and enjoying music in the stern gallery of the East Indiaman *Halsewell*. The *Halsewell* was wrecked off the Dorset coast in 1786.

sixty-one crew and passengers were infected, only one death, the result of an accident, was recorded. The surgeon remarks that 'with so many people confined in a small place with fever it will not appear extraordinary that one should die but that so many should recover.'

The health of passengers and crews was the concern of some regulations established in Great Britain in 1803.

After July 1st 1803 every ship with more than fifty passengers had to carry a surgeon with a medicine-chest properly stocked with medicines, in proportion to the number of persons on board. The bedding of every passenger had to be aired once a day during the voyage by exposure upon the deck, weather permitting, and the vessel had to be fumigated with vinegar at least twice every week. Every ship bound

47

An oil painting by Abraham Storck showing a scene near the toll house on the north bank of the Y. On the right of the picture is a Dutch yacht with a visiting German prince on board; in the centre two bezan-rigged yachts and in the left background a large merchant ship hove to.

for North America had to be stored and furnished with at least twelve weeks' provisions and good and wholesome water sufficient to make an allowance every day during the voyage of not less than half a pound of meat, one pound and a half of bread, biscuit or oatmeal, with half a pint of molasses and one gallon of water, to every person on board,

whether adult or child. Ships of the Royal Navy and East India Company were, however, excluded from these regulations.

Corsairs, Privateers and Pirates
Barbary corsairs, operating from the North African ports,

48

were an almost continuous threat to merchant ships in the Mediterranean until 1830, when the French occupied the coastal regions. The corsairs, who regarded themselves as combatants in a war against the Christian world, were from time to time encouraged by one or other of the Christian powers with the intention of injuring the trade of enemy countries. Using fast, efficient and formidable galleys and chebecs, the Barbary corsairs ranged over the Mediterranean and on occasions even attacked ships in the English Channel.

Privateers were vessels, well armed and equipped by merchants and adventurers who had received a commission — 'Letters of Marque' — from the state empowering them to cruise against and harass the enemy by taking and burning their shipping while, at the same time, exonerating them from charges of piracy. Most of the maritime nations granted commissions for privateers and certain ports were notable for privateering activities. In France, in time of war, Dunkirk, the Channel Ports and Saint-Malo were constantly in use as bases for privateers. The exploits of privateers like Jean Bart, Duquay Trouin and Jacques Crassard, who in the 17th and 18th centuries ravaged English ships in the North Sea, English Channel and Atlantic, have made them the heroes of French maritime history. In England the ports of Liverpool and Bristol were specially associated with privateers. Privateering from Bristol dated from at least the beginning of the 15th century when King Henry IV granted Letters of Marque to two Bristol vessels.

Probably the most remarkable privateering voyage ever made was that of Captain Woodes Rogers who sailed from Bristol in August 1708, with the ships *Duke*, 30 guns, and *Duchess*, 26 guns, on a cruise round the world. No captures were made before the ships rounded Cape Horn but in the Pacific a number of valuable prizes were taken and ports in Spanish colonies were attacked. The *Duke* and *Duchess* returned via the Cape of Good Hope and reached England in October 1711, with their holds filled with treasure.

The following announcement from a Bristol newspaper of 1756 is typical of advertisements for recruits. 'On a Cruise, the *Caesar* Privateer. A prime Sailor and built for the pupose with the best accommodation, Ezekiel Nash, Commander, Burden 360 tons, 20 Nine- and Six-Pounders and 200 men, will sail in 30 days, having a Protection for the Ship's Company. All Officers, Sailors, and able bodied Landsmen, who are disposed to enter on board the said Privateer, let them repair to Mr. Magnis's at the Gibb, where they shall meet with all proper Encouragement.'

More than sixty privateers operated from Bristol during the Napoleonic Wars.

Privateering from Liverpool seems to have commenced in the 16th century. A Liverpool ship, the *Relief,* was granted Letters of Marque in 1586 for a cruise against the Spanish, but it was in the 18th century that privateering from this port reached its zenith. In the short period from August 1778 to February 1779 alone, ninety-nine privateers sailed from Liverpool. William Hutchinson, a Liverpool captain with first-hand experience of privateering advises in his book *Naval Architecture,* published in 1794, that 'privateers should look as little and defenceless as possible, with special port-lids to conceal the guns and so hide their powers and surprise the enemy'.

American privateers have earned well-deserved fame. In the first half of the 18th century large numbers of privateers sailed from Colonial ports to capture many valuable prizes. In one year — 1734 — more than a hundred privateers sailed from the American coast to operate against French shipping.

During the War of American Independence, the privateers commissioned by the Colonies in revolt were so successful that few British merchant ships were able to come in and out of the American ports still under British control. Again during the War of 1812–4 about three hundred American privateers preyed upon the British trade routes. The American privateers of this period were mostly brigs and schooners built and rigged for speed, often armed with a single long-range gun, and designed as commerce raiders which could overtake and destroy merchantmen and usually escape from men-of-war. These American privateers rendered invaluable service to their country by the daring and the extent of their ravages.

During the French and Spanish wars a number of British merchant ships — including East Indiamen — took out Letters of Marque as privateers. Although it was not the intention of their ships to attack enemy shipping, the commission provided some protection from the Press Gang and relieved them of some convoy regulations. Privateering was finally forbidden by international laws in 1856.

Pirates

The true pirate robbed the ships of all nations and it was therefore the duty of all nations to seek out and destroy pirate vessels and bring their crews to trial. During the 16th century piracy was carried on round the British Isles particularly from Ireland and the Scilly Isles. Finally driven from these waters, the pirates moved to the West Indies, the New England coast, the Red Sea and Madagascar. The most interesting period in the history of piracy was between

Ann Bonny *and* Mary Read *convicted of* Piracy Nov.ʳ 28.ᵗʰ 1720 *at a Court of* Vice Admiralty *held at* Sᵗ Jago de la Vega *in* yᵉ Island *of* Jamaica.

Ann Bonny and Mary Read from *The History of Pirates* by Capt. Johnson, 1726. Ann Bonny was an Irish girl with a violent temper, who deserted her husband for a pirate, while Mary Read, who had been brought up as a boy, also became a pirate. Both were sentenced to death but were not executed.

1650 and 1750 when the exploits of famous pirates like John Avery, Bartholomew Roberts and Edward Teach took place. John Avery, known as the 'arch-pirate' after operating in the West Indies and off the Guinea coast, moved to the Red Sea where he captured a treasure ship belonging to the Great Mogul. The Mogul's daughter and 100,000 pieces-of-eight are stated to have been taken. Bartholomew Roberts, born in Wales in 1682, took up piracy in 1719, and is reported to have captured more than four hundred ships. He was killed while fighting against a pursuing warship in 1722. Edward Teach, known as 'Blackbeard', became a pirate in 1716, operating off the New England coast. In 1717 he took a large French West Indiaman which he renamed *Queen Anne's Revenge* and in which he went cruising, after mounting her with forty guns. Beating off a British warship of twenty guns, Teach continued pirate

Contemporary drawing of a section and deck plan of the *Falmouth* East Indiaman, built at Blackwall, 1752. The galley stove is now on the main deck below the forecastle, and chain bilge pumps can be seen amidships.

operations off the coast of Virginia. The position became so bad that local merchants petitioned the governor of Virginia to rid them of the pirates. Two naval sloops were sent to search for Teach and this notorious pirate was killed on November 22nd 1718 in hand-to-hand combat with Lieutenant Robert Maynard, the commander of one of the sloops.

During this period there appear to have been a number of women pirates, the most famous of whom were Ann Bonny and Mary Read (Ill. p. 50). Ann Bonny was the daughter of an Irish lawyer who had settled in Carolina. After an unsuccessful marriage, she sailed with the pirate 'Calico Jack' Rackham, and was one of the more dangerous members of his crew. Mary Read had been brought up as a boy and had fought as a soldier in Flanders, where she married. After the death of her husband she sailed to America on a West Indiaman. The ship was captured by Rackham and Mary Read joined his crew where she became as noteworthy as Ann Bonny. After their capture by a British warship the two women pirates were tried and sentenced to death but were not executed.

pendence this trade was inaugurated when American merchants sent the ship *Empress of China* to China. The *Empress of China*, 360 tons, sailed from New York on February 22nd 1784 with forty-six men aboard and a cargo of goods and specie worth $120,000. She reached Canton

The *Columbia*, of 212 tons, built in 1773, was the first American vessel to sail round the world. Leaving Boston in September 1787 she completed a voyage of more than 40,000 nautical miles and returned to her home port in August 1790. Engraving from *Voyages of the Columbia* by Howay.

Early American Trading Voyages

Because of the monopoly held by the British East India Company, the American Colonies had no direct trade with India and China. After the Colonies had gained their inde-

on August 26th and on the return passage crossed the South Atlantic and sailed up the coast of the Americas to reach New York on May 11th 1785 with a cargo 'that proved America need pay no further tribute for tea or silk to the Dutch or British'.

Another historic voyage—which led the way to Salem, Massachusetts', great trade with the Indies—was that of the American ship *Grand Turk*. Under the command of Captain Ebenezer West, and with a cargo worth £7,000, this merchantman left Salem in December 1785 bound for the

a call was made at Capetown where a quantity of hides were taken aboard. The *Grand Turk* arrived back at Salem in May 1787 and her owner Elias Hasket Derby, a prominent Salem merchant, is said to have doubled his original outlay on the voyage.

A contemporary drawing of the merchant ship *St. Helena*, 240 tons, built in 1766. The vessel is shown with all square sails, staysails and starboard studding sails set. The fore and aft mizen sail is furled and a 'ring tail' is hoisted to the peak of the gaff.

Isle of France (Mauritius). After selling the cargo, Captain West agreed with a French merchant to take a cargo from the Isle of France to Canton. At Canton, where the *Grand Turk* was the third American vessel to reach China, a cargo of tea and chinaware was loaded. On the homeward voyage

The *Columbia* (Ill. p. 52) of 212 tons, built in 1773, was the first American vessel to sail round the world. A syndicate of American merchants decided to undertake an exploratory commercial voyage round Cape Horn, to the fur-trading territory of the north-west. The expedition of two

53

The *Earl of Balcarras* of 1,488 tons burden was built of teak at Bombay in 1815 and was chartered by the Honourable East India Company for a number of successive voyages to the East and home, until 1832 when the Company's trading activities ceased.

ships was placed under the command of Captain John Kenwick in the *Columbia*. The second vessel, a sloop, *Lady Washington*, 90 tons, commanded by Captain Robert Gray, was intended to be used as a tender. The *Columbia* and her tender left Boston on September 30th 1787 and sailed south via the Cape Verde Islands and the Falklands. They rounded Cape Horn and proceeded up the Pacific to Nootka Sound. When a cargo of furs had been taken aboard, the commanders changed ships and, under the command of

Captain Gray, the *Columbia* sailed westward across the Pacific to Canton in China. After selling the furs, a cargo of tea was purchased and the *Columbia* sailed for home on February 12th 1790 and, after calling at St Helena and Ascension, reached Boston on August 16th 1790. The *Columbia* had thus completed a trading voyage in which she had circumnavigated the globe and travelled 41,889 nautical miles. Part of the cargo of tea was damaged by water and the voyage was 'more fruitful of fame than gain'.

III FROM SLAVE SHIP TO CLIPPER SHIP

The Slave Trade

During the whole period of sea travel dealt with in this work the slave trade stands alone in its horror and appalling brutality. Between 1700 and 1800 more than two million negroes were carried in British ships from Africa to the West Indies and America. In addition, during the same century, many thousands of slaves were conveyed by French, Danish, Dutch and Portuguese vessels.

The dreadful trade seems to have been commenced by the Portuguese in 1442 when a number of captured Moors were exchanged for negroes. Regular voyages by ships carrying slaves between Africa and America were taking place early in the 16th century when Genoese merchants obtained the right to supply 4,000 negroes annually to the West Indies. English participation in the trade came later in the 16th century when Sir John Hawkins, the Elizabethan mariner, secured a contract to supply slaves to the Spanish settlements; it was a Dutch ship, however, that brought the first slaves to an English settlement—Jamestown—in 1619. The number of slaves transported annually in English ships increased steadily, reaching the highest figures towards the end of the 18th century. Liverpool, Bristol and London were the principal ports concerned with the trade and in the 1770's, nearly two hundred ships with a total capacity of more than forty-five thousand slaves were based on these ports.

During this period English, French, Dutch and Portuguese merchants maintained factories on the West African coasts where slaves could be assembled for shipment. On the outward journey from their home ports the slavers carried a varied cargo—cotton goods, copper and iron bars, looking glasses, beads, muskets and gunpowder—which could be used to exchange for slaves from the native chiefs. When the slaves were on board, the ships sailed as fast as possible with their 'perishable cargo' on the 'middle passage' to the Americas. The slave ships completed their 'triangular' voyage by returning home with a cargo of colonial produce, such as raw cotton, tobacco, logwood and sugar.

During the early part of the 18th century, many of the slave ships were quite small, often less than 100 tons burden, but by the end of the century much larger ships were being employed. A typical Liverpool slave ship, the *Brook,* built in 1781 was of 300 tons and carried twenty guns. The vessel was 'frigate-built' with the slaves accommodated on the lower deck. The adult male slaves were kept in a compartment, 46 feet by 25 feet; the women in a smaller space, 28 feet 6 inches by 23 feet 6 inches; and the boys' room was 13 feet 9 inches by 25 feet. In these very cramped quarters some six hundred slaves were carried. The 'middle passage' from Africa to the West Indies could be completed in about forty days but often took eight weeks or more. On average $12\frac{1}{2}$ per cent of the slave 'passengers' died during the voyage and it has been stated that of every hundred slaves shipped from Africa only fifty survived for service on the plantations.

As the male negroes came aboard the ship they were fastened together in pairs by irons at the wrists and ankles. They were often stowed so closely together in the compartments that they could only lie on their sides, with very little headroom. To enable additional 'passengers' to be carried, platforms or shelves, about eight feet wide, were fitted in the compartments on either side of the ship. The platforms were placed about half way between the decks, thus leaving only about three feet above and below. Slaves were forced to lie underneath and on these platforms. The sanitary arrangements were of course very primitive. In each of the compartments three or four large conical buckets, about two feet high, nearly two feet in diameter at the bottom and one foot at the top, were placed. In attempting to get to these buckets the shackled negroes had to crawl and stumble over their companions. In this situation they were often unable to get to the buckets and as the necessities of nature could not be resisted, they eased themselves on the spot. At about

DESCRIPTION OF A SLAVE SHIP.

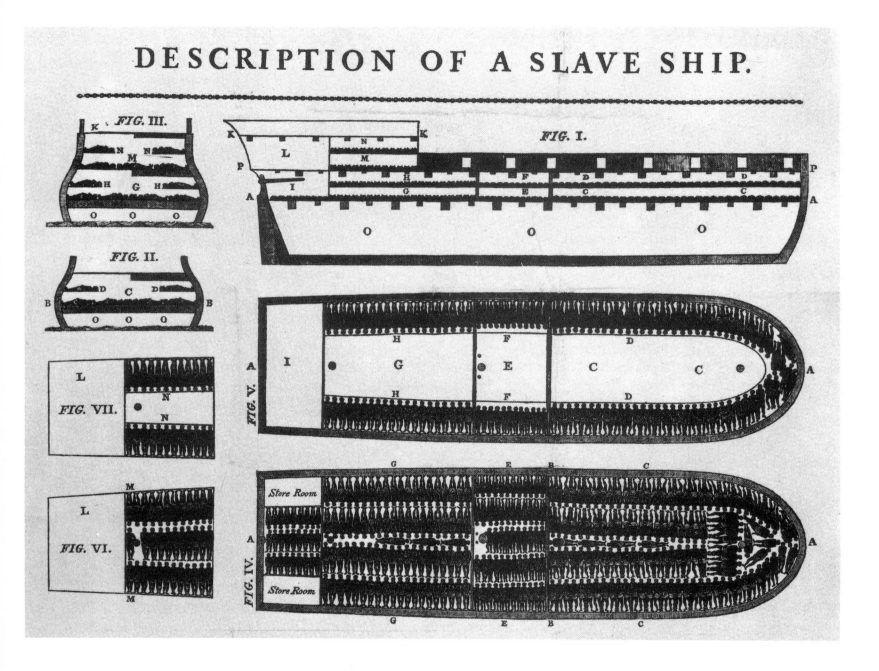

Section and deck plans of the Liverpool slave ship *Brook*, built in 1781. The vessel was 'frigate-built' and the slaves were accommodated on the lower deck. The plan shows less than 500 slaves, but a government investigation showed that more than 600 had been carried.

8 o'clock each morning the slaves were generally brought up to the open deck. Their shackles were examined and a long chain, fastened to a ring-bolt in the deck, was run through the shackles and locked to another ring-bolt in the deck so that fifty or sixty slaves could be fastened to one chain and thus prevented from mutiny or jumping overboard.

If the weather was good the slaves usually remained on deck until the late afternoon. In bad weather, the gratings in the deck, which supplied light and air to the slaves' compartments below, had to be covered with tarpaulins. The conditions in the compartments were then even more terrible, and numbers of the slaves died on these occasions, either from sickness or suffocation. The negroes were usually fed twice a day. The diet consisted of boiled beans, rice and yams, with small quantities of salted or dried beef and pork. The food was prepared in small tubs and about ten

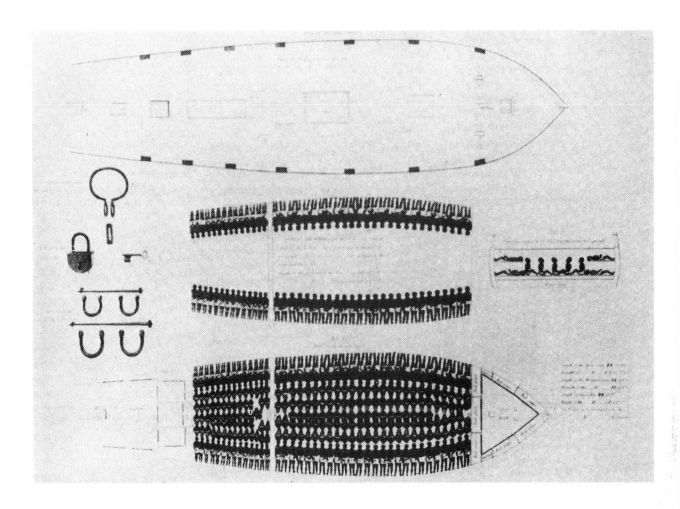

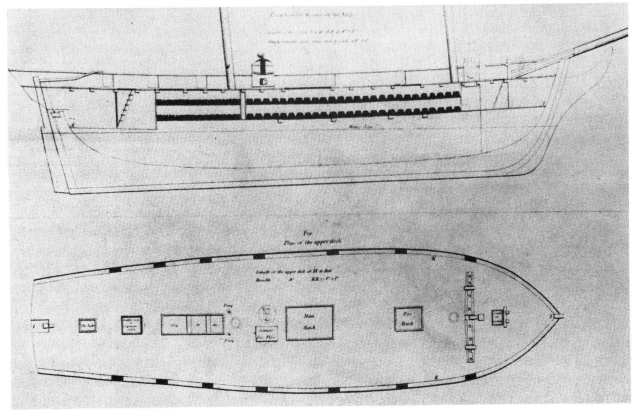

Deck plans and sections of the French slave brig *La Vigilante*, captured in the Bonny River on April 15th 1822. On the left side of the upper plan are shown the shackles, leg-irons and padlocks used to chain the male slave in twos, by wrist and ankle, for fear of revolt. Women and children were not chained. In the hold there was so little headroom that it was impossible for the slaves to sit up and they had to lie on their sides as there was not room to be on their backs. No bedding or cover was provided for the slaves. They were brought up on deck each day for food and exercise if the weather was reasonable. The men were chained to ring bolts in the deck and were made to jump up and down in their chains. It is on record that when a schooner which carried only 140 slaves met with a gale of wind which lasted eighteen hours, no less than 50 slaves perished in that short space of time, possibly due to suffocation as tarpaulins were put over the hatchways in bad weather.

57

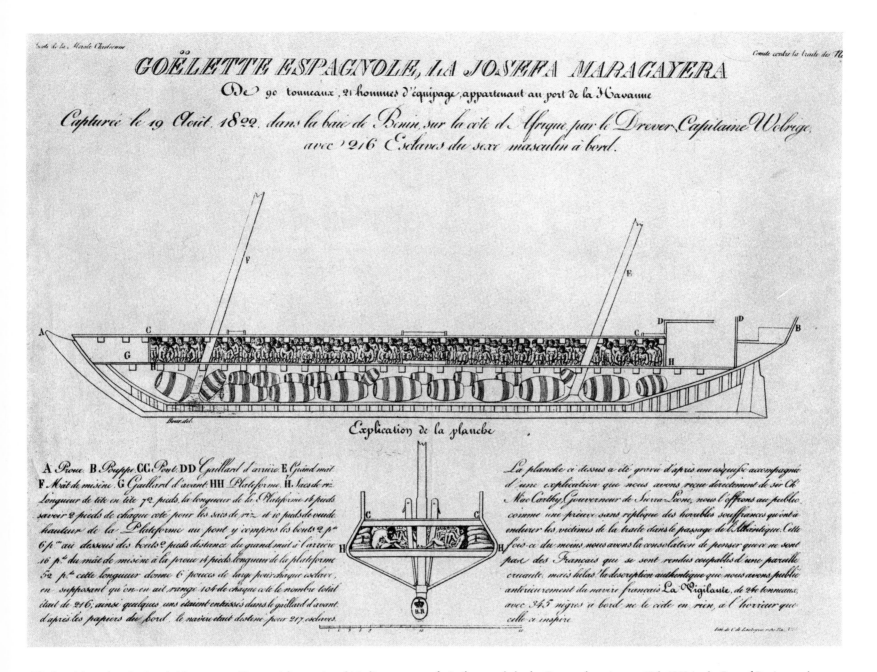

GOËLETTE ESPAGNOLE, LA JOSEFA MARACAYERA
De 90 tonneaux, 21 hommes d'équipage, appartenant au port de la Havanne
Capturée le 19 Août 1822, dans la baie de Benin, sur la côte d'Afrique, par le Drever Capitaine Welrige, avec 216 Esclaves du sexe masculin à bord.

Explication de la planche

The Spanish *goëlette La Josefa Maracayera,* 90 tons. A lateen-rigged Mediterranean craft similar to a chebeck. Captured on August 19th 1822 in the Bay of Benin, on the coast of Africa, with 216 male slaves on board. The slaves were packed in between sacks of rice.

slaves would be placed round each of these tubs, out of which they would feed themselves with a spoon or their hands. Their allowance of water was about half a pint each per meal. If the slaves refused to eat they were beaten or tortured until they died or swallowed the food. Some exercise being considered necessary for their health, they were forced, when on deck, to jump up and down in their chains. Usually slave ships carried many more men than women and, although also very overcrowded in their smaller compartments, the women were not chained.

In Great Britain, from 1788 onwards, a number of regulations were established to try and relieve some of the cruelties of the 'middle passage' but the penalties were not severe and the regulations had little effect. An Act of Parliament laid down that after the first day of August 1799, the whole space between decks, in slave ships, should be allocated to, and properly prepared for, the reception of slaves and that the height between decks should not be less than five feet. The number of slaves carried was limited. The figure was arrived at by multiplying the extreme length of the lower

58

Transporting negroes to the colonies. A wooden palisade divides the men from the women, and a gun, withdrawn from the gunport, is pointing towards the male slaves, while a sailor is about to flog a slave who is shackled in leg irons. Food is being distributed as the captain counts his profits.

deck by the extreme breadth and dividing by eight. Thus in a ship with a lower deck 100 feet long by 30 feet wide the maximum number of slaves allowed on board was three hundred and seventy-five. The Act also stated that a properly qualified surgeon must be on board, that the name of the ship must be painted on the stern, that for every ten slaves there should be at least one mariner or other free person comprising the crew, and that no ship should be cleared outwards, for the purpose of shipping and carrying slaves from the coast of Africa, from any part of His Maj-

esty's dominions, except the ports of London, Liverpool and Bristol.

In times of war, the slaves were in even greater peril. If their ship was in action, the slaves, in their crowded compartments, were in grave danger of death or injury from gunfire. If taken by the enemy they were sometimes murdered. However, a French document of 1795, in the possession of the author, shows that occasionally slaves were released after their ships had been captured. The document states: 'I declare that the Citizen Pierre Olanger, com-

Quarter-deck of H.M.S. *Deal Castle* during a voyage in 1775. Awnings are rigged above the deck to provide protection from the sun. The supply of fresh food was increased by keeping livestock on deck.

ary calendar. Frimaire was the third month of the Republican year and was the period November 20th to December 20th. The use of this calendar lasted till 1805 when Napoleon restored the normal system. It would seem probable that the 'Camp of Liberty' was in the French colony of Saint Domingue (Haiti).

By 1820 many countries had agreed to suppress the slave trade and warships of several nations were cruising off the coasts of Africa and of the West Indies. International treaties gave the commanders of these warships the authority to stop and search vessels for slaves and to capture and confiscate those engaged in the illegal trade. In these circumstances it was even more necessary for the slave traders to use ships capable of fast sailing. The conclusion of the Napoleonic and American-British wars made a number of privateer vessels redundant and these fast schooners were found to be specially suitable for the slave trade. For a few years converted privateers were used for transporting slaves but later schooners were specially designed and built for the trade. Most of these vessels were between 70 and 100 feet in length and were often armed with one centrally-mounted carronade. Crews of between twenty-five and fifty men were usual. As many slaves as possible were carried in these small vessels and their conditions were often even worse than they had been in the 18th century. On occasions, when capture by a warship was imminent, the slaves were thrown overboard by the crew in attempts to avert the confiscation of their vessels. However, the patrolling warships did have spectacular successes, which included the capture of such slave ships as the *Midas* with 400 slaves in 1829, the *Formidable* with 707 slaves in 1834, and the *Matilda* with 529 slaves in 1837. The captures mentioned are of course only selected instances of the excellent work done by the navies of Britain, the United States of America and of other nations over a period of about forty years.

The Post Office Packets and the First Regular Packet Service to America

Although at the beginning of the 19th century a number of sailing ships were making more or less regular voyages to many parts of the world, these voyages cannot be regarded as 'packet' services. In many cases the vessels did not sail on the advertised dates and passengers were kept waiting at the ports until full cargoes were available for their ships. However, the small vessels — mainly brigs — of the British Post Office did maintain some regular services. The Post Office packets sailed at fixed times to Irish, Continental and

mander of the corsair *Le Regulas,* has handed over to me 798 Africans, from the two English prizes, and has requested me to transfer them at once to the General of the Camp of Liberty, in the 19th of Frimaire in the fourth year of the French Republic, One and Indivisible. Signed Partiguinare.' The document is dated according to the French Revolution-

West Indiamen never assumed the size and importance of their contemporaries the East Indiamen. Although similar in general design to the East India ships, in the late 18th century the size of West Indiamen was usually 400 tons or less.

Mediterranean ports as well as to ports in the West Indies and South America.

The Post Office packets to the West Indies, Madeira and the Americas left England at monthly intervals, while more frequent sailings were made to Continental and Mediterranean ports. The packets were fast and armed. In times of war, if the speed of the packet did not enable it to escape, the crews had to be prepared to try and defend their ship against enemy privateers and men-of-war. The passengers, often Army or Government officers, joined in the defence of the packet and on occasions lost their lives in the action. Although the crew and passengers usually fought coura-

61

The brig *Camden,* a former mail packet, was purchased in 1838 by John Williams of the London Missionary Society. The brig was used as a missionary ship in the Pacific until 1843 when she was sent home and sold.

geously, more than thirty Post Office packets were captured by American or French vessels during the War of 1812–5.

The Post Office packets could only carry a few passengers — usually not more than twelve. In 1815, on a packet of about 230 tons, the passengers' quarters, amidships, consisted of a 'dining room' with sideboard and stove. From this compartment sliding doors gave access to six tiny cabins — three on each side — each about six feet long by four feet wide. In addition four open 'bed places' were available for passengers in the small after-cabin.

The first regular transatlantic commercial packet service was founded by a group of New York merchants. On October 27th 1817 it was announced in the Press that 'In order to furnish frequent and regular conveyance for Goods and Passengers, the subscribers have undertaken to establish a line of vessels between New York and Liverpool, to sail from each place on a certain day in every month throughout the year.' It was stated that one vessel would sail from New York on the 5th and one from Liverpool on the 1st of every month.

Four vessels, the *Amity, Courier, Pacific* and *James Munroe,* each of about 400 tons and just over 100 feet in length, were fitted out for this purpose and under the name Black Ball Line became the direct ancestors of the many sailing and steamship lines which were to become famous in the later annals of transatlantic travel.

The first Black Ball ship to leave New York, the *James Munroe,* sailed at 10 a.m. on January 5th 1818 and landed her eight passengers, who had each paid forty guineas for the passage, in Scotland on January 28th. The

Courier left Liverpool on January 4th — three days later than her advertised date! — with six cabin passengers and seven passengers in the steerage, and arrived at New York on February 23rd. Throughout the whole era of the sailing ship, owing to the prevailing westerly winds, the eastward passage across the Atlantic was usually made in much shorter time than the westward. A remarkable feature of the Black Ball Line's regular monthly trips was that sailings were made each way throughout the year, although at this time merchant vessels were often laid up during the winter months. The Black Ball Line, for the first time, gave an efficient and reliable service without regard to season. Their first packet, the *James Munroe,* put up the best consistent sailing performances over the next five years, with a fastest west-bound passage of twenty-three days and average passages over the whole period of thirty-seven days. By 1822 the Black Ball Line had eight ships in service and, from March 16th of that year, dispatched two packets from each side of the Atlantic every month. In the same year, however, two of their packets were lost. The *Albion,* specially built in 1819 for the Line, was wrecked off the Irish coast with a loss of forty-six lives and the recently completed *Liverpool* was lost after running into an iceberg in a fog. In this disaster the passengers and crew were saved in the ship's boats and landed at St. John's, Newfoundland, six days after the accident. Another Black Ball packet, the *William Thompson,* which was employed on the Atlantic service from 1822 to 1830, made the record westward passage, for this period, of twenty days. A contemporary account of a passage in the *William Thompson* relates how the packet left Liverpool on the morning of July 16th 1828 and was towed to the mouth of the Mersey by a steam vessel. On this voyage which was completed in thirty-nine days, the crew consisted of three officers, sixteen seamen, three stewards, two cooks and a boy. There were eleven cabin passengers — eight men and three women — with a maidservant and two steerage passengers. The fare for the cabin passengers from Liverpool to New York was thirty-five guineas inclusive of charges for provisions, wine and spirits.

The size of the packets was steadily increased as new vessels replaced the earlier ships or extra ships were brought into service. The *Canada* of 525 tons, built by Brown & Bell at New York in 1823, for the Black Ball Line, was 131 feet long with a beam of 35 feet. The gentlemen's dining saloon was fitted out with carved mahogany pillars and crimson draperies. The 'dormitories' were large and elegant and the berths were hung round with olive-coloured damask silk curtains, while the ladies' cabins had blue silk curtains.

Aboard the steam packet *Victory,* built in 1818. The artist's impression suggests a spacious saloon with plenty of headroom in a ship so steady as to permit a steward to walk with a tea tray without difficulty. From a print 'Margate pier with steam packets', published by John Hudson in 1821.

At this period the male passengers usually occupied berths in a 'dormitory' and the ladies had a separate room. During the first ten years of its existence the Black Ball Line gained a fine reputation for the excellence of its services. Over the period, the average east-bound passages of their

third between New York and Le Havre in France. The first regular service between London and New York started in June 1824 with the packets *Acasta*, *Crisis* and *Hudson*. By the 1820's ships of more than 600 tons were usual in the Atlantic service. The Black Ball packet *Europe* launched

'Scene on board an East Indiaman showing the effects of a heavy lurch after dinner', a caricature by G. Cruikshank published in 1818. The only persons who do not seem to be worried are the captain and a sailor who is obviously enjoying the fun.

packets took twenty-four days from port to port, equivalent to a mean speed of about 5.8 knots, and an average west-bound voyage took thirty-eight days with a mean speed of about 3.4 knots. The Black Ball Line was without competition for four years but in 1822 three more transatlantic packet lines were founded. Two of the new companies operated services between Liverpool and New York and the

in 1833 was of 618 tons, with a length of 137 feet. In this vessel the dormitory had been replaced by a room 40 feet long and 16 feet wide with enclosed cabins on either side. Each cabin was about 8 feet square and panelled with bird's eye maple. The upper part of the doors and the inboard windows of the cabins were latticed so that when they were closed the occupant could not be seen but air was admitted.

64

The *Ann McKim*, said to be the first real clipper ship. Built by Kennard & Williamson of Fell's Point, Baltimore, in 1832–3 for Isaac McKim, a merchant, she was named after the wife of the owner. This vessel was copper sheathed and mounted 12 brass guns. She was broken up at Valparaiso in 1852.

Each of the cabins was furnished with a washstand containing a double service, a chest of drawers and two berths with mattresses and linen.

The Birth of the Clipper Ship

It has been said that the slave ships were the only merchant vessels of the period designed for speed, but this is an aphorism. Endeavours to improve the design of the sailing ship had, of course, taken place over a very long period. From the 15th century onwards, many of the major problems of naval architecture – strength of structure, stability, weight calculations and the effect of water resistance – were studied. During the 17th and 18th centuries experiments were made with models in tanks of water to ascertain the

Dutch clipper ship with auxiliary steam-engine off Batavia, Java. Lithograph by J.D. Voorn Boers. The artist gives a very clear impression of the rigging and method of furling sails. Native craft in the foreground add interest to the busy scene.

form of solid which would move with the greatest velocity through water. However, it was in the relatively brief period of forty years between 1820 and 1860 that the most remarkable changes in sailing ship design took place. In this period the finely designed fast clipper ship was developed and for many purposes took the place of the heavily-built slow sailing vessel formerly employed. After about 1835, with the increased employment of the now more efficient

steamship, it became clear that the design of large sailing ships would have to be improved and that vessels intended for the conveyance of passengers and some freights would have to be capable of sailing at faster speeds. The earlier vessels of improved design were of much the same length to breadth proportions as the last of the old type of East Indiamen but were designed with finer lines and were without the very large poop usually fitted to Indiamen of the same size. In consequence they only had a single tier of quarter and stern windows. By the 1840's the length to breadth ratio of some new ships had increased to 4.5 to 1, compared to the 4 to 1 proportion of the old Indiamen, and was reduced to 96 days in the 1850's and to 90 days in the 1860's.

The term clipper—meaning 'a thing excellent of its kind'—which seems to have been first applied to fast horses

The clipper ship *Murray* of 903 tons, built by Hall of Aberdeen in 1861, was the last Orient liner to be built entirely of wood. She was considered a fast ship, her best day's run being 325 miles, and was fitted with every convenience for passengers with capacity for a large cargo.

by the mid-1850's this proportion had increased to 5.5 to 1. In the later tea clippers, such as the *Thermopyla* and *Cutty Sark,* the length was still further increased to 5.9 times the breadth. As a result of these improvements in design a clipper ship of the 1860's could, in good wind conditions, sail nearly twice as fast as the Indiaman of the early 1800's, and a very fast passage from China to England, which in the early years of the 19th century took 109 days,

and then to the very fast schooner built on the eastern seaboard of the United States of America, particularly in the Chesapeake Bay area in the early years of the 19th century, became much more renowned when, at the middle of the century, it was used to describe fast square-rigged sailing ships. The exact qualities of design and performance which entitled a vessel to be called a clipper are still a matter of controversy but fineness of hull and speed were the prime

Searching for stowaways. Many people who could not afford to pay for their passage to the New World attempted to travel by this method.

in the shortest possible time. The trade in tea from China to Europe and America was very remunerative and each year the first cargo to reach the dealers fetched the highest price. The discovery of gold in California in 1848 and in Australia two years later also brought about a demand for fast ships to carry men and mining equipment. However, by no means all the sailing ships built at this period were clipper ships. Many thousands of slower bluff-bowed sailing vessels carried goods and passengers to all parts of the world and on coastal voyages, where the ability to transport such cargoes as coal, timber, and general goods in roomy holds was more important than fast sailing qualities.

Indeed, of the vessels designed with finer lines only a small proportion could be classified as the 'sharp' or extreme type of clippers. In most of the larger ships there was now much better accommodation for some passengers in permanent cabins. (The conditions for the emigrants crowded between decks was a different matter and will be described in a later chapter.) A contemporary description of the *Monarch*, a Blackwall 'frigate' launched in 1844, emphasizes the improvement in accommodation. The *Monarch* was provided with twelve cabins each about 10 feet square and a dining saloon 36 feet by 18 feet on the upper deck, with two cabins 18 feet by 16 feet and sixteen smaller cabins on the lower deck.

Advertisements in the newspapers of the period announcing the departures of ships to all parts of the world now usually made a point of describing the passenger accommodation. In the *Times* of November 7th 1837 an advertisement for the New York Line of Packets states: 'The

factors. The title 'the first clipper' has been given to both American and British vessels but it is not possible to particularize to any individual ship. The term was certainly being used to describe British-built square-rigged vessels by 1840.

The aspiration to design and build fast sailing ships was increased by the knowledge that substantial profits could be made by carrying specialized freights from port to port

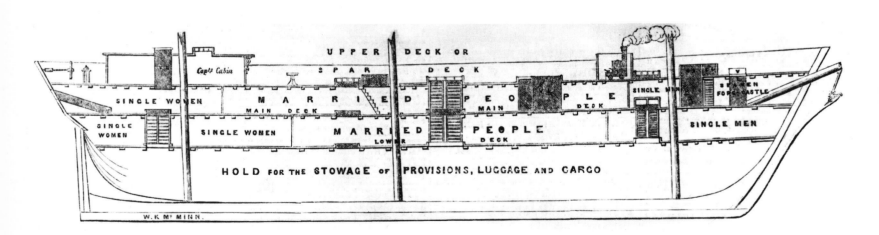

Section of the emigrant ship *Bourneuf* of Liverpool, showing the disposition of passengers, crew, luggage, provisions and cargo on the voyage to Australia. Smoke can be seen coming from the galley chimney where food was cooked for both passengers and crew.

The large clipper *Schomberg* of 2,284 tons, built at Aberdeen for the Black Ball Line of Liverpool, and lost on her maiden voyage to Australia in 1855.

cabins are commodious, elegantly fitted up and provided with everything conducive to the comfort and convenience of the passenger.' The *Vernon* sailing from London to Madeira on October 1st 1841 is described as 'first class, British built, coppered and copper fastened and sails remarkably fast. Her accommodation consists of ladies' and gentlemen's cabins, stateroom, sofas and the convenience of a comfortable airy and superior order, in the arrange-

ment and fitting up of which every attention has been paid so as to render the voyage safe and comfortable for invalids.' Again in the *Times* of March 2nd 1844 the regular packets for Australia—*Lord William Bentinck, Saint Vincent* and *Dale Park*—are described as '…first-class ships and have full poops, with splendid accommodation for cabin passengers for whom a liberal dietary with live stock is provided at the reduced charge of £45 each exclusive of wines, spirits and

The Government medical inspector's office. It was not until 1851, when gold was discovered in Australia, that regulations relating to emigration were enforced. Before this emigrant ships were very poor and the horrors of a long passage resembled conditions on convict ships.

beer.' Further light on conditions for passengers on ships at this period is provided by other advertisements, which, in attempting to attract the prospective passenger to a ship or shipping line, point out that one or other particular vessel 'will carry an experienced surgeon,' 'has seven feet height between decks,' 'carries a full band of music,' 'baths and wash-houses will be erected on deck,' 'a library of 300 volumes will be supplied for the gratuitious use of the passengers' or that 'the cabin accommodations are unequalled, and supplied with beds, bedding and every other requisite, including stewards' attendance and a stewardess for the ladies.'

The clipper *Royal Family* of 1,750 tons, built in 1862 by W. & R. Wright of St. John, New Brunswick, for the Australian trade of Fernie Bros. & Co. of Liverpool. Her figurehead was a three-quarter bust of Queen Victoria. She had accommodation for 20 cabin and 400 steerage passengers.

Before the advent of railways, sea transport was used extensively around Britain for the coastal trades. In the 18th century and early years of the 19th century, cutter-rigged vessels of between 150 and 200 tons, known as 'smacks', were frequently employed for carrying both passengers and goods from ports in Scotland to London. Despite their small size these vessels presented many advantages over the stage coaches and slow-moving goods-wagons. The 'smacks' used for the London to Edinburgh trade were particularly well built and were considered adequate for the purpose until, in the 1830's, they had to face the increasing competition of steam packets. This compe-

In the Atlantic, an artist's impression. It is difficult to imagine that the lady passenger would sit so calmly on the deck while the sea water swirled around her feet.

tition led to the employment of a number of fast schooners.

During the 1830's the shipbuilders James and William Hall of Aberdeen conducted a series of experiments with various scale hull forms in a glass-sided water tank, 10 feet

in length. Following these experiments the Halls designed and built in 1839 a schooner, the *Scottish Maid*, which proved a very fast sailing vessel and because of her design has even been honoured by one historian with the title 'the

The American clipper ship *Comet* built by William Webb, launched in 1851. She became one of Webb's most successful ships, was an exceptional passage-maker and could maintain a relatively high speed in any sailing weather. She is here depicted in a hurricane off Bermuda.

world's first clipper.' The *Scottish Maid* was designed with hollow bow lines and 'a sharpening of the bow by carrying out the stem to the cutwater.' This form of bow was to become well known as 'the Aberdeen bow.' The *Scottish Maid* and other similar schooners were employed on the Aberdeen–London service; the advertised fares for the passage being two guineas for cabin passengers and one guinea for steerage.

The Spanish barque *Porvenir* on a voyage from Barcelona to Havana is shown shortening sail in a storm. Sailors can be seen reefing the main lower topsail. By José Pineda. 1875.

In 1840, one schooner sailed from London every Saturday and one from Aberdeen every Wednesday. The voyage of about 400 nautical miles was frequently completed in less than fifty hours. In addition to the Halls of Aberdeen, other British shipbuilders were also endeavouring to design fast sailing vessels, but there is no doubt that in the 1840's and early 1850's the American-built clipper ships were the fastest and most successful sailing ships of the period.

IV PERILS OF THE SEA

The labouring hull already seems half-fill'd,
With waters thro' an hundred leaks distill'd.
As in a dropsy, wallowing with her freight,
Half-drown'd she lies, a dead inactive weight!
Thus drench'd by every wave, her riven deck
Stript and defenceless, floats a naked wreck;
Her wounded flanks no longer can sustain
These fell invasions of the bursting main.
At every pitch, th'o'erwhelming billows bend,
Beneath their load, the quivering bowsprit-end.
A fearful warning! Since the masts on high,
On that support, with trembling hope rely.
At either pump our seamen pant for breath,
In dark dismay anticipating death.
Still all our powers th'increasing leaks defy:
We sink at sea, no shore, no haven nigh.

These verses are part of a long poem entitled *The Ship-wreck* written by an eighteenth-century mariner William Falconer and first published in 1762. This poem, which provided prospective passengers with a grim account of the perils they might have to endure, aroused much interest and nine editions had been published by 1796 (Ill. p. 45).

While dependent only on sails the ship was at constant risk from the perils of the sea. In the terms of the eighteenth-century insurance broker, everything that happened to a ship in the course of her voyage, by the immediate act of God, without the intervention of human agency, was a peril of the sea. Thus every accident occurring through the violence of the wind or waves, through thunder or lightning, through being driven against rocks, through the stranding of the ship or any other violence which human prudence could not foresee nor human strength resist, was considered a peril of the sea.

Throughout the era of the sail, and despite the often superb seamanship and courage of seamen of all nations, the proportion of disasters in which the vessel became a total loss was very high. Indeed, for some time after the introduction of steam propulsion for ocean-going vessels, the traveller by sea still often found himself at the mercy of the elements. For instance in one year—1850—there were 681 British and foreign vessels wrecked around the coast of the British Isles alone, with more than half the vessels total losses, and more than 700 lives lost. In that year, a north-west gale at the beginning of February caused 47 wrecks, a south-east gale at the end of March caused 73 wrecks, and gales in October and November brought about 62 wrecks. In the month of March a total of 134 wrecks occurred, or more than four a day on average for the whole month. All these disasters took place in the waters around the British Isles or on its shores, and formed a very small part of the total number of vessels lost throughout the world during the same period.

The following accounts of disasters which occurred to eighteenth- and nineteenth-century sailing ships—Indiamen and packets—are only a minute part of the never-ending story of the mariner's efforts to save his ship and the lives of the passengers from the dreadful consequences of gales, faulty navigation, fire and other accidents at sea. On many occasions ships on their maiden voyages have met with disaster. The new Dutch East Indiaman *Amsterdam* left Holland in January 1749, under the command of Captain William Klump, bound for Batavia. On board were three hundred and twenty-nine men, including a number of soldiers, and three women. From the start of the voyage the *Amsterdam* met strong winds and, while off Pevensey Bay on the Sussex coast on January 20th, lost her rudder. The vessel drifted eastward for some miles until brought to anchor. Seamen went out to the *Amsterdam* from Hastings, perhaps to assist in fitting a jury rudder so that the vessel could be got to Portsmouth. A few days later, on January 26th, it would seem that the anchors could not hold the vessel and she was beached, or drifted ashore, at Hastings. In this case the crew and passengers were able to get to

The loss of the East Indiaman *Halsewell*. She left the Downs on January 1st 1786, under the command of Captain R. Pierce, bound for India and China, on her fourth voyage for the East India Company, and five days later was driven on to the rocks near St. Alban's Head.

safety at low tide. The hull of the *Amsterdam* sank rapidly in the quicksands, where it remained until the present day. Recently, trial excavations by nautical archaeologists have recovered many objects from the ship's equipment and cargo, and revealed that the hull was virtually complete up to the main deck. It is hoped that Anglo-Dutch efforts will make it possible to excavate fully and preserve the *Amsterdam* and her cargo to form a unique review of mid-eighteenth-century maritime life, comparable to that of the 17th

century provided by the Swedish warship *Wasa* preserved at Stockholm.

Just thirty-six years after the *Amsterdam* was in distress, the British East Indiaman *Halsewell* (Ill. pp. 76, 77) also found herself being blown on to a lee shore in the English Channel. The *Halsewell*, of 758 tons, commanded by Captain Richard Pierce, outward bound for India with a complement of two hundred and fifty including soldiers and men and women passengers, ran into bad weather on

January 3rd 1786, hove to and anchored off Dunnose on the south-east coast of the Isle of Wight. The topsails were taken in, but in the extreme cold the seamen were unable to reef the frozen main and foresails. In the early hours of the next morning the gale increased and the captain ordered the anchor cables to be cut and the Indiaman sailed away from the coast. During the day the gale further increased in force and the *Halsewell* shipped so many seas that by the next day there was seven feet of water in the hold. In these conditions the Indiaman laboured badly and first the mizenmast and then the mainmast were cut away to ease her. On January 5th, the fore topmast was carried

Scene in the cabin of the *Halsewell* before the vessel was wrecked. Only 79 people survived and Captain Pierce and his two daughters were among those lost.

away and in the strong southerly gale the vessel was driven nearer and nearer the coast of Dorsetshire. In a last effort to save her, attempts were made to anchor but at 2 a.m. on January 7th the *Halsewell* struck the rocks near Seacombe Cliff about two miles east of St Albans Head. It was impossible to launch the boats in the huge waves and, as the *Halsewell* broke up, desperate attempts were made to reach a large cave in the rock cliff opposite the wreck. Most of the passengers perished when the roundhouse at the

(Ill. p. 83). The full story of the catastrophe – 'A Narrative of the Loss of His Majesty's Packet the *Lady Hobart*, on an Island of Ise in the Atlantic Ocean' – was published later by the commander of the packet, Captain William Fellowes.

The *Lady Hobart* left Halifax, Nova Scotia, with the mail for Great Britain, on June 22nd 1803. On June 24th she was intercepted by a French privateer schooner, *l'Aimable Julie*, but in the engagement which followed the privateer was defeated, captured and sent back to Halifax with a

The *Mary* held fast in the ice. Lithograph by Starck and Kramer, *c*. 1868. The crew of the unfortunate vessel are taking to the boats, and salvaging stores before leaving her to her fate.

stern, in which they were sheltering, broke away and was swept overboard. By daylight the wreck had completely broken up and although about one hundred and fifty of the complement managed to get to the cliff during the night more than half of them were unable to hold on and in the morning only seventy-nine survived and were rescued.

Icebergs have always been a hazard to ships on the North Atlantic trade routes and it was an iceberg that caused the loss of the British Post Office packet *Lady Hobart* in 1803

prize crew. Four days later, when about 350 miles from Newfoundland, the *Lady Hobart* (Ill. p. 83) ran into an iceberg which was said to have been a quarter of a mile long with peaks which towered above the packet's masts. The vessel sustained severe damage from the collision and despite efforts to stop the leaks and to lighten her by heaving the guns overboard and dropping the anchors, the decks were soon awash. Before the *Lady Hobart* sank, the passengers, including three women, and the crew were able to

The packet ship *Albion* en route between New York and Liverpool was wrecked off the rocky coast of Ireland on April 22nd 1822. The artist shows the ship being pounded by the heavy seas, while distracted passengers on deck call to the more fortunate ones who have reached the shore.

get away in two boats. Provisions of about forty-five pounds of biscuits and five gallons of water were divided between the eighteen people in one boat and the eleven in the other. After enduring six days of freezing fog, and after being separated and re-united, the two boats reached Newfoundland.

On their return to England, Captain Fellowes and his crew were awarded £200 for their discipline and courage. The fine transatlantic packet service of the Black Ball Line suffered a major disaster in 1822. The packet *Albion* left New York on April 1st 1822 with a crew of twenty-five and twenty-nine passengers. On the night of April 21st, the *Albion* was sailing under reefed sails in a gale, about twenty miles off the Irish coast, when she was struck by a tremendous wave. The mainmast was brought down and the rigging and other masts damaged. The deckhouse, steering wheel and binnacle were swept away and a great deal of water entered the ship. The ship was then unworkable and was driven by the gale towards Ireland. At about 3 a.m. on the morning of April 22nd the *Albion* (Ill. p. 79) struck the rocks at the foot of high cliffs near Kinsale. As the waves broke over the vessel many of the crew and passengers were washed overboard but a few managed to climb from the stern on to the cliff. In the morning light two passengers and six members of the crew were the only survivors.

Fire at sea in the days of wooden ships was a most dreaded

because of the weight of the ammunition stowed in the hold. An officer with a lantern, and two men, went below to see that everything was secure in the hold. The rolling of the ship caused the officer to stumble and drop the lantern into spirit from a broken cask and in an instant the hold was on fire. The crew assisted by soldiers tried to subdue the flames by pumping water into the hold and by spreading wet sails over the hatchways to keep the air out. Despite these meas-

The Return. A lifeboat bringing back survivors from a wreck. One of a series of engravings by Frederick Hunter after paintings by Thomas Brooks. The Royal National Lifeboat Institution of Great Britain was inaugurated in 1824 and maintains now over 168 lifeboats. Service is entirely voluntary.

peril and when the fire occurred during a gale the ship was indeed in great danger. These two perils combined to bring disaster to an East Indiaman in 1825. The Indiaman *Kent* (Ill. p. 84) left England on February 19th 1825, bound for India, with a crew of one hundred and forty-eight and some five hundred passengers, principally soldiers with their families. Part of the cargo consisted of cannon balls and gunpowder for the army in India. When the *Kent* reached the Bay of Biscay she ran into a full gale. The vessel was hove to under a reefed main topsail but she rolled badly probably

ures the fire spread to the cable tier where the rope anchor cable caught fire. In attempting to control this fire so much water was let into the hold that, in the gale conditions, the ship was further endangered. Fortunately a passing brig, the *Cambria,* saw the distress signals and first the women and children, and then the soldiers and crew, were transferred with great difficulty by boat and raft from the *Kent* to the *Cambria.* Before the *Kent* sank, eighty-six lives had been lost but more than five hundred and fifty persons were saved.

Life saving. Emigrants, no doubt Irish, wrecked on the way to St. John's, Newfoundland. The man holding a small girl in his arm is being lowered into the lifeboat by a life-line, while one lifeboatman fends off a ship's boat which has become waterlogged.

It was not only on the ocean that a sudden change in the force or direction of the wind could be a peril. In the 18th century, the passenger travelling in a packet on a Thames river service could meet with trouble, as the following note from the *Times* of September 12th 1791 shows: 'Friday afternoon between three and four o'clock as a Gravesend passenger boat was going down Limehouse Reach, the wind blowing fresh, she carried away her mast close to the board, by which accident a gentlewoman had her arm broken in two places and otherwise so much shattered, that it was

thought an immediate amputation must take place; several other passengers got damage, but not of much consequence, the people were all put on shore at Rotherhithe, the boat being rendered incapable of performing the voyage.'

After these grim accounts of shipwreck, drowning and injury, it would seem appropriate to describe something of the early development of services for giving assistance to the passengers and crews of ships in distress. The first life-boat station in Britain—and probably the first in the world—was established at Bamburgh on the north-east coast of England, where as early as 1771, a charitable trust administered an organization that rendered help in cases of shipwreck. It was soon found that the ordinary boat was not suitable for live-saving in heavy seas and in 1786 the chief officer of the organization arranged with a coachbuilder, Lionel Lukin, to convert a coble—a local type of open beach boat—into a 'safety boat'. Lukin had already patented what he called an 'unimmergible' boat in which bouyancy was obtained by means of watertight boxes and a projecting cork gun-wale. The converted coble served as a life-boat at Bamburgh for a number of years. The first boat in the world to be designed and constructed specially as a life-boat was the *Original* built by William Greathead and launched in 1790. This double-ended boat was thirty feet in length and rose sharply at both bow and stern. The sides were cased with cork, four inches thick, to a depth of sixteen inches downwards. The thwarts, or seats, were five in number, double banked so that the boat could be rowed with ten oars. In addition there was a steering oar at each end. The boat required twelve men to work her, five men on each side rowing and one man at each end to steer, as she could be rowed either way without turning the boat.

By 1809, Greathead had built twenty-three boats for British stations and eight for use in foreign countries. By 1811, more than three hundred lives had been saved by Greathead's life-boat at the entrance to the River Tyne alone.

In 1824, the National Institution for the Preservation of Life from Shipwreck—later the Royal National Life-Boat Institution—was established in Britain. The objects of the society were 'to assist every wrecked person in the Kingdom, by such means as the establishment of life-boats and rocket mortars at all the dangerous parts of the coast, to assist in the forming of local committees at the chief ports to confer rewards in the form of medals, votes of thanks or pecuniary remuneration to all persons risking their life for the sake of others and also to encourage the invention of new and improved life-boats, belts, rocket apparatus, buoys and other means of saving life.' By the middle of the 19th century more than fifty life-boat stations had been set up in the British Isles and life-boat services had been started in Holland and the United States of America. During the next fifty years life-boat services were also established in Denmark, France, Germany, Japan, Norway, Portugal, Russia, Spain and Sweden. In Britain, and in most of the other countries, the service was entirely supported by voluntary donations and subscriptions.

Despite many experiments and trials, there was not a great deal of improvement in the design of life-boats until 1851. In that year the Duke of Northumberland became president of the British Life-Boat Institution and offered a prize of one hundred guineas for the best design for a life-boat. Two hundred and eighty models and plans were sent in for the competition, including three from Holland, two from France and one from the United States of America. The Committee judging the models awarded marks for what they considered the essential qualities of a life-boat and the prize was finally awarded to James Beeching of Great Yarmouth for his design for a self-righting life-boat, thirty-six feet long, pulled by twelve oars. Provisions for righting the boat if it capsized consisted of 2½ tons of water ballast carried in a tank placed in the bottom of the boat amidships, an iron keel weighing ten hundredweight and raised air cases at the bow and stern. Twelve tubes, with valves, through the bottom enabled the boat to be rapidly freed from water. After some modifications the Beeching design was adopted for the Institution's life-boats and the same general principles were long employed for self-righting life-boats (Ill. pp. 80, 81). A further stage in the development of the life-boat took place in 1890, following an accident to two self-righting boats in which twenty-seven out of twenty-nine of the two crews were drowned. For the life-boats in some stations the self-righting principle was abandoned and boats designed by George L. Watson came into use. The Watson life-boats were larger and more stable than the self-righting boats and were able to go a long distance out to sea. In the present century great improvements in the range, power, and efficiency of British life-boats have taken place. Some outstanding stages in this development were: the completion of the first steam life-boat in 1890; the fitting of the first petrol engine in 1904; the installation of the first diesel engine and the use of twin propellers for the smaller life-boats in 1932; the introduction in 1959 of the Oakley self-righting boat in which self-righting was achieved by transferring water automatically from a ballast tank to a righting tank and, in 1969, the adoption of the McLachlan fast rescue boat with a glass reinforced plastic hull.

For the assistance of passengers and crews in danger in ships wrecked close to the shore, the line-throwing apparatus was of great value. The purpose of the apparatus was to put a rope aboard a wrecked ship and so convey the passengers and crew to safety. The line-throwing mortar invented by Captain George Manby at the end of the 18th century remained in use in the rescue service of England and other countries for some eighty years. This mortar could throw a manilla line 293 yards in conditions of strong gale or heavy squalls. The first conception for a rocket life-saving apparatus was claimed in 1802 by a Frenchman C.-L. Ruggieri for his father, but it was an Englishman, Henry Trengrouse, who in 1807 made and used the first practical life-saving rocket. Four rocket stations were established on the coasts of the Isle of Wight in 1824, and in 1855, when the British land rescue service was taken over by the Board of Trade, the rocket life-saving apparatus was officially adopted. A rocket produced by Colonel K.M. Boxer was used for the service from 1865 and in 1878 officially replaced the old Manby mortar for English stations.

The Boxer apparatus, which used a double rocket and had a range of 375 yards, was also in use all over the world. By 1881 there were 288 rocket life-saving stations in Brit-
ain and between 1870 and 1912 these stations were responsible for saving more than 9,000 lives. The rocket carried a light line to the wrecked ship and this was then used to haul in heavier ropes on which the travelling 'breeches-buoy' — an ordinary round life-buoy to which was attached a pair of strong canvas 'breeches' — ran backwards and forwards to bring the passengers and crew one by one to the shore.

When disaster came to a ship at sea far from a life-boat station, the safety of the passengers and crew depended on the number and quality of boats carried by their ship. In the 18th and 19th centuries, on those occasions when sailing ships carried large numbers of passengers, there were never sufficient boats to accommodate all on board. In the 18th century most of the boats were carried amidships and had

The Post Office packet *Lady Hobart* sinking after striking an iceberg on June 28th 1803. The ensign is being flown upside down as a signal of distress. The crew have abandoned ship but two officers still stand at the taffrail.

The *Kent* on fire in the Bay of Biscay. Aquatint after Daniell. The *Kent,* an East Indiaman of 1,350 tons, was on her maiden voyage bound for China with a crew of 148 and nearly 500 soldiers and their wives and children. A lamp was dropped in the hold and fire broke out during a gale. Over 80 lives were lost.

to be hoisted out by tackles from the yards. Davits were introduced early in the 19th century and simplified the launching procedure. The British Merchant Shipping Act of 1854 laid down regulations governing boat accommodation for all British ships and for foreign ships carrying passengers between ports in the United Kingdom. The number of boats required was based on the tonnage of the vessel and vessels of 1,000 tons and over had to carry at least seven boats. Further regulations in 1890 required that in cargo ships boat accommodation should be sufficient for all on board and that in steamships the boats should be carried under davits

on each side of the vessel. In addition the compulsory boat accommodation for passenger and emigrant ships was increased by 50 per cent and life-belts had to be available for all persons on board. After the *Titanic* disaster in 1912, public concern brought about a further revision of the regulations in 1914, and in sea-going passenger steamers sufficient boats had to be carried for all persons on board, while the length of the steamer governed the number of sets of davits required.

An international safety convention in 1929 finally ensured that all sea-going passenger ships had sufficient boats.

V EMIGRATION UNDER SAIL

Tiburnia. A three-masted barque on a voyage to China.

Emigration — the departure of the inhabitants of one country or state to another for the purpose of residence — what hopes and fears the term must have aroused in people who, for economic, social or religious reasons decided to leave the country of their birth and settle in a distant land! Migration by sea had taken place since prehistoric times, but the tremendous flood of people, who, in the 19th century, crossed the Atlantic from Europe and Britain to settle in North America, was perhaps the greatest mass movement across the sea of all time. In the first half of the 17th century the emigration of the Puritans and their successful establishment of New England served as an example to all the peoples of Europe. Towards the end of the 17th century and during the 18th century many emigrants left Germany and settled in what is now Pennsylvania; the Dutch colonized New York; the Swedes Delaware; and the French were established in Canada and Louisiana, but the flow of emigrants was slow when compared with that at the end of the 18th century and during the 19th century. It is believed that on average about 6,000 people settled in the United States each year during the twenty years between 1790 and 1810 but in the period between 1819 and 1859 nearly 5,000,000 immigrants arrived in the United States of America from Europe. Of this number about 2,600,000 came from Great Britain and Ireland; about 1,600,000 from Germany and Austria; 200,000 from France and small contingents from Belgium, Holland, Italy, Portugal, Russia, Scandinavia and Switzerland.

Emigration to Canada, from Britain and Ireland alone, amounted to about 500,000 people in the years between 1846 and 1860. At first most of the emigration to Australia was forced and between 1793 and 1838 about 74,000 convicts were transported there. After 1837 free emigration increased and between that date and 1859 about 600,000 people took passages to Australia and New Zealand.

Until the middle of the 19th century the vast majority of emigrants were carried in sailing ships, but from 1860 onwards the sailing ship was rapidly replaced by the steamship for the emigrant trade, particularly for the Atlantic crossings. The tremendous increase in the numbers of passengers carried by sailing ships during the 19th century made legislation necessary to provide safeguards against the evils of overcrowding and the insufficient provisions sometimes carried for the sustenance of the emigrants. The British regulations of 1803 have already been described in Chapter II. In 1819, the United States Congress approved laws providing that if the master of any vessel should take on board or transport between the United States and any foreign port a greater number of passengers than two for every

5 tons of measurement, he should forfeit $150 for each passenger above that number. Children under one year of age were not counted, and two children under eight years of age were counted as one passenger. The vessel itself was forfeited if the number of passengers in excess of that allowed by law amounted to twenty. The law also required that an allowance should be made for a voyage between North America and Europe of at least 60 gallons of water, 100 lbs. of salted provisions, 1 gallon of vinegar and 100 lbs. of wholesome ship-bread for each passenger, and a proportionate amount for a shorter or longer voyage. In case the passengers were put on short allowance at any time, a payment of $3 a day for each passenger for every day of the restricted allowance had to be made. Ship captains were required to make under oath lists of passengers arriving on their vessels, designating in each list the age, sex, occu-

pation, and nationality of each passenger, and setting forth the number of deaths on the voyage.

In Britain further regulations relating to conditions on board emigrant ships came into force in 1828, 1838 and 1842, and an appreciation of the improved conditions is provided by the account of a typical emigrant ship, *St Vincent*, which was published in the *Illustrated London News* in April 1844. The *St Vincent*, of 628 tons, with accommodation for about 240 emigrants, took on board 165 emigrants at Deptford on the Thames, preparatory to sailing to Plymouth where emigrants from the western part of England would embark and would then proceed to Cork for the Irish emigrants, before starting the long voyage to Sydney in Australia. The *St Vincent*, in common with some other emigrant ships at that time, was specially fitted out for the voyage under the supervision of an agent of the Colonial Land and

'Crossing the Channel.' The deck of a paddle-steamer on a stormy day could be a very uncomfortable place; there was very little room for passengers below and those who suffered from sickness often preferred to remain on deck in spite of the elements.

The Ostend packet in a squall. Etched by Cruikshank. Published 1824. The discomfort of the diners is increased by that of the passengers in the bunks.

Emigration Commissioners. The lower or 'between' deck of the *St Vincent* was 124 feet long, 25 feet 3 inches wide amidships with a height between decks of 6 feet 4 inches. From the stern of the ship right away to the stem on the port side and back again to the stern on the starboard side the space was occupied by a double tier (one above the other) of fixed sleeping places. The bed places for two persons were each 6 feet by 3 feet and those for a single person 6 feet by 2 feet. Each bed place was divided from the one adjacent by a partition of stout planks extending from the deck below to the deck above. Pegs, on which clothes could be hung, were provided on each stanchion. The bed places for single women aft and those for single men forward were divided off by bulkheads and separated by the beds of the married couples. Water-closet latrines were provided for the women but men had to use the facilities on the upper deck. A hospital for females, at the stern, was fitted up with six beds, one of which was specially prepared for accouchements, and the hospital for men, with four beds, was forward. Along the length of the decks, between the port and starboard rows of sleeping places, tables were placed, with fixed seats on each side, and beneath which were plate-racks and battens to hold the small casks containing the daily water ration. Seats were also fixed to the ends of the bed places. Numerous scuttles admitted light and air and the bulkheads were constructed so as to allow a free circulation

Ladies' saloon on board a Hamburg-America Line ship, 1894. The elaborate furnishings and atmosphere of luxury and comfort are in sad contrast with the lot of the steerage passengers.

of the breeze from windsails arranged on the upper deck. The scale of provisions to be supplied on the *St Vincent* was described as follows:

'We now give the following statement of weekly allowance, made to each adult during the voyage: — children being victualled at one half the scale, and of course the provision is served out in proportions daily: — 4²/₃ lb. of bread, 1 lb. beef, 1¹/₂ lb. of pork, 1 lb. preserved meat, 1³/₄ lb. flour, ¹/₂ lb. raisins, 6 oz. suet, 1 pint of peas, ¹/₂ lb. of rice, ¹/₂ lb. preserved potatoes, 1 oz. tea, 1¹/₂ oz. roasted coffee, ³/₄ lb. of sugar, 6 oz. of butter, 5 gallons and 1 quart of water, 1 gill pickled cabbage, ¹/₂ gill of vinegar, 2 oz. salt. This, taken singly, is adequate food, but when united in messes (say of ten) where appetites are not equal, is certainly not bad living, and we have not heard any complaints against the respectable agents on account of the quality of the victuals

supplied. After the emigrants have arrived in the colony, they are allowed ten days free access to the ship, with all its advantages, should they not be hired or obtain employ before the expiration of that time.'

Despite the apparently reasonable facilities on the *St Vincent*, and perhaps a few other vessels, in general the conditions for emigrants during the 1830's and 1840's were appalling. The regulations laid down by successive Passenger Acts, American and British, were not enforced or were unenforceable and deaths from overcrowding and poor and insufficient food reached dreadful proportions. Unscrupulous ship-owners took advantage of the many thousands of people who wished to leave their homeland and packed them between the decks of sailing ships with sometimes three layers of bunks fitted in the height of only six feet. Often the ships were in a filthy state as the passengers

The living conditions between decks in early emigrant ships were dark, crowded, and squalid. Rats, lice, and fleas were the wretched peoples' constant companions. In bad weather the hatches were battened down so that cooking, which was done on deck, became impossible. Sanitation was primitive.

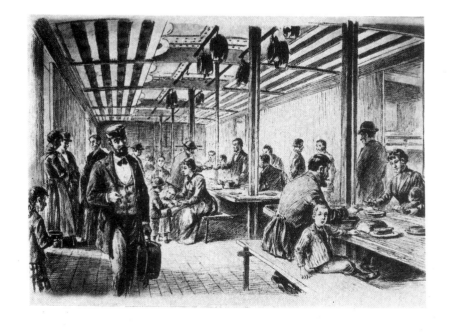

Steerage dining-saloon on a Hamburg-America Line vessel, *c.* 1894.

refused to clean the decks after meals or to use the proper places for the needs of nature. It has been said that, after a period of bad weather, when the hatchways were opened 'the steam rose and the stench was like that from a pen of pigs'. At this time the emigrants were expected to cook their own food on deck and in bad weather when this was impossible had no hot food. A social worker, Stephen de Vere, made the following report to the British Emigration Commissioners in 1847:

'...Having myself submitted to the privations of a steerage passage in an emigrant ship for nearly two months, in order to make myself acquainted with the condition of the emigrant from the beginning, I can state from experience that the present regulations for ensuring health and comparative comfort to passengers are wholly insufficient, and that they are not, and cannot be, enforced, notwithstanding the great zeal and high abilities of the Government agents.

'Before the emigrant has been a week at sea he is an altered man. How can it be otherwise? Hundreds of poor people, men, women and children, of all ages from the drivelling

Emigrants to Australia. Sadness, fear, hope, despair, and tranquillity are all depicted by the artist, who seems to have understood the human problems of those leaving their native land.

idiot of ninety to the babe just born, huddled together, without light, air, wallowing in filth, and breathing a fetid atmosphere, sick in body, dispirited in heart; the fevered patients lying between the sound, in sleeping places so narrow as to deny them the power of indulging, by a change of position, the natural restlessness of the disease; by their agonized ravings disturbing those around and predisposing them, through the effects of the imagination, to imbibe the contagion; living without food or medicine except as administered by the hand of casual charity; dying without the voice of spiritual consolation, and buried in the deep without the rites of the Church. The food is generally ill-selected, and seldom sufficiently cooked, in consequence of the insufficiency and bad construction of the cooking places. The supply of water, hardly enough for cooking and drinking, does not allow washing, in many ships the filthy beds, teeming with all abomination, are never required to be brought on deck and aired; the narrow space between the sleeping berths and the piles of boxes is never washed or scraped, but breathes up a damp and fetid stench, until the day before arrival at quarantine, when all hands are required to "scrub up", and put on a fair face for the doctor and

Children playing on deck. An awning has been erected for the comfort of passengers as the ship is evidently in the tropics.

Government inspector.'

Perhaps as a result of this report further legislation was passed in 1848 and the Colonial Land and Emigration Commissioner laid down the following rules for emigrant ships:

1. Every passenger to rise at 7 a.m. unless otherwise permitted by the surgeon.
2. Breakfast from 8–9 a.m., dinner at 1 p.m., supper at 6 p.m.
3. Passengers to be in their beds by 10 p.m.
4. Fires to be lighted by passengers' cook at 7 a.m. and kept alight by him till 7 p.m., then to be extinguished.
5. Three safety-lamps to be lit at dusk; one to be kept burning all night in main hatchway; two others may be extinguished at 10 p.m.

Passengers embarking on a Hamburg-America Line steamship. In the background can be seen a forest of masts of sailing ships. The top left-hand picture shows the steerage accommodation. Some of the passengers are obviously the worse for drink; one is brandishing a bottle.

Dancing on the deck of a pleasure steamer, c. 1825.

A first-class cabin aboard the sailing ship *Deutschland* in 1848. This was the first ship of the Hamburg-American Packet Company's fleet.

6. No naked light to be allowed at any time or on any account.

7. The passengers when dressed, to roll up their beds, to sweep the decks, including the space under the bottom of berths, and to throw the dirt overboard.

8. Breakfast not to commence till this is done.

9. The sweepers for each day to be taken in rotation from the males above 14, in the proportion of 5 for every 100 passengers.

10. Duties of the sweepers to be to clean the ladders, hospitals, and roundhouses, to sweep the decks after every meal and to dry, holystone and scrape them after breakfast.

11. The occupant of every berth to see that his own berth is well brushed out.

12. The beds to be well shaken and aired on the decks, and the bottom boards, if not fixtures, to be removed and dry scrubbed and taken on deck at least twice a week.

Passengers on the poop deck of a Peninsular & Orient Company's steamer which is passing through the Red Sea on its way to China.

13. Two days in the week to be applied by the master as washing days, but no clothes to be washed or dried between the decks.
14. The coppers and cooking vessels to be cleaned every day.
15. The scuttles and sternports, if any, to be kept open from 7 a.m. to 7 p.m., and the hatches at all hours.
16. Hospitals to be established with an area, in ships carrying 100 passengers, of not less than 48 superficial feet with 2 or 4 berths.
17. On Sunday the passengers to be mustered at 10 a.m., when they will be expected to appear in clean and decent apparel. The day to be observed as religiously as circumstances permit.

18. No spirits or gunpowder to be taken on board by any passenger.
19. No smoking allowed between decks.
20. All fighting, gambling, riotous behaviour, swearing or violent language to be at once put a stop to. Swords and other offensive weapons, as soon as passengers embark, to be placed in the custody of the Master.
21. No sailor to remain on the passenger deck among the passengers except when on duty.
22. No passenger to go to ship's cook-house without special permission of the Master.

The amount of food to be provided during the voyage was also defined by regulations. Each adult passenger had to be provided per week with 2½ lbs. of biscuits, 1 lb. of wheaten flour, 5 lbs. of oatmeal, 2 lbs. of rice. Potatoes might be given in lieu of oatmeal or rice at the rate of 5 lbs. of potatoes for 1 lb. of oatmeal or rice. In vessels sailing from Liverpool, or from Scotch or Irish ports, oatmeal might be given in equal quantities for rice. Twenty-one quarts of water had to be supplied to each passenger every week and one lb. of molasses twice a week. In 1851 an alternative scale allowed the substitution of beef, port and salt fish for breadstuffs. At the same time more stringent regulations for the protection and welfare of the emigrant was also enforced by laws passed by the United States Congress. An Act of 1847 states that the space allotted to each passenger should not be less than fourteen superficial feet on the lower deck, if the vessel

was not to pass within the tropics. If it was to pass within the tropics, twenty superficial feet were to be allowed to each passenger, or thirty feet on an 'orlop' deck. A year later, legislation compelled the proper ventilation of passenger vessels and the victualling of them so that each passenger might have on his voyage, if needful, 15 lbs. of good navy-bread, 10 lbs. of rice, 10 lbs. of oatmeal, 10 lbs. of wheaten flour, 10 lbs. of potatoes, 1 pint of vinegar, 60 gallons of fresh water, and 10 lbs. of salted pork; which was considered provision for ten weeks. The space allowed to each passenger was increased, and regulations made respecting cleanliness and good discipline.

With the stricter enforcement of these regulations and the keen competition between ship-owners to attract passengers

'Turning in' on board a yacht en route from Portsmouth to Lisbon, from the *Journal of a Landsman*. Engraved by R. Seymour and published by McLean. 1831.

94

to their particular ships, conditions gradually improved and with better accommodation and victualling, and stricter discipline on board, the sickness and deaths of emigrants during the passage became less and less. A contemporary account of the routine aboard the emigrant ship *Eagle*, owned by a Liverpool firm Gibbs & Bright, during a voyage to Australia in 1853 provides evidence of these improvements. The emigrants on board the *Eagle* were divided into messes and each mess elected two of its members as messmen for one week. The messmen drew the provisions for the week from the purser and were expected to make puddings for the mess three times a week, as well as oatmeal cakes and bread. Fresh water was served out by the third mate to every messman once a day. Each adult was allowed three pints per day

and the same amount was given to the cooks for the tea, coffee and soup for each person on board. The *Eagle* had two cooking galleys with two cooks and four assistants. Breakfast was at 8 a.m., dinner at 1 p.m. and supper at 6 p.m. The messmen carried the cooked food from the galleys to their respective messes. Each week two days were set apart for washing clothes; if the passengers had not saved up enough fresh water, or collected rain water, the clothes had to be washed in salt water. The clothes were dried by hanging them in the rigging. Each passenger had to have two suits of clothing, one for hot, and one for cold weather.

The improved conditions on emigrant ships were also reflected in a report published in the *Times* in March 1854. The report, by Train & Co. of Liverpool, states that out of

'Breakfast' on board a yacht. Another engraving from the series in *Journal of a Landsman*. The weather has become rough and the passenger does not appear to be in a fit state to eat even if the steward had not dropped the tray of food.

'The embarkation,' Waterloo docks, Liverpool, 1850. Emigrants boarding a sailing ship carrying huge boxes which probably contained their only possessions. Cooking utensils are strewn round those waiting on the quayside. Emigrants had to cook their own food on board. Bare-footed children play among the crowd.

more than 13,000 passengers carried by their vessels from Liverpool to Boston in 1853, there were only 38 deaths during the voyage, which occupied a period ranging from 24 to 48 days. The firm stated, as the result of their experience, that the health of passengers must mainly depend upon the good discipline enforced in the ship, and especially upon the maintenance of cleanliness. It is remarked that the passengers whose fares are prepaid in America are, as a class, far superior to those who in many cases emigrate as a last resource from the pressure of necessity, starting in poor condition, and without adequate strength for a voyage; and among such emigrants disease and death will wreak fright-

Mr. Hardy-Lee, his yacht. 'Mean! – Mr. Lee (to friend opposite). Come wake up Fred! and have a sardine and a glass of Porter.' Lithograph after Dr. Charles Ellery Steadman. 1857.

Emigrant ship between decks. The artist gives the impression of height whereas in fact there was very little headroom, passengers were crowded together and there was no privacy. The American Red Cross Line clipper *Dreadnought,* built in 1853, could take 200 emigrants in her 'tween decks.

ful havoc unless the police of the ship is good, the 'tween decks cleaned and fumigated, and the passengers turned out on deck at all hazards.

In America, the provisions of previous laws were partly suspended by an elaborate Act of 1855 which provided that only one passenger should be carried for every two tons of vessel, fixed the space that should be appropriated to each passenger at not less than sixteen superficial feet on the main or poop decks, or in the deck houses, and eighteen superficial feet on the lower deck—no passengers were to be carried on any other deck nor where the height or distance between the decks was less than six feet.

A hospital must be provided, berths constructed of sufficient width, and not occupied by more than two passengers. Ventilation must be secured by the erection of wooden houses or booby-hatches. Each vessel must have a sufficiently large cooking range, and an ample supply of provisions must be placed on board. Discipline and cleanliness must be maintained. The captains of vessels who failed to furnish sufficient well-cooked provisions were subject to a fine of not more than $1,000, and imprisonment for not more than one year. Money penalties could be collected for other violations of the act. A payment of $10 must be made for each death on board during the voyage. Vessels were subject to inspection and examination and lists of passengers, with designations of age, sex, occupation, nationality, and so on, had to be delivered on the arrival of the vessel.

The British Passenger Act of 1855 gave even more protection to the emigrant than the American laws just

97

described. Increased space was allowed for the passengers and their number was further limited, while the dietary scale was improved. The enforcement of these regulations afterwards became the duty of the Board of Trade and an extract of the Act had to be posted up in every emigrant ship. The Emigration Commissioners reported in 1857 that the Act was having good effects and that the regulations had added materially to the comfort and health of the passengers. Mortality in ships which sailed to Australia in 1857 with 18,758 emigrants amounted to only 62. Of 16,467 emigrants who proceeded to Boston in the first nine months of 1857 only 22 died on the voyage while among 4,939 emigrants who sailed for Philadelphia, in the same year, there were only eight deaths.

When disaster did come to sailing ships carrying emigrants there was usually great loss of life. In 1848 the sailing ship *Ocean Monarch* left Liverpool with 338 emigrants bound for Boston. A group of emigrants started a fire in a ventilator to boil a kettle. The fire spread and the efforts of the crew to fight the flames were hampered by the passengers who panicked and made it impossible for the fire fighters to overcome the flames. Although other vessels were able to rescue many of the passengers and crew the death roll was 178. On January 19th 1854 the iron sailing ship *Tayleur* left Liverpool on her maiden voyage to Australia, with a crew of 80 and 496 emigrants on board. Although the compasses had been fitted with compensating apparatus suitable for an iron vessel, they gave false readings and three days later, while sailing in a gale, under topsails, mizen topsail and foretop staysail, the *Tayleur* struck the rocks of Lambay Island off the east coast of Ireland. On January 25th the *Times* published the captain's report:

'…The shock was tremendous, shaking the vessel from stem to stern. She rose on the next wave, and drove in rather broadside on, and when she struck again, still heavier, the sea made a clean breach over her amidships, setting everything on deck afloat. After two or three more shocks the ship began to sink by the stern, and the passengers rushed up the hatchways screaming and imploring help. The ship's quarter drifted on towards one side of the creek, and one of the cook's assistants (a black man), two lascars, and three seamen, contrived to jump across on shore, and thus saved their lives. A rope and a spar were afterwards got across, and by this means a number of lives were saved, chiefly through the activity and devoted gallantry of two or three young men, passengers, whose exertions in saving the lives of their fellow-sufferers deserve the highest praise. Those who attempted to escape by the bows of the vessel, all, or nearly, met a miserable fate. The moment they fell into the water the waves caught them, and dashed them violently against the rocks, and the survivors on shore could perceive the unfortunate creatures, with their heads bruised and cut open, struggling amidst the waves, and one by one sinking under them. The surgeon of the doomed ship, Dr. Cunningham, was remarkable for his efforts in endeavouring to save first the lives of his own wife and child, and also the lives of his fellow-passengers; and it is one of the most melancholy features of the disastrous occurrence that this intrepid man lost his life in the attempt to save the lives of others. When the vessel struck, amid the dire confusion and dismay that prevailed, Surgeon Cunningham was seen everywhere trying to restore confidence and courage among the passengers and endeavouring to preserve order and coolness…'

Altogether 297 people were drowned in this disaster. The fate of the *Ocean Monarch* and the *Tayleur* are examples of a number of similar tragedies in which hundreds of emigrants lost their lives.

VI STEAM CHALLENGES SAIL

After the discovery of gold in California, American clippers carrying gold-seekers sailed westward round Cape Horn to San Francisco, then across the Pacific, in ballast, to China where cargoes of tea were taken aboard for New York and Boston. Following the repeal of the British Navigation Acts in 1848, when British ports were opened to ships of all nations, American clippers also brought tea to London.

In the early 1850's the demand for ships, particularly fast ships, brought about a very large increase in shipbuilding in America, and clippers were built which by their performances at sea won world-wide admiration (Ill. p. 129). Donald McKay, the most renowned American shipbuilder of the period, built four fine clippers at Boston in 1853–4 for the British Black Ball Line (Ill. p. 132). This shipping company, founded by James Baines of Liverpool in 1851, which had no connection with the earlier American Black Ball Line, had already become one of the leading Liverpool firms carrying emigrants from that port to Melbourne, Adelaide and Sydney in Australia. Adults were charged sixteen guineas for an 'enclosed berth' on Black Ball ships for the passage from Liverpool to Melbourne and those who only wished to make a short stay in Australia could obtain tickets at half-fares 'allowing sixty days in the colony'. The four ships built by Donald McKay for the Black Ball Line were the *Lightning*, *Champion of the Seas*, *James Baines* and *Donald McKay*. These clippers, in common with other American clippers of the period, were built almost entirely of wood and completely sheathed with copper sheets below the waterline. The *Lightning*, the most famous of the quartet,

The *Charles-Philippe* on the Seine in 1816. The first steamboat built in Paris in 1816 by Marquis Claude D.-E. d'Abban Jouffroy, the inventor. From a coloured engraving attributed to C. Dolfuss after De Lucourt, exhibited in 1951 on the occasion of the bicentenary of the birth of the Marquis.

A watercolour sketch by Baroness Hyde de Neuville of a cabin on board *L'Eurydice*, May 16th 1816. The steward is cleaning the deck under the watchful eye of the nurse, while the child in the cot plays with her doll. A bell pull hangs over the head of the bunk.

was 244 feet long, with a beam of 44 feet and was 1,468 tons register. The design of the hull proved to be most successful and the vessel is said to have had more 'hollow' at her bows than any other clipper. The following extract from a contemporary journal provides an excellent description of the *Lightning*:

'The whole height of her bulwarks is 7 feet, and she has a full topgallant forecastle, which extends to the fore-rigging; and its deck is connected with the top of a house, which is continued aft, and is 48 feet long, and 19 wide at the after-end. The top of this house is connected with the poop by two gangways, so that the men can pass forward and aft without descending into the waist. She has a full poop-deck 90 feet long, the outline of which is protected by a mahogany rail, on turned stanchions of the same wood.

'There is a spacious house over the wheel, designed, in part, for a smoking-room; and it also protects a staircase on the starboard side, which leads to the captain's state-room and the after-cabin.

'The after-cabin is 34 feet long, 12 wide, and 7 high, and is wainscoted with mahogany, enamel, polished ash, and other fancy woods, relieved with rosewood pillars, papier-

A cabin aboard *L'Eurydice* with a self-portrait. A watercolour sketch by Baroness Hyde de Neuville. 1816. The doors appear to fold across the bunk, totally enclosing the occupant. Both doors have locks and keys.

mâché cornices and flowered gilding. It has four state-rooms, two sofa-recesses and other apartments, a splendid sofa aft, rich carpeting, a circular marble table in each recess, and a mahogany extension table amidships. All the state-rooms are furnished differently, for the sake of variety, we suppose, and their furniture is of the choicest kind, arranged with consummate skill. Every state-room has a square window in the side, and a perforated ventilator between the beams; so that, for light and air, all has been done that could be desired. There are four stern windows, and a large oblong-square skylight in the after-cabin, and similar skylights over the dining-saloon, which is connected with the after-cabin. The skylights are set on mahogany frames, and nearly all the windows are of stained glass. In the recesses and partition of the after-cabin are plate-glass mirrors, which give reflected views of every part of the cabin. A more beautiful cabin, or one more richly furnished, is seldom seen.

'The dining-room, which leads from the cabin—also wainscoted—is painted pure white, like enamel, and is taste-fully relieved with gilded mouldings and flower-work. It is 48 feet long, 13 feet wide aft, and 14 forward, and has a large mahogany table its whole length, with settees along

101

The Victory, built 1818. 'View of passengers' from 'Margate pier with steam-packets,' published by John Hudson, 1821. When carrying 400 excursion passengers she collided with a collier brig on the Thames but luckily kept afloat.

View of the interior of the saloon of a paddle-steamer. A projected design by Borrodall Robert Dodd, civil engineer of Newcastle-on-Tyne. Published 1818. (Dodd built the *Victory* paddle-steamer 1818.)

its sides. It has spacious state-rooms and other apartments on each side its whole length, and these rooms are admirably designed for the accommodation of families. In richness of furniture, light and ventilation, they are equal to those of the after-cabin. At the forward partition there is a costly side-board of marble, and rising from it is a large mirror. Another mirror and sofa ornament the after part, so that

poop-deck projects about five feet and shelters the entrances to the saloon.

'The accommodation for her second-cabin passengers are in the house before the main hatchway, which has an entrance amidships, aft. It is 36 feet long, and has a passage amid-ships 5 feet wide, which leads to six state-rooms on each side, and these rooms are well lighted and ventilated, and

'Margate pier with steam-packets.' The *Victory* was built at Rotherhithe under the direction of George Dodd. The picture shows the ship from two angles; this type of double portrait was not unusual. Two cutters, probably belonging to the revenue service, are also shown.

the saloon is reflected from both ends.

'The Chief-officer's state-room is on the starboard side forward, and the pantry opposite; and between them are two doors which lead to the quarter-deck. The front of the

tastefully furnished. The forward part of this house contains the galley, and before it, on each side, are staircases which lead to the between-decks. Her crew's accommodations are under the topgallant forecastle, and are neatly fitted up.

'The between-decks are designed for the accommodation of passengers, and have ten plate-glass air-ports on each side, skylights and ventilators along the sides of the house above, so that they are well supplied with light and ventilation.

'As the top of the house projects three feet on each side, a waterproof awning will be spread from it to the rails, so as to shelter the waist, that the passengers may always have an opportunity of coming on deck without exposure to wet weather.

'Her accommodation forward and aft are upon a liberal scale, and are most admirably designed for health, comfort and safety.

'The ship herself is amply found in the best of ground tackle, has a good, substantial windlass, three capstans, a patent steering apparatus, and copper-chambered pumps; and below she has an iron water-tank of 5,000 gallons capacity.'

The accommodation for emigrants between decks, where there was headroom of eight feet, was fitted up when the vessel arrived at Liverpool.

On her maiden voyage from Boston to Liverpool the *Lightning* made a day's run of 436 miles and her first passage for the Black Ball Line, from Liverpool to Melbourne — a distance of about 14,000 nautical miles — was made in seventy-seven days. On her homeward voyage the *Lightning* completed the passage in sixty-four days, three hours and ten minutes, setting up a record which was not exceeded by other sailing vessels. The *Lightning* remained on the Australian service until 1857, when, together with other clippers, she was used to take troops to India as quickly as possible to suppress the Mutiny. After this Government service, the vessel returned to the Australian trade until she was lost by fire at Victoria, Australia, in 1869.

The competition of the large American ships which were serving so well with British companies led to an increased effort by British shipbuilders, and, encouraged by alterations in the British laws relating to tonnage measurement in 1854, fast sailing ships were built at many places in the British Isles including London, Sunderland, Liverpool and on the Clyde. The vessels built in the British yards during this period were usually smaller than the typical American-built clippers, but were able to compete in the Australian and China trades. In the 1860's many of the British shipbuilders were constructing bigger and better clippers while in America the financial crises of 1857 and the effect of the Civil War led to a decline in shipbuilding.

Thus it will be seen that the prospective passenger to America, Australia or the Far East, who could afford to pay for a cabin — and fares were by no means cheap for the period — could expect a reasonably comfortable and fast voyage in a British- or American-built sailing ship which could be expected to leave on a specified date, although the date of arrival at the destination would depend on wind, weather conditions, and the seamanship of the officers and crew.

Steam takes to the water

From early times it was man's ambition to drive his boat through the water without using his own muscles, by relying on the vagaries of the wind. In the simplest sense the mechanically propelled vessel originated when man first applied muscular power to oar or paddles. It is not possible to give an exact date for the introduction of the paddle-wheel for the propulsion of a vessel, but a bas-relief of the 6th century A.D. shows what is believed to be a Byzantine war vessel fitted with small paddle-wheels driven by three pairs of oxen. Warships with two paddle-wheels on each side, perhaps driven by man-power, are reported to have been used in China in the 8th century A.D., and in Europe fifteenth-century documents show designs for vessels driven by paddle-wheels turned by men or animals. The early steam engines worked by the pressure of the atmosphere, which was made available by condensing steam in an enclosed space, usually a cylinder. The potential value of the steam engine as a power to drive ships was soon recognized and, as early as 1690, the French physicist Denis Papin made proposals for the propulsion of a boat with paddle-wheels driven by an atmospheric engine. Twelve years later Thomas Savery writing about his steam engine said: 'It may be very useful to ships, but I dare not meddle with that matter and leave it to the judgement of those who are the best judges of maritime affairs.'

The first really successful steam engine was introduced by Thomas Newcomen, in about 1712, for use as a land-engine. It consisted of a cylinder placed above a boiler. The piston was connected to one end of an overhead oscillating beam, the other end of which carried a counter-weight. Steam was admitted to the underside of the piston; when this steam was condensed by a jet of water it produced a partial vacuum, with the result that the pressure of the atmosphere above the piston forced it down. The next step in the application of steam to marine engineering was the

Rigging plan of the *Savannah*, auxiliary paddle ship. She was the first steamer to cross the Atlantic from Savannah, Georgia, to Liverpool, in 1819. Although she took thirty-five days for the passage, she was only able to use her engines for eighteen days. After this voyage the engines were removed owing to fuel problems.

patent taken out by Jonathan Hulls in 1736 for an arrangement of a steam-propelled vessel, to be used as a tug, in which a paddle-wheel at the stern was driven by a Newcomen engine. The steam engines of that time were, however, too heavy in relation to their power for practical trials to be made. The first boat actually to be driven by steam

power was that used by J.-C. Perrier on the River Seine near Paris in 1775.

The method of passing steam under pressure into a cylinder and then cooling it by means of a jet of water was very wasteful of heat and its equivalent energy, and it was not until James Watt introduced in 1765 the separate condenser and, later, methods to prevent the loss of heat from the cylinder and other improvements, that any practical efforts in marine steam propulsion were possible.

In France, the Marquis de Jouffroy d'Abbans carried out experiments with steam propulsion, and in 1783 his vessel Rumsey of Virginia employed a form of hydraulic jet propulsion in which a steam pump was used to draw water in at the bows of a vessel and force it out at the stern. Rumsey's first experiments were with a model, but in 1785 he built a boat, which, powered by his jet principle, made a voyage

In 1807 Robert Stevens launched his paddle-steamer *Phoenix*. This vessel went from New York to Philadelphia in a gale and afterwards plied on the Delaware river for six years as a passenger ship. It is interesting to note the pile of logs on the paddle sponson.

the *Pyroscaphe* was propelled for fifteen minutes against the current of the River Saône, near Lyons, by paddle-wheels driven by a steam engine. Early experiments with marine steam propulsion were also taking place in America. James on the River Potomac. Another American, John Fitch of Pennsylvania, was conducting experiments at the same time. In 1786, he designed a vessel with six paddles on each side which were driven by a steam engine. The boat was completed in 1788 and made a voyage of about twenty miles from Philadelphia to Burlington. Two years later he started a service on the River Delaware, between Philadelphia and Bordentown with a boat fitted with a beam engine driving paddle-boards at the stern. This service was advertised in

early development of the steamboat was a Scot, Patrick Miller of Edinburgh. Miller first experimented with various vessels driven by paddle-wheels turned by manual power, but in 1787 he engaged a young engineer, William Symington, to design a steam engine for one of his vessels. The

The Dutch paddle-wheel steamer *Prinses Marianne*.

the papers but was not commercially viable, perhaps because the vessel was too small to carry an economic payload of passengers and cargo.

Another inventor who played an important part in the

engine was constructed and in 1788 fitted to one portion of a double-hulled boat and the boiler was placed in the other portion. The engine was connected by gearing to two paddle-wheels, arranged fore and aft between the two hulls.

During trials on a lake near Dumfries the boat attained a speed of five miles an hour and, in the words of a spectator, 'it answered Mr. Miller's expection fully and afforded great pleasure to the spectators present'.

After the success of his engine in Miller's boat William two loaded barges, each of 70 tons burden, were successfully towed by the *Charlotte Dundas* on the Forth and Clyde Canal for a distance of nearly twenty miles in six hours. However, it was an American, Robert Fulton, who first used a steamboat with some financial success. Fulton

Paddle-steamer *Curaçao* built of wood at Dover by J.H. & J. Duke in 1825 under the name of *Calpe*. Intended for trade between Britain and the West Indies by the American & Colonial Steam Navigation Co., she never sailed in their service, but was sold to the Dutch and became the first steamship in the Netherlands Navy.

Symington was employed from 1801 to 1803 by Lord Dundas in experiments into the possibility of employing steamboats instead of horses for towing barges on canals, and the first practical steam vessel, the *Charlotte Dundas*, was built and powered by a Symington engine. In 1802, was born in America in 1765 and came to Europe in about 1786. During the last decade of the 18th century he became very interested in the development of marine steam propulsion. After successful trials with a steamboat on the Seine, Fulton returned to America and ordered a steamboat to be built in New York. Named the *Clermont,* this paddle-steamer was 133 feet long and was powered by a 20 h.p. engine, built by Boulton and Watt in England, and shipped out to America in 1805. After trials on the River Hudson, the *Clermont* sailed from New York on August 17th 1807

In Europe, Henry Bell's *Comet* was the first steamboat employed on a regular passenger service. Encouraged by the reports of the success of steamboats in America, Bell had a vessel built at Glasgow in 1811–2 for service on the Clyde and named after the famous comet of 1811. The *Comet,*

Queen of the West, Morning Star, and another side-wheeler 'rounding a bend' on the Mississippi river, 1866. 'The parting salute.' These boats only drew about 3 feet to 4 feet when loaded. After F. F. Palmer. Published by Currier & Ives, New York.

and reached Albany, lying nearly 150 miles away, in thirty-two hours, the return voyage being made in thirty hours. Later in the year the *Clermont* was used as a packet on this route and regular services were maintained, thus definitely establishing steam navigation on a commercial basis.

built of wood, was 51 feet long, with a breadth over the paddle boxes of 15 feet. The engine of 4 nominal h.p., with a single upright cylinder, was placed on the port side of the vessel and the boiler set in brickwork on the starboard. At first experiments were made with two sets of radial paddles

The *William Fawcett*, 206 tons gross, built in 1829 by Caleb Smith and engined by Fawcett & Preston, both of Liverpool, for use on the Mersey as a ferry boat, she later became the first ship of the Peninsular & Orient Co. There is no record of her ultimate fate.

on each side, driven by a spur gear, but as this arrangement gave trouble, one paddle-wheel on each side was substituted, giving a steaming speed of about 6.7 knots. There was a single tall thin funnel, which served also as a mast and carried a yard and square sail. In the forepart of the *Comet* there was a second-class cabin, about 7 feet long, fitted with wooden benches on each side, but with only 4 feet headroom. The first-class, or 'best' cabin aft was about 9 feet long and had standing headroom throughout its length under the central deckhouse, but only sitting headroom under the side

decks. The service of the first steamer to run commercially in Europe was announced, on August 14th 1812, as follows:

The Steamboat *Comet*.
Between Glasgow, Greenock, and Helensburgh.
For Passengers only.

'The subscriber, having, at much expense, fitted up a handsome vessel to ply upon the River Clyde from Glasgow, to sail by the power of air, wind, and steam, intends that the

The arrival of royalty in Holland in the steam yacht *Lion* on July 23rd 1846.

vessel shall leave the Broomielaw on Tuesdays, Thursdays, and Saturdays about mid-day, or such an hour thereafter as many answer from the state of the tide, and to leave Greenock on Mondays, Wednesdays, and Fridays in the morning to suit the tide.

'The elegance, safety, comfort, and speed of this vessel require only to be seen to meet the approbation of the public, and the proprietor is determined to do everything in his power to merit general support.

'The terms are for the present fixed at 4/– for the best

cabin and 3/– for the second, but beyond these rates nothing is to be allowed to servants, or any person employed about the vessel.

'The subscriber continues his establishment at Helensburgh Baths, the same as for years past, and a vessel will be in readiness to convey passengers by the *Comet* from Greenock to Helensburgh.

'Passengers by the *Comet* will receive information of the hours of sailing by applying at Mr. Houston's Office,

Broomielaw, or to Mr. Thomas Blackney's, East Quay Head, Greenock.

HENRY BELL.'

some months. In 1816 the *Margery* was sold to a French firm and in March of that year became the first steam-propelled vessel to cross the English Channel. Renamed

Caricature of a German paddle-steamer. Top left: the journey takes between twenty and seventy hours; top right: for bed and all passenger comforts we give the Best, below: the quick runner (except Sundays and weekdays). There is no fare increase for passengers helping to pull the boat.

The early steamboats, by their size and capabilities, were really only suitable for inland waters and when the P.S. *Phoenix* (Ill. p. 106) made a coastal voyage from New York to Philadelphia in June 1808 it was the first occasion that a steamboat had been navigated on the open sea. A steamer service was first established on the River Thames on January 23rd 1815 with the P.S. *Margery*. This vessel had been built at Glasgow in 1814 and served on the Clyde for

Elise the paddle-steamer served for a time on the Seine, in competition with a French-built paddleboat the *Charles Philippe* (Ill. p. 99) designed by Jouffroy d'Abbans.

In America, after the success of Fulton's *Clermont*, the potential value of steamboats for communications on the west seaboards, rivers and lakes was soon realized and, by the late 1820's, large numbers of paddle-steamers were in use. The P.S. *Pocahontas* built at Baltimore in 1829 for the

112

The *Britannia* paddle-steamer, built 1840. Her dimensions were 207 length on keel, beam 34.2 feet inside the paddles and her tonnage 1,156. Her engines took up 70 feet of her length and used 38 tons of coal a day. She could only carry 225 tons of cargo.

Sail plan of *Britannia*, paddle-steamer built 1840. The first ship of the Cunard Line fleet, she was constructed of wood by R. Duncan & Co. of Glasgow. Her engines were built by R. Napier & Co. and had a nominal horse-power of over 400, capable of driving her at a speed of 8.5 knots.

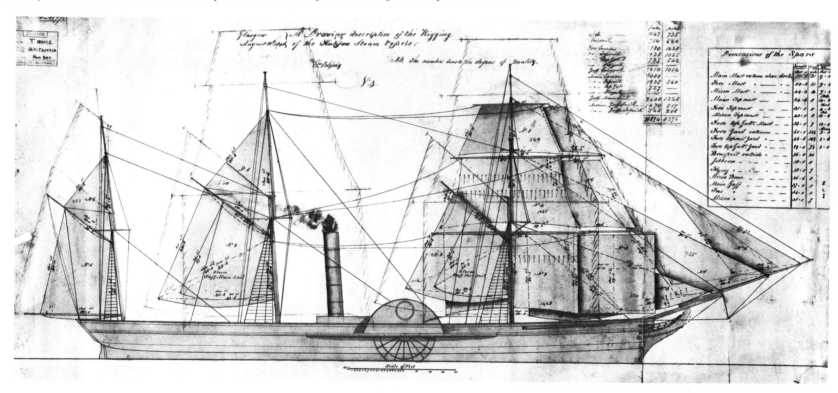

The paddle-steamer *Leipzig*, 1840, sailing between Hamburg and Magdeburg. Printed and published from a lithograph by Chs. Fuchs.

services between Baltimore, Norfolk and Richmond was an example of a typical American passenger steamer of this period. The *Pocahontas*, of 420 tons, was 138 feet 6 inches long, with an extreme width over the paddle-wheel guards of 54 feet, and a contemporary description of the vessel states:

'She is in all respects a boat of the first class, and being intended exclusively for the transportation of passengers, combines the most improved arrangements, as well on the score of elegance as comfort. . . . In her construction particular attention has been paid to strength of frame, as well as excellence and durability of materials. The principal cabin or dining room is below deck; it is a spacious, light and airy apartment, handsomely finished and furnished, and contains thirty-two commodious berths. One hundred persons may here be accommodated at table. The centre of the

A scale model of the *Britannia*, 1840. The ship in which Charles Dickens was a passenger and which he described in such unflattering terms. She had accommodation for 115 cabin passengers. She had two decks, on the upper the officers' cabins, galley, bakery, etc., and on the main deck, two dining-saloons and passengers' accommodation.

boat below is occupied by boilers and machinery, the former (of copper) having been placed below in order to ensure perfect safety in navigating the Chesapeake in rough weather. The front cabin contains twenty sleeping berths, a bar-room, dressing room, etc. The cabin appropriated for the use of ladies exclusively is an elegant apartment on the main deck. It is richly furnished and decorated, and contains twenty sleeping berths and two state rooms. An upper deck, the loftiness of which affords abundance of light and a free circulation of air to the main deck and lower cabins, extends the extreme length and width of the boat, and presents a safe and delightful promenade of the most ample dimensions. The engine is of one hundred horses' power, and is remarkable for the ease of its operation. When pro-

115

The steamship *Washington* arriving at Bremerhaven on June 19th 1847. This event seems to have created quite a sensation judging from the number of small boats crowded with sightseers. The very small paddle-steamer in the foreground is particularly interesting. Lithograph after C. J. Fedeler.

Drawing of cycloidal paddle-wheel fitted to the *Great Western,* designed by I. K. Brunel. In 1838 she crossed from Bristol to New York at an average speed of 8.2 knots. Her length was 212 feet, beam 35.3 feet, and her tonnage was 1,340. Her paddles were driven by two simple engines working with a steam pressure of 15 lbs.

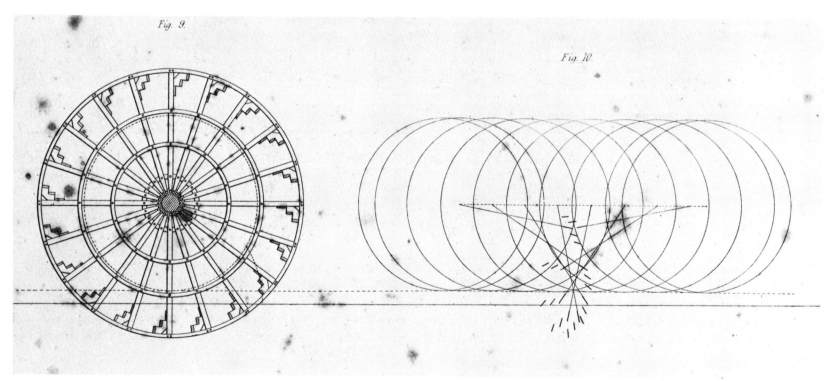

Fig. 9.

Fig. 10.

116

pelling the boat at the rate of twelve miles an hour, the motion is scarcely preceptible.'

Steam propulsion was soon established as an alternative to sail for river and coastwise traffic but ocean-going steamships were to retain a large spread of sails for many years. A steam packet service was started across the Irish Sea, in November 1817. The first steamer built in Germany was the P.S. *Prinzessin Charlotte*. This important double-hulled wooden vessel was constructed near Spandau for the Patentierte Dampfschiff Gesellschaft, fitted with an engine supplied by the British Boulton Watt Company, and launched on September 14th 1816. The *Prinzessin Charlotte*, intended

Now 'The Cunard Royal Mail Steamship *Britannia* (John Hewitt, Commander),' she was caught in the ice in Boston in February 1844. The inhabitants of that city cut a passage through the ice, 7 miles long, to enable her to reach the open water, and they refused to have the cost of the work refunded to them.

between Holyhead and Howth, in 1816, and six years later a cross-channel steamship service was established between Dover and Calais. In October 1817 the P.S. *Caledonia* crossed the North Sea to Rotterdam and then became the first steamer to sail on the River Rhine, reaching Coblenz for service on the rivers Elbe, Havel and Spree, had a large deck over the two hulls, with accommodation for passengers in each hull. The engine drove a paddle-wheel fitted between the hulls and the tall thin funnel may have carried a sail, in the same way as the earlier *Comet*.

The Mediterranean saw its first steamship the *Ferdinando Primo* in 1818. This paddle-ship built in Italy had side-lever engines of 50 nominal h.p. and a speed of about 6 knots. In a saloon forward, there was accommodation for fifty passengers and sixteen small private cabins were also provided.

Sketch of the cabin which Charles Dickens occupied on board the *Britannia* when he went to America in 1842. On this ship the first recorded stowaway in a steamer was discovered.

Steam crosses the ocean

The honour of being the first steamboat to cross an ocean goes to the American paddle-steamer *Savannah* (Ill. p. 105). This wooden ship of 320 tons, with a length of 110 feet, was built at New York in 1818 as a sail-packet, but before completion was bought by the Savannah Steamship Company and fitted with an auxiliary engine of 58 nominal h.p., with

one cylinder 40 inches in diameter by 5 feet stroke. The paddle-wheels, 15.25 feet in diameter, were so constructed that they could be folded up like a fan and taken on deck when not in use. The tall funnel was fitted with an elbow at the top, which could be turned as necessary, to direct the smoke and sparks away from the sails. The paddle-steamer left Savannah in Georgia on May 24th 1819 and arrived at Liverpool on June 20th. Although the *Savannah* was provided with staterooms with thirty-two berths, no passengers were carried on the historic voyage across the Atlantic. Her speed under sail alone was about 6 knots but on this passage the engines were only used for about eighty-five hours in all. Steam power was still so new that when the *Savannah* was seen off the coast of Ireland she was reported as a ship on fire. The *Savannah* later went to Russia, from whence she returned to New York under sail. Her engine was then removed and she was used as a coastal sail-packet until wrecked in 1821.

With the idea of speeding the mails to India, the Government of India in 1823 offered a prize of 20,000 rupees for the establishment of permanent steamship communication between England and Calcutta before the end of 1826, with the condition that the voyage should not take more than

Model of the *Great Britain*. This ship was built at Bristol in 1843 for the Great Western Steamship Co. and was the first iron vessel fitted with a screw propeller to cross the Atlantic Ocean.

The American paddle-steamer or side-wheeler, *Iron Witch*. Painted by V. Cornell, 1846. On the lower Ohio and on the Mississippi the side-wheeler was popular, on the upper Ohio and on the tributaries the stern-wheeler was preferred.

seventy days. In an attempt to win this prize the P.S. *Enterprize* left Falmouth on August 16th 1825, with seventeen passengers on board. This paddle-steamer had one flush deck with a raised poop and carried three masts fitted with fore and aft sails. The side-lever engines of 120 nominal h.p. were supplied with steam from a copper boiler. It was hoped that this copper boiler would stand up to the long service on the voyage better than an iron boiler. A very heavy load of coal was carried, much of it in iron tanks which, when emptied, could be filled with sea water to ensure that the vessel remained properly ballasted and the

paddle-wheels properly immersed. The *Enterprize* reached Capetown on October 13th and Calcutta on December 7th. The 13,700 miles from Falmouth took one hundred and thirteen days of which sixty-four were under steam. As the conditions of not more than seventy days for the voyage had not been fulfilled only half the prize money was awarded. The *Enterprize* was purchased by the Indian Government but does not appear to have been used for the mail service, and was broken up in 1838.

In the 1830's the small steamers, built for service on ensure that the vessel remained properly ballasted and the

Fair weather on the deck of a clipper ship carrying gold seekers to California in 1849. Gold was discovered in California in 1848 and in Australia in 1850. Hundreds of people rushed to stake their claims, travelling in the most appalling conditions on board clipper ships.

Gentlemen's first-class saloon on board the steamship *Deutschland*, 1848. The passengers having finished dinner are enjoying their port and cigars.

capable of making long ocean voyages. One of these small vessels, the P.S. *William Fawcett* (Ill. p. 110), built at Liverpool in 1829 for use as a ferry-boat on the River Mersey, was later placed on the Belfast, Dublin and London service of the Dublin and London Steam Packet Company. In 1837 the *William Fawcett* was purchased by the newly formed Peninsular Steam Navigation Company in connection with their contract mail service between Falmouth and Gibraltar, and used on the Madeira run. The *William Fawcett*, of 206 tons, was 87 feet long and only had accommodation for twelve passengers, in cabins and a saloon, under the raised quarter-deck. The vessel was rigged with two masts; the

The *Hamburg* – like the *Leipzig* – belonged to the River Steamers Company, Hamburg. Lithograph 1839. They were powered by 60-h.p. engines and were said to have been beautifully decorated and to have had a piano and other musical instruments, a library, newspapers, and games for use of passengers.

The Lloyd Triestino paddle-steamship *Africa*, 1849. This ship was employed on the Mediterranean and Orient service.

foremast carried three square sails and the mainmast a gaff sail. In fair weather the engines of 60 nominal h.p. gave a speed of about 8 knots. In 1840 the name of the company was altered to the Peninsular and Oriental Steam Navigation Company — now the familiar P. & O. Line — and the service extended first to Alexandria and later to India, China, Japan and Australia. The service which began on September 1st 1840 was announced as 'Steam conveyance from London and Falmouth to Vigo, Oporto, Lisbon, Cadiz, Gibraltar, Malta, Greece, the Ionian Islands, Egypt and India'. Five paddle-steamers were employed, leaving London every Friday, and Falmouth every Monday, with the

mail for Portugal, Spain and Gibraltar. The Company's ships ran every alternate week from Gibraltar to Malta and from Malta to Corfu. The vessels from Malta to Alexandria ran once a month, to connect with a line of steam communication through the Red Sea to India. It was, of course, necessary for passengers for India to travel overland from Alexandria to the Red Sea port. The average time in which the steam vessels made the passage was: from Falmouth to

After the historic voyage of the P.S. *Savannah* in 1819, the Atlantic was crossed, eastward and westward, by a number of steamers — British, Canadian, French and Dutch — but on each occasion only part of the passage was under steam. The first vessel to cross to America under continuous steam power was the P.S. *Sirius*. Built of wood in 1837 and intended for the packet service between London and Cork, in Ireland, the *Sirius* was chartered by the newly formed

Screw steam packet ship *Labrador* belonging to the Compagnie Générale Transatlantique, 1860. This longitudinal section gives a very clear impression of the way in which the ship was divided into passenger accommodation, cargo, including horses, crew space, and engines, fuel and boilers.

Lisbon, 84 hours; to Gibraltar, including 24 hours stay at Lisbon and 6 hours at Cadiz, 7 days. The passage from Gibraltar to Malta took about 5 days and from Malta to Alexandria about 4 days. The first class fare from London to Gibraltar was £18.

◄ Midship section of *La Champagne*, 1886, showing the engines.

British and American Steam Navigation Company because their own vessel, the P.S. *British Queen* would not have been ready in time to compete with the P.S. *Great Western* owned by a rival company. The *Sirius*, of 703 tons, was 208 feet long and propelled by side-lever engines of 320 nominal h.p. She was the first steamer on the Atlantic crossing to be fitted with surface condensers, which enabled her boilers to be supplied with fresh water and thus avoid the frequent engine stops necessary when salt water was used so that the accu-

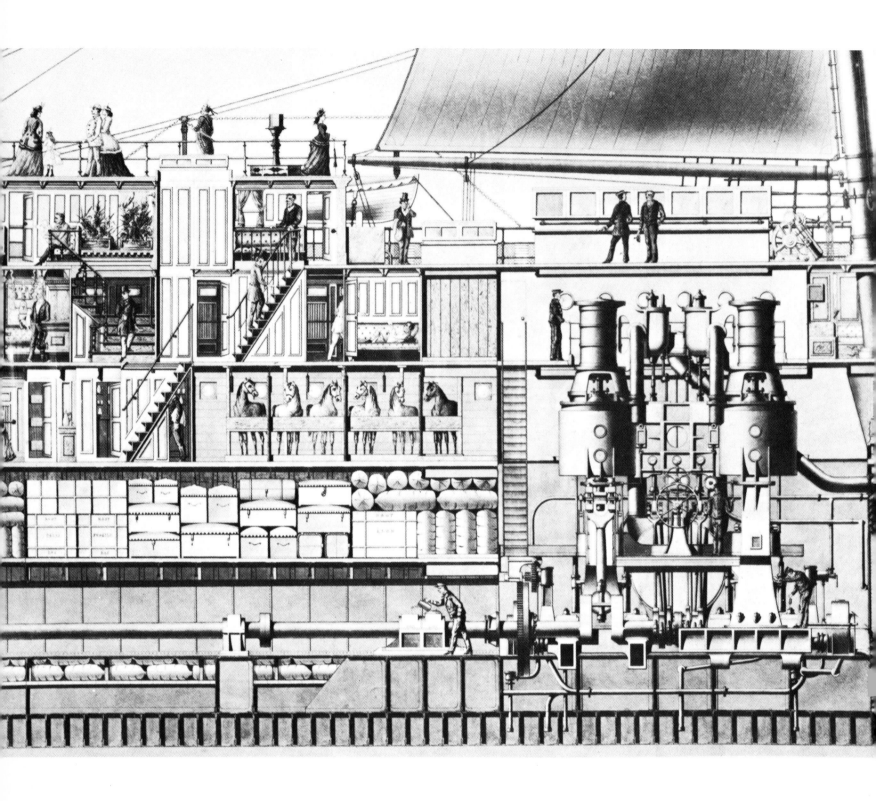

A close-up view of the midship of the screw steam-packet ship *Labrador* showing engineers and greasers at work and passengers enjoying their enforced leisure.

Another view of the interior of the steam packet *Labrador* showing the forecastle with some of the crew resting in their hammocks. A little further aft can be seen the bunks of the second-class passengers. Cargo is stowed in the hold and huge coiled hawsers in the bows.

mulated salt could be cleared from the boilers. The *Sirius* left Cork harbour, with forty passengers, on April 4th 1838 reaching New York in eighteen days, ten hours at an average speed of 6.7 knots. Her arrival caused great excitement in New York and the newspapers gave great prominence to the event. One announcement stated: 'Nothing is talked of in New York but about this *Sirius*. She is the first steam vessel that has arrived here from England, and a glorious boat she is. Every merchant in New York went on board her yester-

day.' Another newspaper commented: 'Yet certainly to the *Sirius*, to her gallant Commander and gallant crew, was reserved the fame of first shooting boldly from Europe over the broad Atlantic in defiance of winds and waves, and first bringing into our city the flag of Great Britain upborne on the masts of a steamship.'

Before 1838, the steam vessels employed for the Atlantic crossings had been built for use in coastal waters or the narrow seas, but the *Great Western*, launched in 1837, was

Darien, a paddle-steamer belonging to the Compagnie Générale Transatlantique, was built in Hartlepool by Pile Spence & Co. in 1866. In 1870, the first year of the Franco-Prussian war, the company transported 15,000 soldiers to ports in north-west France, but the *Darien* was lost in this year when she went aground.

An agency poster advertising the Services Maritimes des Messageries Nationales packet boat *Périclès*, 1859.

constructed specially for the Atlantic Ferry service. This paddle-steamer was designed by the great engineer Isambard Kingdom Brunel for the Great Western Steamship Company, and built at Bristol. The hull, 236 feet long, was constructed with very heavy frames and internal bracing of iron and wood trusses, giving great longitudinal strength. The paddle-wheels, 28¾ feet in diameter, were of the cycloidal form (Ill. p. 116) and were driven by side-lever engines of 450 nominal h.p.

As could be expected, special attention was given to the passenger accommodation, and the saloon, 75 feet long, 21 feet wide, and 9 feet high, was said to have been the largest and most luxurious room in any vessel of the period. The decorations included panels painted by the artist Edward Thomas Parris R.A., and large pier-glasses fitted in richly ornamented frames in imitation of Dresden china. The prevailing colour of the apartment was a light flesh or salmon colour, with richly gilded ornaments and decorations. A

127

Poster advertising the clipper ship *Fearless* of 1,700 tons, built in 1853. She sailed from Manila to Boston in 86 days, arriving on May 21st 1855.

small apartment at one end of the saloon was fitted up with sofas and draperies as a withdrawing room exclusively for the use of lady passengers. The cabins on each side, communicating with the saloon, each contained two sleeping berths, so arranged that in the daytime they could be turned

Poster advertising the clipper ship *California*, built by Samuel Hall of East Boston. Hall was a prominent shipbuilder of the 1850's.

up against the side of the vessel and conceal the bedding, thereby forming a small sitting-room 7 feet by 8 feet. The *Great Western* could accommodate one hundred and twenty first-class passengers, twenty second-class and if necessary berths for a further one hundred could be provided, but when the steamer left for her maiden voyage on April 8th 1838 there were only seven passengers aboard, including one lady. After a passage of fifteen days, five hours, at a mean speed of 8.8 knots, the steamer arrived in New York harbour on April 23rd. The arrival only three and half hours after the *Sirius* showed that steam was really practicable for the Atlantic, for the *Great Western* had more than forty tons of coal left while the smaller *Sirius* had to burn spare spars and other woodwork, and refuel at Sandy Hook. On the return voyage the *Great Western* carried 68 cabin passengers, 5,500 letters and 1,760 newspapers. She continued on the Atlantic service until 1846. In 1847 she was sold to the Royal Mail Steam Packet Company and for ten years ran between Southampton and the West Indies.

The term 'liner' could for the first time be applied to a transatlantic steamship in 1840, when the British and North American Royal Mail Steam Packet Company, later the famous Cunard Steamship Company, used four sister-ships, the paddle-steamers *Britannia*, *Acadia*, *Caledonia* and *Columbia*, to establish a monthly mail service from Liverpool to Halifax and Boston, subsidized by the British Government. The *Britannia* (Ill. p. 113, 115), the first of the quar-

The clipper ship *Empress of the Seas*, 1853–64. One of the many ships built by Donald McKay at East Boston. Painted by F. Todgeg.

tet to go into service, was built of wood at Greenock and launched on February 5th 1840. She was a three-masted vessel, with two decks, propelled by side-lever engines of 440 nominal h.p. giving a service speed of about 8½ knots.

The *Britannia* left Liverpool for her first crossing of the Atlantic on July 4th 1840. A contemporary newspaper account states that 'the fine vessel is so large that it was necessary to swing her out into mid-stream and place her passengers aboard from a tender owing to her immense size.' She arrived at Halifax in eleven days, four hours, and com-

pleted her run to Boston in fourteen days, eight hours. The return crossing was made in a little over ten days; the best steaming was 280 miles in one day.

The *Britannia* had accommodation for one hundred and fifteen passengers, with a dining saloon and cabins on the lower deck. This accomodation (Ill. p. 118) was described in advertisements in the usual glowing terms but one passenger had a very different opinion. The famous author, Charles Dickens, who crossed the Atlantic in the *Britannia* in 1842, states in his *American Notes:*

129

STAR LINE
FOR
JAPAN !

THE A. I. CLIPPER BRIG
" LEVERET, "
R. N. WARNER, Esq., Commander,
Having part of her Freight and Passengers engaged, will
leave for the port of
HAKODADI,
ON OR ABOUT THE 15TH INST.
For Freight or Passage, apply to
SWAN & CLIFFORD.
Honolulu, March 1, 1855.

Graham & Morton Transportation Co.

St. Joseph and Benton Harbor Division. The elegant side wheel steamers **City of Chicago** and **City of Milwaukee,** with the **Screw Steamer Soo City,** keep this division open the entire year, excepting January and February, making three trips daily between **Chicago, St. Joseph and Benton Harbor,** during June, July and August. Excursion fare $1.00 Round trip. Close connections are made at St. Joseph with the Pere Marquette Railway, Indiana, Illinois and Iowa Railway, at Benton Harbor with the "Big Four" and Milwaukee, Benton Harbor and Columbus Railway.

Holland Division. Navigation is open during the entire season on this division excepting January, February and March. The elegant **Screw Steamers, Puritan** and **Argo,** make two trips daily during July and August. Close connections are made with the Pere Marquette Railway for Grand Rapids and all northern and eastern Michigan and also with the Inter Urban Electric Railway for Saugatuck and other points reached by them. Lake tickets can be secured from all railroad agents. Freight and passenger rates lower than all rail.

J. S. MORTON, SECRETARY.　　　　J. H. GRAHAM, PRESIDENT.
CHAS. B. HOPPER, Pass'r and Freight Traffic Manager.
Dock--Chicago, foot of Wabash Avenue.　　　Telephone, 2162 Central.

Poster advertising the 'clipper brig' *Leveret* of the Star Line. The ship depicted on the poster is not a brig, but appears more like a ship of war.

Graham & Morton Transportation Co. poster advertising their fleet of paddle- and screw-steamers which they appear to have run at competitive fares.

'Before descending into the bowels of the ship, we had passed from the deck into a long and narrow apartment, not unlike a gigantic hearse with windows in the sides; having at the upper end a melancholy stove, at which three or four chilly stewards were warming their hands; while on either side, extending down its whole dreary length, was a long, long, table; over which a rack, fixed to the low roof, and stuck full of drinking-glasses and cruet-stands, hinted dismally at rolling seas and heavy weather.'

The following advertisement, from the *Times* of May 25th 1842, provides further information about this early transatlantic steam service: 'Steam from Liverpool to Boston, calling at Halifax to land Her Majesty's mail and passengers. The British and North American Royal Mail Steamships will leave Liverpool twice every month as under:

Britannia	Capt. J. Hewitt	Sat. June 4th
Caledonia	Capt. E. G. Lott	Sun. June 19th

Stage coaches are established between Halifax and Picton, and Quebec, in connection with the above vessels carrying the mails and passengers for Canada. The above steamers will take a few tons of measurement goods on freight for Boston, if shipped three days before the time of sailing.

'Passage including provisions, to Halifax and Boston 38 guineas, but without wines or liquors which can be obtained on board. Steward's fee one guinea. Dogs charged £5 each. All letters and newspapers intended to be sent by these vessels must pass thro' the post office. Passengers will be charged freight on their personal luggages when it exceeds half a ton measurement.'

A cartoon lithographed and published by N. Currier in 1849 entitled 'The way they come from California' which suggests that although gold was plentiful, food and berths on board ships could not be so easily come by.

The *Britannia* completed forty Atlantic crossings before being sold to the German Government in 1849.

In the 1840's the great proportion of passengers—the emigrants—still crossed the Atlantic in sailing packets, although wooden paddle-steamers, by making regular and fast passages between England and New York, proved the reliability and advantages of the steam engine for ships making ocean voyages. The desire to win some of the valuable passenger trade from the sailing packets led to a decision by the directors of the Great Western Steamship Company to allow their chief engineer Isambard K. Brunel to design a steamship, which was to be the first ocean vessel

Alexandre Dumas leaving the port of Marseilles on board the yacht *Monte Cristo* on May 9th 1860. After a sketch by M. Crapelet.

BLACK BALL LINE

OF

BRITISH & AUSTRALIAN EX-ROYAL MAIL PACKETS,

With branches to Tasmania and New Zealand.

Parties desirous of forwarding Letters and Newspapers by these Clippers, must send them through the Post, marked *per "Black Ball Line,"* via *Liverpool.* Newspapers require to have a Penny Postage Stamp attached, but payment of Letters is optional, except to New Zealand, for which Colony they must be paid in advance.

This Line since its establishment has conveyed more passengers to Australia than any other in the Kingdom, and made the Quickest Passages on record, namely—'Lightning' from Melbourne 12 days less, and the 'James Baines' to Melbourne 8 days less than any other Ship in the world.

FROM		FROM	
LIVERPOOL TO MELBOURNE.		MELBOURNE TO LIVERPOOL.	
JAMES BAINES	63 days.	LIGHTNING	63 days.
LIGHTNING	69	JAMES BAINES	69
OCEAN CHIEF	72	MARCO POLO	75
Champion of the Seas	73	OCEAN CHIEF	76
MARCO POLO	74	INDIAN QUEEN	79
INDIAN QUEEN	79	Champion of the Seas	85

The "BLACK BALL" is the only regularly Established Line of Clippers sailing between

LIVERPOOL & MELBOURNE,

On the 5th of EACH MONTH.

FORWARDING PASSENGERS BY STEAM, AT SHIP'S EXPENSE, TO ALL PARTS OF

AUSTRALIA, TASMANIA, AND NEW ZEALAND.

Carries full Bands of Music, as well as Chess, Backgammon, and Draught Boards for the Amusement of the Passengers.

Vessels.	Tons.	Captains.	Vessels.	Tons.	Captains.	Vessels.	Tons.	Captains.
JAMES BAINES,	3000	M'Donnell.	MARCO POLO,	3000	Clarke.	GREAT TASMANIA,	3500	Brewer.
LIGHTNING,	3500	Enright.	DONALD M'KAY,	3000	Warner.	CONWAY	2000	Duguid.
SALDANHA,	3000	Watts.	OLIVER LANG,	2300	Murdle.	FORTUNE,	1200	Sandford.
OCEAN CHIEF,	2500	Tobin.	MONTMORENCY,	1200	Kiddle.	SWITZERLAND,	2000	Doherty.
TUDOR,	3000	Anderson.	Commodore PERRY,	3500	Webb.	DAVID M'IVER,	2500	Bailie.
JOSEPH TARRATT,	2300	Hamer.	AMERICA,	1500	Foote.	JOHN & LUCY	2000	Miller.
Champion of the Seas	4500	M'Kirdy.	INDIAN QUEEN,	2500	Joines.	VOCALIST,	2500	Gardyne.
WAVERLEY	1400	Rose.	ALMA,	2000	Ross.	PANAMA,	1400	M'Donald.

AND OTHER FIRST CLASS VESSELS.

The above Line is composed of the LARGEST, the FINEST, and FASTEST MERCHANT SHIPS IN THE WORLD, and have been built by the most celebrated Builders of the day, including M'Kay of Boston, and Hall of Aberdeen. They are commanded by men who have already rendered themselves famous; and their equipments and accommodations are unequalled by any Line of Ships afloat. The Provisioning is of the best quality, and is supplied under the inspection of Her Majesty's Emigration Officer. Each Vessel carries an experienced Surgeon, whose diploma is approved of by the Government Medical Inspector.

Agents in Melbourne, MACKAY, BAINES & CO., Hall of Commerce.

LOADING IN COBURG DOCK,

Extra Packet for the 12th JANUARY,

THE BEAUTIFUL ENGLISH-BUILT CLIPPER

WAVERLEY,

Captain ROSE, 730 Tons Register, 1400 Tons Burthen.

This fine Ship is classed A 1 at Lloyd's for 12 years, and is one of the fastest ships afloat, having made the passage out to Sydney in 76 days. The accommodation for all classes of Passengers are most excellent, combining convenience, space and ventilation. Passengers' Luggage will be received at the Company's Depot, Coburg Dock, on the 10th January, and all Passengers must be on board by 9 o'clock on the morning of the 12th, to pass the Government Inspector, otherwise they cannot proceed in the ship.

For further particulars, &c., apply to ☞ *For Rates of Passage, &c., see other side.*

JAMES BAINES & Co.,

6. COOK STREET. LIVERPOOL.

1855.—During this year 21 "Black Ball" Clippers, of the aggregate tonnage of 31,453 tons, sailed from Liverpool for Australia, carrying 9624 Passengers.

1854.—During this year 25 "Black Ball" Clippers, of the aggregate tonnage of 37,014 tons, sailed from Liverpool for Australia, carrying 8959 Passengers.

Poster advertising the famous Black Ball Line, 1854. This line was founded by James Baines of Liverpool in 1816. They became the owners of many famous ships.

Drawing of a Western Ocean packet ship (Black Ball Line) by John Leavitt. 1854.

built of iron and the first screw-propelled iron vessel to cross the Atlantic. The *Great Britain* (Ill. p. 118) was built at Bristol and launched in July 1843. The hull, with iron framing, bulkheads and plating, was 322 feet long. Five transverse bulkheads divided the hull into six watertight compartments. The original engines of 1,000 nominal h.p. had four inclined cylinders each having a diameter of 88 inches with a stroke of 6 feet, working upwards on to the crankshaft from which the motion was taken down to the propeller shaft by four sets of flat pitch chains. A six-bladed pro-

Dinner plate as used on board the clipper ship *Dreadnought*, built in 1853 for the American Red Cross Line. She was one of the fastest of all sailing ships.

The P & O steamship *Himalaya*, built in 1853 by Mare & Co. at Blackwall. She was designed as a paddler but was altered to screw on the stocks. The largest merchant vessel of her time (3,438 tons gross). During the Crimean War she was chartered for trooping. The *Himalaya* was converted to a coal hulk in 1920 and finally sunk by a bomb during an air raid in June 1940.

peller was fitted and on trials the vessel attained a speed of 11 knots. The six masts were rigged with wire rope. The mainmast carried square sails and was stepped on the keel but the other masts, hinged at the deck, carried fore and aft sails.

The following description of the passenger accommodation appears in a special supplement to the *Liverpool Standard* published on July 1st 1845: 'The *Great Britain* has 26 state rooms with one bed each, and 113 with two, so that in addition to her crew, officers, firemen, etc., she can accommodate 252 passengers, each of whom can be provided with a single bed, and that without making up a single sofa, or any other temporary convenience.

'The walls of the after or principal promenade saloon are painted in delicate tints; and along the sides are several fixed chairs of oak. A row of well-proportioned pillars, which range down the centre of the promenade, serve the double purpose of ornament to the room and support to the deck. In this saloon, on either side, is a range of exceedingly comfortable state-rooms and sleeping berths. About twelve of with the deck is of iron. The stairs are far more wide and commodious than is generally met with on ship-board. From this promenade you descend into the main or dining saloon, which is 98 feet 6 inches long, by 30 feet wide. This is a really beautiful room. A large sum of money has not been uselessly squandered in procuring for it gaudy decorations, not harmonising with its uses, but its fittings are alike chaste and elegant.

'Down the centre are twelve principal columns of white and gold, with ornamental capitals of great beauty. Twelve similar columns also range down the walls on either side. Between these latter and the entrances to the sleeping berths are (on each side of the deck) eight pilasters, in the Arabesque style (of which character the saloon generally par-

The American paddle-steamer *Adriatic*, 1855. Owned by Edward K. Collins, she once ran from St. Johns, Newfoundland, to Galway, Ireland, in 5 days, 19 hours, forty-five minutes. After a sketch by M. Barbin.

The ladies' saloon on board the *Great Eastern* during a storm in September 1861. A large mirror has been smashed and a cow appears to be plunging through the deck light.

these on each side of the deck will be reserved for ladies, as they are made to communicate with two commodious ladies' boudoirs, or private sitting rooms, measuring 17 feet by 14 feet. The advantages of this arrangement must be obvious, as ladies who may be indisposed, or in negligee, will be enabled to reach their sleeping berths without there being the slightest necessity for their appearing in public. The framework of the staircases communicating from the saloon

takes), beautifully painted with oriental birds and flowers. On either side are seven doors, which open into as many passages, each of which communicates with four bedrooms. The archways of the several doors are tastefully carved and gilded, and are surmounted with neat medallion heads. Some looking glasses are so arranged as to reflect the saloon lengthways at two opposite sides, from which a very pleas-

Preparations for launching the *Great Eastern*, 1857. Unfortunately she stuck fast on the launching ways and it took about three months to get her afloat.

The *Great Eastern* off Holyhead. Lithograph by McGuire. Published by Read, 1859. Designed by Isambard Brunel and John Scott Russel, she was laid down at Scott Russel's yard at Milwall on the Thames and was 692 feet long, 83 feet beam, and her tonnage according to builders' measurements at that time was 22,500.

ing illusion is produced. The walls of this apartment are of a delicate lemon tinted drab hue, relieved with blue, white, and gold. At the stern-end are a number of sofas, which range one above the other, nearly up to the stern lights. At the opposite extremity is a large room for the steward's use. The saloon is fitted with rows of dining tables, of sufficient capacity to admit of 360 passengers sitting down to dinner at one time, with perfect convenience and comfort. On each side of the forward promenade saloon there are 36 berths, or sleeping places, and in the saloon below it 30 on each side,

making in all, forward 132. To the state rooms there are passages leading from the saloons, and running athwart the ship.'

The *Great Britain* left Liverpool for New York on July 26th 1845 with sixty passengers and over six hundred tons of cargo. The crossing took fourteen days, twenty-one hours at a mean speed of 9.3 knots. Her fifth voyage to America ended in 1846 when she went aground on the coast of Ireland. She remained on the beach through the winter but was refloated in 1847 and taken to Liverpool. After repairs,

The paddle-steamer *Spirit of the Age, c.* 1860. A proposed design for the Trans-Atlantic Express Steam Packet Company to be built under the patents of Messrs. Silver & Moore. The vessel was to have been of great length in comparison with her beam and have very little freeboard, though she was never actually built. Lithograph by T.G. Dutton.

Design for the interior decoration of the Royal saloon on board the *Great Eastern*.

the vessel was refitted with geared engines having two oscillating cylinders and a three-bladed propeller.

On August 21st 1852 the *Great Britain* started her first voyage to Australia, with six hundred and thirty passengers. The following extracts are from the diary of an after-saloon passenger on this voyage:

'Liverpool Aug. 21 — At 4 p.m. the last steamer left us, no service; the crew too busy to attend. Saloon crammed. At 9 p.m. service again. At 11 p.m. went over the ship. Thermometer as low in second cabins as in my own berth. The Captain has a great deal of tact with his passengers, his manner and arrangements on Sunday made a great impression on us all.

The Prince Napoleon and Princess Clotilde about to embark on the *Jérôme-Napoléon* at Marseilles in 1862. Engraved after J. Gailoreau.

The launch of the paddle packet-boat *L'Impératrice-Eugénie* belonging to La Compagnie Transatlantique at Saint-Nazaire. She was the first ship to go to China via the Suez Canal (1869). After a sketch by M. Duclos.

'Aug. 23 — J. Clark, a second-cabin passenger, reports he is robbed of 35 l. At night, singing and dancing on deck.

'Aug. 24 — Clark finds his money. Passengers wanted to duck him; Matthews interfered. Passengers deposit several sums of money with Cox.

'Aug. 25 — After-saloon passengers pleased with fare. Whilst music, Shakespeare readings, chess, draughts in saloons, dancing and singing. In the fore-saloon there are many passengers who seem well able to pay for after-saloon berths; I think they seem to expect more than they ought to get for what they pay — 44 l. 11 p.m. — the second cabins same temperature as after-saloon.

'Aug. 26 — Steaming ten miles per hour.

'The Postal Agent,' Messageries Maritimes. Sketch by Patrick Demanceau.

'Aug. 27—Disconnected screw, but it takes a ten knot sailing breeze to beat the engines.

'Aug. 28—Weather warmer. Thermometer—aft saloon berths, 76 deg; midship, 81 deg; fore saloon, 72 deg; second cabin forward, 75 deg; aft, 80deg.

'Aug. 29 (Sunday)—Passed Palma, distance about four miles. At 1 a.m. a squall, and bright moon.

'Aug. 30—Weather hot, and all less inclined to do anything.

At 11 o'clock p.m. thermometer in aft-saloon, 80 deg; fore saloon, 80 deg; second cabin aft, 79 deg; forward, 82 deg. The notices on the mainmast were as follows:

"By permission from Capt. M. a Sunday school for children will be commenced next Sunday Aug. 29; hours, 3 to half past 4. Parents are invited to send their children, and the assistance of ladies as teachers is requested." "Found, at 4 p.m. a silver watch, apply to Chief Officer." "Divine service will commence at 10.30 a.m.; all passengers are requested to attend. The Secretary has prevailed upon the following gentlemen to take the management of the readings

The iron floating bridge *Alexandra*. This Portsmouth and Gosport ferry was built by Lewis & Stockwell, iron shipbuilders of London, and engined by James Watt & Co., Birmingham, in 1864. She was designed by F.H. Trevethick and was still in service in the 1930's.

from Scott, Dickens, Shakespeare, etc., and trusts the passengers will give them their cordial support (names, etc.).''

'Sept. 1 — Stewards have hard work, 2,040 plates have to be washed, 2,720 cups and saucers, 900 knives, 900 forks, etc.

'Sept. 6 — (Sunday) — Service at 10.30 and at 8 p.m. saloon crowded.

'Sept. 7 — Was asked to dine in fore saloon by a passenger;

'Sept. 16 — Blowing fresh. All very much excited about a ball and concert to be given today, wind increased, and night rough and stormy.

'Sept. 17 — Wind ahead, blowing hard, S.E. heavy sea on, ship rolling and pitching very much, one of the sails forward blown away.

'Sept. 18 — Blowing hard, and heavy sea on, no one could sleep, very heavy seas continually striking the vessel. Capt.

The Brazilian paddle-steamer *Presidente*, built in 1864 by John Maylor & Co. at Rio de Janeiro. She was wrecked in South American waters in 1883. Lithograph after T.G. Dutton.

had a capital dinner. At 9 p.m. Neptune and his satellites came on board, and shaved all the new ship's company and myself.

'Sept. 14 — Jews, thirteen on board, hold a synagogue in officers' mess room.

Matthews put the ship round for St. Helena to take in more coal.

'Sept. 19 — Sunday Service at 10.30 and 8 p.m.

'Sept. 20 and 21 — Going before the wind, expect to be at

St. Helena by Wednesday night; all comfortable. The detention will be a greater loss to the owners than ourselves.

'Sept. 22 — Rushing before the wind, fresh from S.E. and occasionally v. squally.

as comfortably through the latter as we have through the former part of her journey; indeed, there has been no grumbling on board, with the exception of some of the fore-saloon passengers, which, however, was of no moment, and was at once put to rights by the Capt. or first officer, I forget which,

The *Allemania*, built for the Hamburg-America Steam Packet Co. in 1856 by C. A. Day & Co., of the Northam Ironworks, Southampton. She was on mail service until 1883 when she was sold to W. Hunter of Liverpool and renamed *Oxenholme*. She was sold again in 1894 and abandoned at sea in that year.

'Sept. 23 (Wednesday) — Blowing very fresh, ship going eight knots with screw disconnected. At 10 p.m. connected the screws again....

'The *Sydney* put into Ascension short of coal and proceeded, and we hope to follow her, and trust we shall get on

but I must say the stewards were very green at first and waited very badly, but are better now.

'I believe that had the consumption of coal been a 150 tons less, which I suppose, it would have been but for these confounded head winds, or had we had a change of a fair wind and been able to set out sails, I should now have been writing from the Cape, instead of from St. Helena, for we went along famously when we had a wind, and, curiously enough, hardly any person on board was seasick, the motion was so easy.'

Except for breaks for troop-carrying service, the *Great Britain* continued on the Australian route for many years. In 1882, her engines were removed and she was converted into a sailing ship. From 1887 until 1937 she was used as a coal hulk at Port Stanley in the Falkland Islands but was then beached at Sparrow Cove, Port William. In April 1970 the *Great Britain* was repaired and refloated. A pontoon was submerged and when the *Great Britain* had been positioned above it, the water was pumped out and it rose to the surface thus lifting the former steamer out of the water. The pontoon carrying the *Great Britain* was then towed the short distance to Port Stanley and prepared for the tow of some 7,600 miles across the South Atlantic to Bristol. The pon-

On the bridge of a ship of the Hamburg-America Line, *c.* 1894. The binnacle, engine-room, telegraph, and other instruments are on the open deck.

toon arrived at Avonmouth on June 23rd, the *Great Britain* was refloated, towed up the River Avon to Bristol and on July 19th entered a dry dock. Work is now in progress to restore enough of the ship to its original appearance in 1843 to enable the visitor to visualize what life was like on this famous Victorian liner.

About ten years after he designed the *Great Britain*, Isambard Kingdom Brunel suggested to the Eastern Navigation Company that a steamship five or six times the size of any existing vessel be built for their Indian and Australian trade. It was known that large vessels were specially suitable for long voyages and it was estimated that a vessel of the dimensions proposed would be able to maintain a speed of 15 knots with less power per ton than ordinary ships of the period. The great size would also allow better passenger accommodation and cargo capacity, with an ability to carry enough fuel to make calls at coaling stations unnecessary. So the *Great Eastern* (Ill. p. 135) was built, 692 feet long with a breadth of 82.7 feet and, for thirty years, remained the largest vessel afloat; indeed it was not until 1899 that her dimensions were exceeded.

The keel of this huge vessel was laid down in 1854 at Milwall on the River Thames and after delays, the *Great Eastern* was finally afloat on January 31st 1858. The construction of the vessel was undoubtedly a triumph for nineteenth-century British shipbuilders. From the keel to the waterline, the hull was double, while the deck was also cellular, factors which contributed to the longitudinal strength of the hull. The safety of the ship was increased by transverse bulkheads dividing the hull into watertight compartments. The *Great Eastern* was also unique in that she was propelled both by paddle-wheels and a screw propeller. In addition the six masts could carry 6,500 square yards of sail. There were cabins for eight hundred first-class, two thousand second-class and one thousand two hundred third-class passengers. It has been said that the accommodation (Ill. pp. 134 and 136) on board the *Great Eastern* was ruled by considerations of quantity rather than quality but the following contemporary description shows that this was not altogether true:

'The chief saloon is situated forward of the engine rooms, an advantage not usual in other ships, is 62 feet long by 36 feet wide, and 12 feet high; adjoining it is the ladies' cabin, 20 feet long. The arrangements for ventilating and lighting the lower cabins from the skylight above necessitated the railing off of open space on each side of the saloon. Besides this, two of the enormous funnels find their way upwards through this room. These pecularities all presented consid-

The screw steam vessel *Buenos Aires* of 2,438 tons, built at Sunderland in 1872 for the Hamburg-South American Steamship Company. She was lost in 1890. Painted by A. Jansen, 1888.

erable difficulties to be overcome in the decoration. The open spaces on each side are treated as arcades, resting on light iron columns; and between these are ornamental balustrades, also of iron, of very delicate design. Both these were cast by the Coalbrookdale Iron Company, and are beautiful specimens of their work. This ironwork is all treated by a peculiar process in imitation of oxydised silver relieved with gilding.

'Above, the columns appear to support, by means of brackets, the iron beams of the ship. There is no attempt at concealing these, but they are decorated alternately in blue and red, the under-side being gilt. The spaces between these beams are divided into panels which are very lightly decorated in colour and gold.

'The walls are hung with a rich pattern in raised gold and white, divided into panels by green stiles and pilasters in imitation of oxydised silver, to correspond with the columns.

'The two large funnel-casings, which occupy considerable space in the room, are octagon in plan. The four larger sides of these have been covered with mirrors, which continue the perspective of the saloon, and almost do away with the

143

appearance of obstruction which before existed. On the four smaller sides, at the angles, are arabesque panels ornamented with children and emblems of the sea.

'Mirrors are also placed on the large airshafts at the sides of the saloon, and on each side of them are other arabesque

prevailing colour being maroon, assist in giving effect to the other decorations.

'The sofas are covered with Utrecht velvet, and the buffets are of walnut wood richly carved, the tops being of a fine green marble.

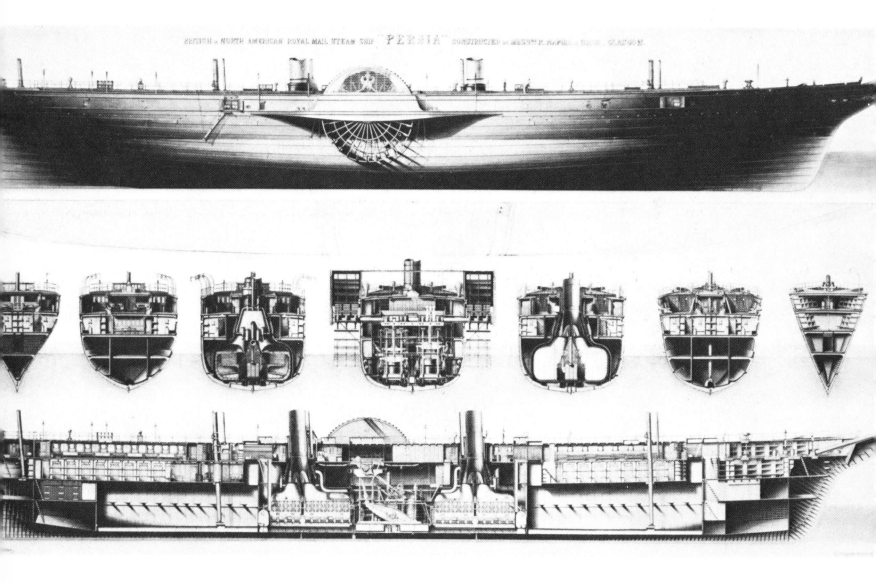

The first iron Cunard liner, *Persia*, built and engined by Robert Napier & Sons in 1855. She was 376 feet long, 45.3 feet beam, and her tonnage was 3,300. Her engines were capable of driving her at nearly 14 knots. She captured the Eastbound Blue Riband in July 1856, and was finally broken up on the Thames in the early 1870's.

paintings with children personifying the arts and sciences connected with the building and navigation of the ship.

'There are portieres of rich crimson silk to all the doorways; and the carpet, of which the pattern is simple, the

'A very peculiar feature in this unique saloon is the mode by which it is lighted and ventilated at the sides—by large openings railed off with gilt balustrades, and reaching to the upper deck, where they are met by skylights, which can be left up or down at pleasure. Besides the great additional light which these openings give, they are invaluable as securing at any moment currents of fresh air — a luxury which will only be fully appreciated when the *Great Eastern* is steaming majestically across the Indian Ocean. Next to this berths of the passengers are skilfully arranged, the amount of accommodation being regulated, of course, by the price paid for the passage. But it is hardly fair to call them mere berths, seeing that they are, generally speaking, rather suites of apartments, comprising sleeping, sitting, and dressing

The wreck of the *Atlantic*. A White Star screw liner built by Harland & Wolff, Belfast, in 1870. On April 1st 1873 she became stranded on the Moris Rock near Halifax, Nova Scotia, and broke up with the loss of over 500 lives. Three hundred were saved by Quartermaster Owen who swam ashore with a line. Lithograph by Currier & Ives.

imperial saloon is another and still longer one, which is to be appropriated to the ordinary first-class passengers, the other being exclusively devoted to the extra first and the ladies. Around these two principal saloons the sleeping-rooms, all self-contained, and offering to females as complete seclusion as if they were in their own homes. The smallest of these berths is larger than the best cabins in any other vessel; and they have the peculiar advantage of being

The wooden paddle-steamer *St. John*, built in 1863 by John Englis of Brooklyn for the People's Line Service between New York and Albany. Her length was 417 feet, beam 85 feet and she was fitted with a vertical beam engine. She was totally destroyed by fire in 1885 while laid up in the ice season at New York.

at least double the height, and possessing most ample and ready means of ventilation.

'The cabins are not all arranged alike, but some are constructed as "family cabins", and some in the usual "two-and-two" fashion; whilst others, by a combination of both the above styles, can be turned into a suite of one large and two small ones, making up eight bed places altogether, all opening into each other, and capable of being shut out completely from the passage and the rest of the

ship. Each family cabin measures 18 feet by 7 feet 6 inches, and is 7 feet 6 inches high, and is furnished with every necessary convenience. The berths are so constructed that by a very simple process they can be made to collapse and fold together against the sides of the cabin, leaving a space of six inches between the two, so as to admit of stowing away the bed-clothes; this done, curtains are drawn across, and so kept until night, the consequence being not only that the bed arrangements are entirely concealed all day, and the cabin

The National Line steamer *Spain,* an iron-screw vessel built and engined by Laird Bros. of Birkenhead in 1871. She was designed for service between Liverpool, Queenstown, and New York, principally carrying steerage passengers. She was sold to French shipbreakers in 1896.

turned into a snug little drawing-room, but that Space is gained equal to about one-third of the whole area. The tables are so arranged as to be capable of extension or diminution in size. The cabins are floored with oilcloth, with Turkey rugs above.

'Under one of the settees is a bath, which can be easily supplied with hot, fresh or salt water, by the aid of what are called the "donkey-engines" or some of the multitudinous shaftings which are to work everything all over the ship.

Some idea will be formed from this attempt at description of the accommodation for passengers afforded by the vessel, and which are carried out on much the same scale in every class and department, the difference consisting merely in the degree of plainness or ornamentation, as the case may be.

'The second-class saloons extend along the centre of the vessel immediately beneath and exactly corresponding to the first-class saloons, and form in truth the ground floor of the magnificent hotel, of which the others are the first; or perhaps it would be still more accurate to say that the lower saloons, with their flanking cabins, are the ground and first floors, the first-class saloons and their cabins thus becoming the second, for the superior height of the lower saloons enables two tiers of cabins to be one above the other; round them, short flights of stairs leading to the upper tier. It will be recollected that, in describing the principal saloon and passenger accommodation, we pointed out that an open space

equally of course the fittings of the lower saloons are of a far simpler and less magnificent character than those which adorn the upper, yet to our mind the toning down and subduing of light, combined with the great loftiness, produce an almost more pleasing and tranquilising effect. In the lower saloon, surrounded by all the substantials of comfort, and without any pomp and glitter to put folks on their "best company" behaviour, one seems to feel even more

The grand saloon of the *Bristol,* a steamer of the Fall River Line, employed on part of the U S mail route between New York and Boston via Newport and Fall River. 1866.

some six or seven feet wide was left on each side of the floors of the upper saloons, and was crossed by bridges leading to the cabins. The object of these spaces we stated to be the admission of light to the lower saloons and though of course the quantity of light cannot be so great as that admitted through skylights opening direct into the air, and though

at home, more at one's complete ease, more as a man does at his own fireside than even when lolling on the velvet cushions of the grander apartments. The lower saloons, too, are the furthest from deck noises; and we much doubt whether between the tropics they will not prove the cooler, and, even if there were to arise in them a demand for more air, think what a breeze would pour down a windsail from the deck of a vessel tearing across the water at twenty miles an hour! The dimensions of these saloons correspond with those of the upper ones, the space on each side beneath that through which the light is admitted being occupied, as already described in those appropriated to the first-class passengers, only of course less luxurious and less smart, and accommodating on the whole more passengers. In fact, many of them, when their living contents are all berthed for the night, will present very much the appearance of cup-

The American paddle-steamer *Tolchester*, 1866. She was powered by a vertical beam engine, visible in the picture. This type of vessel was very popular for short river excursions and also they were often used as river packets.

shown in the illustration, by a row of cabins with lean-to roofs constructed of hammered glass, which will admit plenty of light without permitting any curious first-class passenger to pry into the secrets of the cabins below by peeping over the balustrade above. The interior arrangements of the cabins are much on the same plan as those boards full of prostrate people laid round on the shelves.'

The *Great Eastern*'s first voyage across the Atlantic was made in June 1860 at an average speed of 14 knots. The great ship was not a commercial success either as a passenger or a cargo vessel, and has been described as 'the greatest failure in the whole history of marine engineering;

149

a premature leviathan conceived and built forty years in advance of practical experience'. However, the *Great Eastern*'s most useful service was between 1865 and 1873 when she was engaged in laying a number of submarine cables, an employment for which her great size made her specially suitable.

With hulls constructed of iron instead of wood and more efficient engines, steamers increased in size and the disadvantages of the paddle-wheel was slowly realized. Although the *Great Britain* showed how successful screw propulsion would be, paddle-steamers continued to be built for the Atlantic service until the 1860's. The *Scotia*, launched in 1861 for the Cunard Atlantic service is said to have been the finest paddle-steamer built for this purpose and made a record crossing in eight days, three hours. The *Scotia* was the last of the British paddle-steamers on the North Atlantic service and held the Blue Riband from 1862 to 1867.

VII   STEAM AND SAIL IN THE 1870's

By the 1860's, the steamships had won an almost complete victory over the sailing-packets for the passenger trade on the transatlantic routes and for other comparatively short voyages. However, the sailing ship was able to compete for many years with passengers on the very long voyages to Australia and the Far East.

The great flow of emigrants across the Atlantic continued and, during the eleven years from 1860 to the end of 1870, more than two million people left ports in the British Isles and north-west Europe to settle in the United States of America. The majority of these passengers sailed in steamships with a hull form and accommodation very similar to

The steamship *Germania* of the International Line trading between Trieste and New York, *c.* 1875. She was owned by Ward & Holzapfel, Newcastle-on-Tyne.

that of the sailing-packet. During 1870 there were eight principal lines of European steamship companies operating to America. The 106 steamers owned by these companies made 555 round voyages conveying 302,148 passengers and nearly 1,700,000 tons of freight. Iron was replacing wood construction which influenced the construction of later passenger steamships for the Atlantic routes. For the blockade-runners, strong construction, high speed, shallow draughts and a low silhouette were necessary. One of the first steamers to be specially designed for use as a Confederate block-

The *City of Rome,* a liner brought out by the Inman Line in 1881. She was intended to be a record breaker, but she proved to be much slower than was expected and was returned to her builders. After changing hands many times she was broken up in 1902.

in the construction of steamships, while the propeller was taking over from paddle-wheels.

Although the Civil War had a disastrous effect on merchant shipbuilding in America, the special requirements needed for ships ordered from British yards by the Confederate States brought about experiments in design and ade-runner was the paddle-steamer *Banshee,* built at Liverpool in 1862. This steamer, 214 feet long, with a beam of 20 feet, was constructed with steel plates on iron frames and was the first steel ship to cross the Atlantic. Engines of 120 h.p. gave the *Banshee* a speed of 11 knots. Another Liverpool-built blockade-runner, the paddle-steamer *Colo-*

nel Lamb, reached a speed of 16¾ knots on trials in 1864, and again the shipbuilders used steel for a strong but relatively lighter construction. Sixteen years later the first steel liner went into service on the North Atlantic.

In 1871 a new type of steamer was introduced on the At-

the steamer was 420 feet long, with a beam of only 41 feet. Instead of the usual bulwarks and narrow wood deck-houses, the *Oceanic* had an extra iron upper deck with open iron railings. Another innovation was the positioning of the main saloon amidships. From the earliest times, the place of

The Royal Mail Steam Packet Co.'s wooden paddle-steamship *Orinoco,* built by Pitcher of Northfleet in 1851. Engines by Maudslay of 800 h.p. were capable of driving her at 12 knots. She was broken up at Vauxhall in 1859.

lantic. This new era was inaugurated when the Oceanic Steam Navigation Company (White Star Line) brought into service the *Oceanic, Celtic, Baltic, Republic, Atlantic* and *Adriatic.* .The first of this new type of vessel, the *Oceanic,* launched in 1870, represented a major advance in the development of the great multi-decked luxury liner. Built of iron,

honour had always been at the after part of the ship, but it was now accepted that the motion due to the waves was greater at the ends of the vessel and with the introduction of the propeller, the vibration was felt more at the stern. The midship saloon extended the full width of the vessel, with light and air from the side-lights. Separate chairs in the

The North German Lloyd steamship *Adler*, 1864. Oil painting by Jaburg (1830–1908).

The steamship *Prins van Oranje* on the quayside, 1871.

154

The steamship *Hermann* of Bremen. 1865–96. One of the Norddeutscher Lloyd Line ships. Painting by Weltering, *c.* 1870.

St. Carlo Quay, Trieste. An important port on the Adriatic, Trieste was founded by the Romans.

The steamship *Oranje Nassau* of the Dutch West India Mail Service, 1884.

saloon, larger cabins and the provision of electric bells to call stewards were other new features in the ship. Like all other ocean-going steamships of the period, the *Oceanic* carried a large spread of sail, and this liner was rigged as a four-masted barque. The propelling machinery consisted of two sets of four cylinder compound engines, each of 500 h.p., driving a single-screw propeller. About 65 tons of coal were used daily to obtain an average speed of 14 knots. In this class of vessels, the *Adriatic* held the record passage with a westward crossing of 7 days, 13 hours, 17 minutes in 1872, while disaster struck the *Atlantic* when she went ashore near Halifax, on April 1st 1873, and quickly broke up, with a death roll of 546 (Ill. p. 145).

The saloon of the *Atlantic*, a paddle-steamer of the Collins Line, built in 1849. Her tonnage was 2,800, which was considerably more than that of the contemporary Cunarders. The Collins Line failed in 1857 when the United States Mail subsidy was withdrawn.

The steamship *Rotterdam*, painted by A. Jacobsen in 1887, was a passenger ship of the Holland-America Line. The house flag shows the initals N.A.S.M. as the company's Dutch name is Nederland-Amerikaansche Stoomvaart Maatschappij.

The grand saloon of the famous American river steamer *Grand Republic*, 1876.

As rivals to these White Star liners the Cunard Company ordered the *Bothnia* and *Scythia*, both of 4,500 tons. The two steamers were placed on the Liverpool to New York service in 1874 and 1875 respectively but they were slower than the White Star ships although slightly larger and carrying 300 cabin and 1,100 other passengers compared to the *Oceanic*'s 166 cabin and 1,000 other passengers. The following rules and regulations of the Cunard Company were applicable to the cabin class in the *Bothnia* and *Scythia*:

'It being obvious that, on a passage of some days' duration, the comfort of a numerous body of passengers must very much depend upon the manner in which they themselves assist in promoting it, a cheerful acquiescence is ex-

157

The Mississippi river paddle-steamer or 'side wheeler' *J.M. White*, 1878. Notice the gang planks hanging over her bows, suspended by a derrick ready for disembarking passengers and cargo. This vessel was burned in 1886.

The *Grand Republic*, 1876. The very tall smoke stacks helped to keep the smoke from the boiler fires away from the passengers.

pected in the following regulations and suggestions, which, if in any instance at variance with the opinions or inclinations of the few, are framed with a regard to the comfort of the whole.

1. In case of dissatisfaction with any of the servants, it is requested that the head steward may be informed, and, if the grievance be not immediately redressed, that the captain be appealed to, and, if of a serious nature, that it be represented in writing, in order that it may be brought before the agents at the conclusion of the voyage.

The Hamburg paddle-steamer *Königin Maria*, one of the early steam vessels in use possibly on the river Elbe.

2. The stewards and boys are engaged on the express understanding that at table they attend in becoming apparel.
3. The state-rooms to be swept, and carpets to be taken out and shaken, every morning after breakfast. To be washed once a week, if the weather is dry.
4. The saloon and ladies' cabins to be swept every morning before breakfast, beginning at 5 o'clock.
5. Bedding to be turned over as soon as passengers quit their cabins. Slops to be emptied and basins cleaned at

The floating theatre *Temple of the Muses,* New York, *c.* 1848. Show-boats were the only entertainment available to people living alongside the rivers.

A scheme suggested in 1884 for transporting ships overland by railway as an alternative to the construction of the Panama Canal.

9. The stewardess only is to enter the ladies' cabin and state-rooms, and to make the beds at the time stated.
10. The wine and spirit bar will be opened to passengers at 6 a.m., and closed at 11 p.m.
11. Breakfast to be on the table at half past 8, and cloths removed by half past 9.
12. Luncheon to be on table from 12 to 1 o'clock.
13. The before-dinner bell to be rung at half past 3 — dinner to be on the table at 4 — the cloths to be removed the instant it is over.
14. Tea to be on the table at half past 7.
15. Supper, if required and ordered, to be before 10 o'clock.
16. Lights to be put out in the saloons at half past 11, and in the state-rooms at 12.
17. As the labour of the servants must be very great, and the space required for a larger number absolutely preventing an increase, the passengers are requested to spare them as much as possible between the meal hours, and particularly preceding dinner.
18. No passenger is allowed to change his state-room or berth without the knowledge of the purser; and it is understood that the passage tickets are to be given up to him before the termination of the voyage.
19. With or without their owners, *dogs* are not allowed to come abaft the foremast.'

the same time. Beds to be made once a day only, except in cases of illness, etc., and within one hour after breakfast.
6. Bed linen to be changed on the eighth day. 'Boots and shoes to be cleaned and put back into the state-rooms every morning at 8 o'clock.
7. Two towels to be hung up for each passenger, and to be changed every other day, or as often as required.
8. Passengers are requested not to open their scuttles when there is a chance of their bedding being wetted. The head steward to see that the scuttles are open when the weather will permit.

Design for a turntable for use with the overland ship transporter. The route proposed was across the isthmus of Tehuantepec, north of the Canal Zone.

The *Normandy,* launched 1882, renamed *La Normandie* in 1886, and broken up in 1912. She was owned by the Compagnie Générale Transatlantique, one of the oldest French shipping companies, often called the French Line.

On the routes to the Far East and Australia the great distance between coaling stations put the steamer at a disadvantage until the opening of the Suez Canal in 1869 made the long haul round the Cape of Good Hope unnecessary for steam-propelled vessels. Even after the opening of the Suez Canal the sailing ships were able to compete with steamers for cargo-carrying in certain specialized trades and for the passenger trade. While the *Oceanic* and her sister ships opened a new era on the Atlantic in the 1870's, Devitt & Moore's famous Australian Line of sailing packets were making regular and scheduled voyages from London to Melbourne and Sydney. One of their Company's finest ships and one of the largest sailing ships afloat, the *Sobraon,* was designed to carry a large number of passengers in partic-

ularly commodious accommodation. The *Sobraon,* launched in 1866, was a 'composite' ship, that is one built with iron frames and beams but planked with wood, and, with a length of 317 feet and a beam of 40 feet, the *Sobraon* was the largest composite vessel to be built. She had a flush deck with a very small poop, containing only the officers' quarters. There was a deck-house containing a smoking-room, two bathrooms and a handsome staircase leading to the saloons. The principal saloon, 100 feet long, was panelled in polished teak and maple, and could seat seventy people for dinner. The ladies' saloon, suitably decorated, was near the stern. The sleeping cabins were arranged in the usual manner on either side of the saloon and both the second and third-class cabins were said to have been particularly well ventilated. About a

161

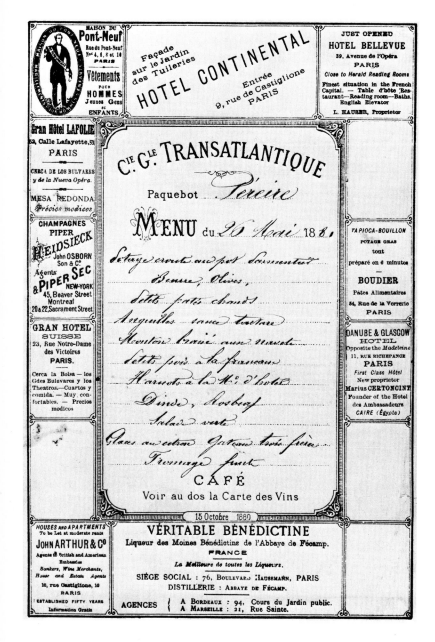

Menu from the steam packet *Pereire*. Built on the Clyde in 1865 she made a record run from Le Havre to New York in nine days in 1866.

The *Sobraon* was also fitted with an icebox with a capacity of ten tons of ice and a condensing plant to provide fresh water from salt water. She made her maiden voyage to Australia in 1867 and was employed as one of Devitt & Moore's regular Australian packets for twenty-five years. The outward passages usually took about seventy-five days, but homeward voyages took longer as the *Sobraon* always returned via the Cape of Good Hope, calling at Capetown and St. Helena. The following extracts from a newspaper published on board the *Sobraon* during the passage from Melbourne to London in 1875 provides a first-hand account of life and events in a large sailing ship:

'1875, February 12, Friday — The *Sobraon* being anchored in the bay, some two miles from Sandridge, the passengers, with a few exceptions, came on board in the tug at about 4 p.m., amidst deluges of rain. One unfortunate individual

hundred passengers were usually carried on the outward passage, with somewhat fewer on the return voyage. The following list of supplies taken aboard for a homeward passage shows that the passengers were not likely to be put on short rations: 173 sheep, 30 pigs, 18 sucking-pigs, 720 fowls, 420 ducks, 144 geese, 1 cow; flour, 12 tons; sugar, 2½ tons; butter, 1 ton; biscuits, 3 tons; preserved meat, 6,000 lb.; salt meat, 6,200 lb.; soup, 1,200 lb.

Menu from the packet ship *La Normandie*, dated August 18th 1889.

A wine list as used on board ships of the Compagnie Générale Transatlantique.

A passengers' contract ticket for the Orient Line steamship *Garonne*. The cost of a steerage passage from Melbourne to London was £15.15 in 1881.

fell from the paddle-box into the sea, and was, with some little difficulty, rescued. There was great confusion on board during the evening.

'February 13, Saturday — Weighed anchor at 9.30 a.m., and were towed to Queenscliff, where we remained for the night.

'February 14, Sunday — Were towed through the Heads at about 8.30 a.m. After we were cast off by the tug, we made but little progress, as it was almost a calm during the day. No services.

'February 16, Tuesday — A general meeting of the passengers was convened to consider the subject of amusements. Three subcommittees were formed, viz., Musical, Dramatic and Literary.

'February 18, Thursday — Dancing on deck in the evening. An albatross and a mollyhawk caught.

'February 24, Wednesday — An evening concert given by the Musical Committee in aid of the Merchant Seamen's Orphan Asylum. Admission 1s.6d. Amount realised, between £4 and £5.

'February 28, Sunday — Prayers on deck in the morning. Evening Service with Sermon in the Saloon.

'March 1, Monday — First performance of the Christy Minstrel Troupe on the main hatch.

'March 6, Saturday — Dancing on deck in the evening.

'March 10, Wednesday — Second Christy Minstrel Entertainment on the main hatch.

'March 12, Friday — A gale, probably a cyclone or circular storm, lasting about fourteen hours, with a heavy confused sea. There were severe squalls of wind, which reached their climax at 3.30 p.m., when the jib was blown into ribbons. Six hats went overboard.

'March 13, Saturday — Wind and sea moderating. In the evening a second concert was given under the auspices of the Musical Committee. Admission free.

'March 15, Monday — St. Valentine's Day was kept today, the editor's box of the *Sobraon Gossip* being temporarily used as a post-office. Nearly a hundred valentines were posted, and were distributed at breakfast-time by a special postman. In the evening a trial was held on the main hatch in a case of breach of promise of marriage.

'March 16, Tuesday — Second evening of the trial. Verdict for the plaintiff.

'March 20, Saturday — A waterspout was visible early in the morning. It was about six miles from the ship.

'March 24, Wednesday — First chess handicap tournament commenced. Each player to play forty-eight games.

'March 26, Good Friday — Prayers on deck in the morning. Flying fish to be seen.

'March 27, Saturday — A second circular storm or small hurricane. The gale commenced with torrents of rain, and afterwards the wind shifted very rapidly, and the ship was taken aback. The foretopsail carried away, also a large boom. For several hours the ship was under main lower topsail only. There was a heavy confused sea, and a good deal of water was shipped. The gale lasted about nine hours.

Passengers on the promenade deck of a Hamburg-America Line ship, 1890.

The decks of the Inman liner *City of Rome*, 1881.

In the first decade of the 20th century, travellers who crossed the Arctic Circle on a ship of the 'Hapag' line were awarded a baptismal certificate signed by Neptune, ruler of the ocean, and the seal 'Robb Robbes.'

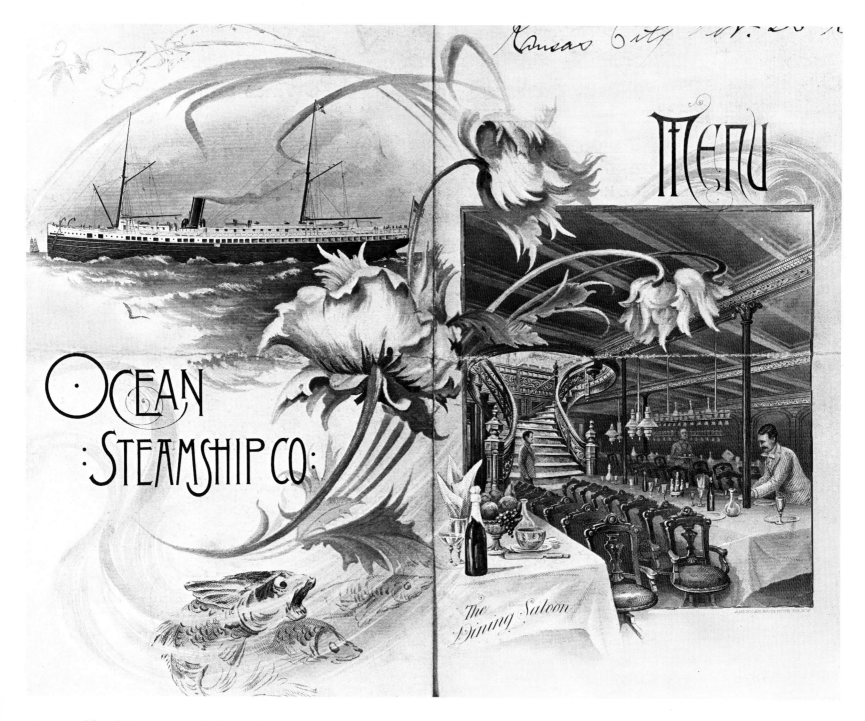

A menu card from S.S. *Kansas City*, dated November 25th 1895. This ship was owned by the Ocean Steamship Company and was built in 1889 by Delaware River Iron Ship and Engine Building Co., Chester, Pennsylvania.

'March 28, Easter Sunday—Service in the saloon, morning and evening.

'March 30, Tuesday—Shark seen but not caught. Dramatic entertainment in the evening on the main hatch. The piece played was *Little Toddlekins*.

'April 2, Friday—Longest run—274 miles.

'April 3, Saturday—Severe squall in the night in which the ship was taken aback. It blew hard all day with a heavy sea.

'April 4, Sunday—Service in the saloon morning and evening.

'April 5, Monday—Nearing land. Colour of sea changed. Final performance of Christy Minstrels.

'April 6, Tuesday—Severe thunderstorm in the night with

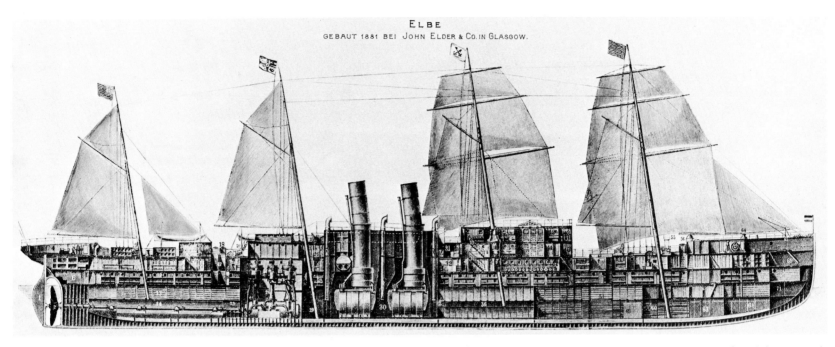

ELBE
GEBAUT 1881 BEI JOHN ELDER & CO. IN GLASGOW.

A profile section of the screw steamship *Elbe*, built in 1881 by John Elder & Co. in Glasgow for the Norddeutscher Lloyd Line, the famous Bremen firm founded in 1857. The crossed key and anchor on the house flag are taken from the arms of Bremen.

The dining-saloon on board one of the Hamburg-America Line ships in 1894. In the years previous to 1912, 'Hapag' decided that larger, very luxurious, but less speedy ships would be profitable on the Atlantic run.

squalls of wind and rain and a heavy sea. In the morning there was an almost total eclipse of the sun, lasting from about 5.30 to 7.30 a.m. In the Agulhas current.

'April 7, Wednesday—Sighted the coast of Africa in the morning. Passed Cape Padrone and the lighthouse on Bird

'April 11, Sunday—Came in sight of land about 2 o'clock p.m. Sighted the Cape of Good Hope late in the afternoon, and were close to the lighthouse on its extreme point by nightfall. We had nearly reached the light on Green Point (marking the entrance to Table Bay) by 10.30 p.m., with a

Chart and log, kept by Charles Desgras, on the Messageries Maritimes Line's steamer *Salazie*. The ship left France on December 16th 1885 and arrived in Australia on April 3rd 1886.

Island before evening. After dark the light on Cape Recife was visible.

'April 9, Friday—Land only visible towards evening in the distance. Fished for cod on the Agulhas Bank, but caught none. Passed a brigantine. Sighted the light on Cape Agulhas about 10 p.m.

very strong breeze blowing off the land, when the ship was suddenly taken aback in a sudden shift of wind under the lee of a mountain, and we put out to sea again for the night. Prayers in the saloon in the morning; none in the evening.

'April 12, Monday—Again attempted to enter Table Bay, early in the morning, but the wind failed before reaching

A poster advertising Ballin's Imperial Mail paddle-steamers *Prinzessin Heinrich, Prinzess Elisabeth,* and *Balder* sailing daily between Hamburg and Borkum via Heligoland, Sylt, Amrum, and Norderney from June to September.

Green Point, and the ship drifted about until the afternoon, and was once in some danger of going upon a large rock— the "Whale Rock". About 3 o'clock a light wind took us into the bay, where we anchored at 4 p.m. Most of the passengers went ashore.

'April 15, Thursday—Re-embarked in the *Sobraon* at noon, and weighed anchor at 3 p.m. Left Table Bay with a favourable wind by the North Passage, between Robben Island and the northern extremity of the bay.

'April 27, Tuesday—Off St. Helena by daybreak. The majority of passengers went on shore at about 8.30 a.m. The ship did not anchor, but stood on and off during the

An afternoon in the tropics; the *Hindostan* in the Indian Ocean on her way to China. Some passengers are playing 'Bull' or deck quoits, on the paddle box a Mohammedan is saying his evening prayer; several ducks and a pig look out from their pens in an enquiring way.

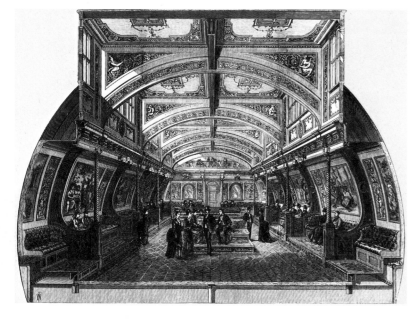

The *Bessemer*, built 1874 by Earle of Hull. She was double-ended and her saloon was pivoted amidships in an attempt to overcome sea sickness.

day. Having spent a pleasant day on the island, we all re-embarked by 4 p.m., and set sail about an hour later.

'May 1, Saturday — Several whales to be seen in the distance. Second chess tournament commenced.

'May 2, Sunday — Island of Ascension in sight all day, about 25 miles off to the east of us. Prayers on deck in the morning; evening service with sermon in the saloon.

'May 7, Friday — Passed the Equator about 9.30 a.m.; almost a dead calm all day. We saw a large school of porpoises in the evening and soon afterwards a shark made his appearance, and was caught in the usual way. His length was about six feet.

Some of the steamers navigating the rivers and bays of the United States were constructed on a scale of magnificence unknown in European waters. This illustration shows the grand saloon of an American steamer in 1875.

'May 8, Saturday—This morning we were boarded by a boat from the barque *Cameo* (London to Adelaide). Her Captain wished to send a letter by us.

'May 18, Tuesday—Mr. Barwick, a saloon passenger, died early this morning and was buried at sunset. The Rev. J. B. Smith read the funeral service.

'May 21, Friday—The Captain's gig, with a crew of 18 passengers and midshipmen, under the charge of Mr. Seaborne, put out to a brig for newspapers and potatoes. She was the *Britannia* from Liverpool, for the Island of St. Thomas, thirty-one days out.

'May 25, Tuesday—Third chess tournament commenced.

The music-saloon aboard a passenger ship, *c.* 1886.

Immigrants on the steerage of the SS *Pennland* in 1893. The liner was built for the Cunard Line in 1870 and first named *Algeria*. From 1881 until 1895 she was owned by the Red Star Line.

'May 26, Wednesday—Two vessels in the distance. A large swordfish was seen near the stern of the ship; it was said to be about 14 feet long.

'May 30, Sunday—Three or four ships in sight—two were signalled; they were the *Flying Fish* and the *Nereid;* all outward bound. Service in the saloon morning and evening.

'June 1, Tuesday—Mrs. Sturgess, a second-class passenger, died at 3 o'clock this morning.

'June 5, Saturday—In the forenoon the Captain sent his gig with a crew, under the command of the second officer, to investigate a large log of timber which was seen floating at some little distance from the ship. The boat returned after an absence of about an hour with two turtles and five fish—the latter are called "Old Wives", and are usually found under all old floating timber. They are good eating.

The log was supposed to be part of the deck cargo of a North American timber ship, and was covered with barnacles.

'June 6, Sunday—In the afternoon the gig with a crew of twenty went off to a large barque. She proved to be a German vessel, the *D. H. Watjen,* 1,200 tons register, bound from Newcastle to Singapore with coals; twenty-one days out. She was a fine vessel with a poop 83 feet long. We obtained from her some newspapers and potatoes. Service morning and evening in the saloon.

'June 7, Monday—The gig with several passengers, including four ladies, put out to a small brigantine, the *Edith Grant,* 200 tons, from Belfast for Charlestown; eleven days out.

'June 8, Tuesday—Several passengers witnessed the cu-

172

Father playing ball with his little girl on board SS *Circassia* in 1896. This ship belonged to the Anchor Line. Built of iron, and launched in 1878, she was of 4,250 tons, with a length of 401 feet, a beam of 42 feet, and a speed of 13 knots.

rious spectacle of a whale in difficulties. He was being attacked by his enemy the thresher-fish — a kind of shark. An outward bound barque in sight.

'June 9, Wednesday — Crossing the Bay of Biscay. The sea is no longer blue. Several vessels in sight during the day. A closing concert was given in the evening in the Saloon, in aid of the Merchant Seamen's Orphan Asylum.

'June 11, Friday — Sighted Start Point at 6.30 p.m.

'June 12, Saturday — Abreast of St. Catherine's Point. Isle of Wight at 4.30 a.m., and stood in to Dungeness, for a Pilot, towards noon. After a splendid run up Channel, we anchored off Margate about 5 p.m., being unable to enter

Deck scene aboard the 6,500-ton Peninsular & Orient steamship *Arcadia*, built in 1888. This photograph was taken in 1894.

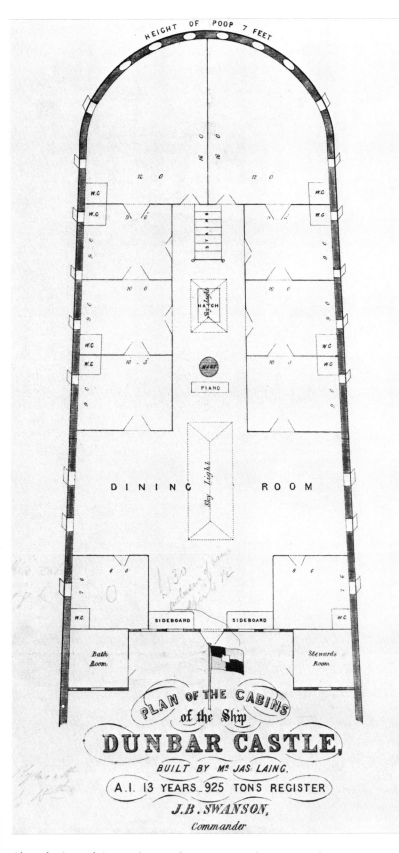

Plan of cabins of the *Dunbar Castle*, 925 tons, built by Laing of Sunderland. This ship was ordered just before Duncan Dunbar died, and was one of the ships that Devitt & Moore bought. She went into the Sidney trade and was always known as the last of the *Dunbars*.

the Mouth of the Thames on account of the westerly gale that was blowing.

'June 13, Sunday—Weighed anchor at 3 a.m., and were towed up the river. Were moored at Gravesend at about 10 a.m.'

The Early Years Of Some Famous Steamship Lines

The middle decades of the 19th century saw the foundation of many of the British and foreign steamship lines which were later to become so well known to all who travelled by sea. The early steamers of the Peninsular & Oriental Steam Navigation Company, the Cunard Steamship Company and the White Star Line have already been described. Other famous British steamship lines established during this period were the Liverpool, New York & Philadelphia Steam Ship Company (Inman Line) (Ill. below) founded in 1850 with the steamer *City of Glasgow*, the Anchor Line founded in

Poster advertising the Liverpool, New York & Philadelphia Steam Ship Company's sailings between Liverpool and New York in 1861.

1856 and the Royal Mail Steam Packet Company established in 1839. The Inman liner *City of Brussels* made a record eastbound Atlantic crossing in 1869 and their *City of Berlin* won the Blue Riband in 1875 with passages eastbound in 7 days, 15 hours, 28 minutes and westbound in 7 days, 18 hours, 2 minutes. This steamer of 5,490 tons was 489 feet long, and was the largest vessel on the Atlantic service at that date, with accommodation for 1,700 passengers. In 1879 the *City of Berlin* became the first Atlantic liner with internal electric lighting when a generator was fitted to supply current to lamps in the dining-saloon. The *City of Rome* (Ill. pp. 52, 164), launched in 1881, was one of the last steamers to be built for the Inman Line.

The Hamburg-Amerikanische Packetfahrt-Aktien-Gesell-schaft (Hamburg America Line) and the Norddeutscher Lloyd (North German Lloyd), two of the more famous German steamship lines, were founded in 1847 and 1856 respectively. The Hamburg America Line's service to America was commenced in 1848 with sailing ships each carrying

Passengers aboard the S S *Circassia* enjoying a dance; music is provided by a passenger perched on top of a deck house, playing a concertina.

A state-room on board S S *Puritan*, 1889, owned by the Fall River Line. Built with a double hull and watertight bulkheads, she was said to be unsinkable.

about two hundred passengers, and the Company did not employ steamers on this route until 1856 when the *Borussia* and *Hammonia* were brought into service. The North German Lloyd Company was founded at Bremen in 1856 and started its service from Bremerhaven to New York in 1858 with the steamer *Bremen* of 2,674 tons. A weekly service to America was commenced in 1867 with the *Hermann* (Ill. p. 155) and three other steamers and in that year 33,427 passengers were transported across the Atlantic. Until 1888 the North German Lloyd steamers were built in Britain and their first so-called 'express' liner, the *Elbe* (Ill. p. 167), built at Glasgow, made a record time of eight days for a passage from Southampton to New York in 1881. The *Elbe* was lost after a collision in the North Sea in 1895.

In France, the Compagnie Générale Maritime started business in 1855 with sailing ships and small steamers but in 1861 the firm's name was changed to Compagnie Générale Transatlantique (French Line), and a contract was made with the French Government to carry the mail from Le Havre to New York, and from Saint-Nazaire to the West Indies and Central America, for an annual subsidy. In addition the Company was granted a large loan without interest so that

A poster called 'The passenger from number 54' after a sketch by Lautrec, drawn on board the Messageries Maritimes line's steamer *Chile* during a voyage between Bordeaux and Lisbon in 1895.

176

The grand saloon on board the S S *Puritan*, 1889. One of the fleet forming the Fall River Line between New York and Boston via Newport and Fall River.

one of the British-built steamers, left Le Havre for New York. Six weeks later another British-built ship, the *Lafayette*, joined the service and the two steamers carried on a regular schedule until May 1865 when they were joined by the *Europe*, the third British-built vessel. These three steamers were each 345 feet long, with accommodation for 330 passengers, and were propelled by paddle-wheels. The earlier ships built in France for the French Line were also paddle-steamers, but the success of the British screw-driven Cunard and Inman liners made it very apparent that the propeller was superior to the paddle-wheel for large vessels. The French Line's liner *Napoleon III*, completed in 1866, was the last paddle-steamer to be built for the transatlantic service, and with the famous Cunard paddle-steamer *Scotia*, launched in 1861, and the American Pacific Mail Company's *America* of 1868, represented the final development of the ocean-going paddle-steamer. The directors of the French Line ordered that the designs of the three ships still on the stocks, the *St-Laurent*, *Ville-de-Paris*, and *Pereire*, should be altered so that they could be fitted with screw propellers. Between 1867 and 1874 the other French Line Atlantic steamers were converted to screw propulsion. The *Lafayette* and *Washington* were each fitted with two propellers in 1867, and thus became the first twin-screw liners to operate on the Atlantic.

The Messageries Maritimes Line, another historic French Company which has become world famous, obtained in 1851 the first overseas contract with the French Government for the conveyance of mail to Italy, Greece and the Middle East. A direct weekly line of steamers from Marseilles to Naples was started in 1855. Two years later the Messageries Maritimes steamers carried the French mail to South America, and from 1861 to India and China. After the opening of the Suez Canal, the Messageries Maritimes competed with the British P & O Line for the trade to the East and by 1875 were the largest steamship Company in the world. In 1881, the French Government awarded the Company a subsidy for a mail service to Australia and New Caledonia. This service was inaugurated with the new iron screw steamer *Natal*, of 3,800 tons, and by 1884 six more steamers were operating on the route.

The New York and Liverpool United States Mail Steamship Company (Collins Line), founded by E. K. Collins, was one of the more famous early American steamship lines. Four paddle-steamers, the *Atlantic*, *Pacific*, *Arctic* and *Baltic* were built at New York, in 1849–50, with the help of a subsidy from the United States Government, and their service provided the first serious competition with British

new ships could be built in France and abroad. In 1862–3 the French Line ordered five iron steamers from its own ship-building yard (later Chantiers de l'Atlantique) and three more from a British yard. The transatlantic service was inaugurated on June 15th 1864 when the *Washington*,

First-class lounge of the *Lucania*. This ship was owned by the Cunard Line and was placed in service together with her sister ship *Campania* in 1893. Both ships held the Blue Riband record.

steamships on the fast Atlantic routes. These schooner-rigged vessels, of nearly 3,000 tons, were 282 feet long—larger than their Cunard rivals—and were the first Atlantic steamers with straight stems. Each had two sets of side-lever engines and the coal was delivered to the stokeholds by mechanically-driven buckets. They were the most luxuriously fitted steamers of the period (Ill. p. 156), with accommodation for two hundred first-class passengers. The cabins, with improved ventilation, were heated by steam, and bathrooms and a barber's shop were available for the passengers. The *Atlantic* made her maiden voyage to Liverpool in May 1850 and in July of the same year made a record crossing from New York to Liverpool, a distance of 3,058 miles, in 10 days, 8 hours, 20 minutes.

The *Atlantic* was refitted in 1851. A new dining-saloon, in which two hundred persons could be conveniently seated at dinner, was built and communicated directly with a pantry connected with the kitchen and its offices, affording every facility for culinary operations. The windows of the saloon were of stained glass, outside of which were 'glass lights' to be drawn over them as occasion required, and also 'dead lights' to be used in heavy weather. At the after part of the saloon were the wheel-room, smoking-room and apartments for the captain and officers. The old dining-saloon was converted into a fore-cabin so that eight additional passengers could be accommodated.

The Collins Line enjoyed the confidence and the patronage of the travelling public. A testimonial from the passengers on the *Baltic*, dated November 27th 1851, reads: 'Resolved — that without instituting any comparison, but on the contrary, with best wishes for all the other lines between the United States and Europe, we have no hesitation in declaring that as far as we are competent to judge, there is not a safer, more agreeable steamer or one better entitled to the public confidence than the good ship *Baltic*.'

The Collins Line steamers were a little faster than the Cunarders and able to make the transatlantic crossing in about one day less than their British competitors. From January to November 1852 they carried 4,306 passengers to the 2,969 who went by the Cunard Line and in eight years the Collins Line passenger traffic increased fivefold.

In 1852 the *Arctic* crossed from New York to Liverpool in 9 days, 17 hours, 30 minutes at an excellent average speed of 13¼ knots. Unfortunately the *Arctic* was lost with 322 passengers after a collision with a French steamer in September 1854 and the *Pacific* disappeared without trace in 1856. These misfortunes put a severe strain on the Company and although a larger paddle-steamer, the *Adriatic* (Ill. p. 204), of 4,144 tons was brought into the service in 1885, the United States Government did not renew the mail contracts when they expired in 1857 and the Collins Line came to an end in 1858. Another important American line, the Pacific Mail Steamship Company, was founded in 1848 and started the first regular steamship service along the western coats of America and across the Pacific. The paddle-steamers *California*, *Oregon* and *Panama* were put into service between Panama and San Francisco and carried thousands of passengers making their way to the newly

A menu card from the *Normannia*, a ship of 8,200 tons, belonging to the 'Hapag' line. She was built by Fairfields on the Clyde in 1890.

179

MAIL STEAMERS to NEW-YORK

every tuesday

HAMBURG-AMERICAN STEAMSHIP-COMPANY.

A poster advertising the Hamburg-America Line or 'Hapag,' as it is known from the initials of its German title. The line was founded in 1847.

found Californian goldfields. By 1865 the Pacific Mail Company owned twenty steamers and the *America,* of 4,450 tons, launched in 1868, was the last paddle-steamer built for the Company. This vessel is stated to have been the largest wooden ocean-going merchant steamer ever built. The *America* and three other paddle-steamers were used to operate a monthly service from San Francisco to the Far East. In 1873–5, eleven iron-screw steamers were built for the Company and the sailings to the Far East were made every two weeks. In 1875 the governments of New South Wales and New Zealand granted mail contracts to the Pacific Mail Company and a monthly service was operated from San Francisco to Sydney and Auckland.

The great maritime traditions of the cities of Venice and Genoa were continued when Italy was united under one government, and the 1860's saw the beginning of the development of the modern Italian merchant navy. In 1861 a number of steamers were employed by the newly formed Società in Accomandita Piroscafi Postali—Ignazio & Vincenzo Florio (I. & V. Florio) and in the 1870's a direct passenger service was started from Italy to New York. The opening of the Suez Canal in 1869 gave an added impetus to Italian shipping with the establishment of services to the Middle and Far East. In 1881 I. & V. Florio amalgamated with another Italian shipping firm, R. Rubattino of Genoa, to form the Navigazione Generale Italiana, and three screw steamships *Vincenzo Florio, Washington* and *Archimede,* each of about 2,800 tons, were employed on a service to New York. Two further ships of about the same size were built for the service in 1883. The Navigazione Generale Italiana took over two more Italian shipping companies in 1885 and started sailings to South America.

American River Steamboats

During the 19th century the great waterways of the United States of America served as important commercial highways and it is perhaps appropriate, even in a book devoted primarily to sea travel, to provide a brief description of the unique stern and side paddle-wheel vessels used on these waterways. The rivers Mississippi and Missouri have a combined length of 3,760 miles and the River Ohio, which joins the Mississippi, is 960 miles long. The Mississippi and its tributaries drain an area of about 1,250,000 square miles, embracing a number of States. The steamboats designed for use on these waterways were of a very specialized design; they had to be of very shallow draught and yet large enough to carry powerful engines and a large payload of passengers and cargo. The first steamer on the Mississippi was the paddle-boat *Orleans,* built in 1811 by Robert Fulton, in association with Nicholas Roosevelt. The *Orleans,* with a speed of about three miles per hour, served as a packet between New Orleans and Natchez, until she sank in 1814 after striking a rock. The *Washington,* said to have been the first Mississippi boat with two decks, was built in 1816. The engine which in previous boats was in the hold was brought up a deck, a position it usually occupied in later river boats. The early Mississippi paddle-boats had such low-power engines that they could only be employed on the lower Mississippi and Ohio when the current was less than three miles an hour, and they could never get up the swifter rivers after having once gone down. The *Washington,* however, was a powerful boat for her day, and was able to make

Three posters designed by Laurie Taylor, Bernard Lacheur, and Gilbert Galland, for the Messageries Maritimes. These advertised the Mediterranean and Far East routes between the wars, where the company still operated, although nearly half their passenger fleet had been lost during the First World War.

a round trip from New Orleans to just below the falls at Louisville and back in forty-five days.

In 1818 the *General Pike* was built for passenger traffic between Louisville, Cincinnati and Maysville. She was 100 feet long on the keel, 25 feet beam, and had a cabin built on the deck between the engines. The central hall was 40 by 18 feet, with eight state-rooms at one end and six at the other.

Up to 1818 the fastest trip from New Orleans to Louisville was made by the *Shelley* in nineteen days. She carried fifty-one passengers with a cargo of freight, and stopped at ten places *en route*. The usual time was from twenty-five to thirty days. The fast steamer *Cincinnati* made the round trip in about forty days. After 1830 determined efforts were made to improve the speed, and in 1838 the *Diana* ran from New Orleans to Louisville in less than six days, winning a premium of $500 from the United States Post Office Department.

As the size of the river-steamers increased they suffered from hogging and sagging. With a shallow draught boat of the type used on the Mississippi and other American rivers there was not sufficient longitudinal stiffness and an elaborate system of short thick masts, struts and iron ties was introduced to provide the hull with greater longitudinal strength. The *Sultana*, built in 1843, was 250 feet long with a beam of 35 feet and had a speed of 15½ miles per hour. Speed and comfortable accommodation for a large number of passengers were of the greatest importance for the river boats. The *Eclipse*, built at New Albany in 1852, was for many years one of the most popular and fastest boats on the river. She cost $300,000, was luxuriously fitted up with a richly furnished saloon and was 360 feet long.

When fast boats became popular there was a fierce rivalry, and races frequently took place. Boats were sent over the course stripped of every possible weight that could be dis-

In these three posters Lloyd Austriaco advertise a regular paddle-steamer service between Trieste and Venice; while the Orient Line, now P & O, offers enticing cruises to the Mediterranean and Constantinople, or a sixty-day cruise to the West Indies via Madeira, Teneriffe, and the Azores.

pensed with, and without any cargo, driven at the full power of the engines, simply to beat previous records and establish a reputation for speed. Until legislation regulated the strength and pressure of boilers, this passion for fast time led to great loss of life and property on account of explosions.

In 1853 the *Eclipse* raced the *Shotwell* also built in 1852. Both vessels were stripped for the race and did not carry passengers or cargo. Furniture, landing-stages and fenders were sent on shore and even the bulkheads in the wheelhouses and parts of the decks were removed. The *Eclipse* won the race making the journey from New Orleans to Louisville in four days, nine hours, thirty minutes.

The *Empire State,* a steamer employed on the Fall River, Massachusetts, but very similar to the Mississippi steamers, is described by an English traveller writing in 1853 as follows:

'The word "boat" gives a very imperfect idea of this float-ing palace, which accommodates at the very moderate charge of four dollars each, from five to six hundred American citizens and others, of all classes, in a style of splendor that Cleopatra herself might envy. There is little to remind one of machinery, for the paddle-wheels are covered, and the engine is rendered invisible by being surrounded with glass and drapery. However, one thing is certain, the vessel moves smoothly and quickly through the water. I followed a crowd of five hundred up a handsome staircase, through splendidly furnished saloons covered with carpet of velvet pile, to the upper deck.

'Tea being served, we all adjourned to the gentlemen's cabin. The apartment was very large, with berths three deep all around it; the curtains of these being drawn, covered the sides with drapery of different colors mixed with lace shades. At the entrance we were met by tall swarthy figures, clothed in white linen of unspotted purity, who conducted us to our seats. There were three tables, the entire length of the room,

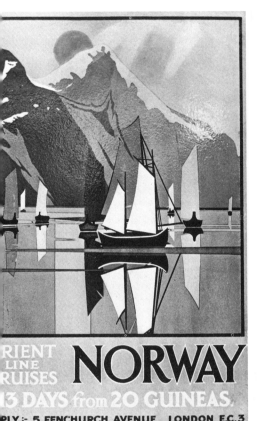

Orient Line posters dated 1910 (right), 1913 (centre), and 1925 (left). It is interesting to compare the fares and note the increase of £8.8.0 after the First World War. Modern cruising began in 1889 when the Orient liner *Chimborazo* sailed to the Mediterranean.

covered with everything that was beautiful; but nothing that seemed eatable, except the pineapple and some small delicate, delicious-looking things that, for want of a better word, I shall call rolls, though it vulgarized them sadly. Notwithstanding this unreal appearance, you no sooner wished for anything than a ministering spirit was at your elbow to gratify you. At his touch, pineapples became butter, pyramids tea cakes, and magical boxes of savory pies; tongue, ham, all kinds of delicacies issued from their flowery retreats at his bidding. At the end of the banquet you heard whispered in your ear, "half a dollar". It was produced and silently disappeared… not a clink was heard.'

The American Civil War seriously interrupted traffic on the River Mississippi and a number of the older boats disappeared. However, after the end of the war new and superior boats were soon built. Two of these new vessels, the famous *Robert E. Lee* and the *Natchez*, built in 1866 and 1869 respectively, raced from New Orleans to St. Louis, a distance

of 1,200 miles, in 1870. Both boats were stripped for the race and steamed at about 17 miles per hour. For long periods during the race they were close together, sometimes abreast. The *Robert E. Lee* arrived at St. Louis in 3 days, 18 hours, 4 minutes and the *Natchez* 6 hours, 33 minutes later. The steamers *Great Republic* and *J. M. White* (Ill. p. 158) were typical examples of the vessels used on the Mississippi in the post Civil War period.

During the 1920's, the United States Government sponsored the Inland Waterways Corporation, and many large steam- and diesel-powered river craft were built. In the 1970's, the last of the stern-wheel river-boats to carry overnight passengers, the *Delta Queen*, still cruises on the Mississippi. Built in 1926, with a steel hull and wood superstructure, the steamer *Delta Queen* is 285 feet long, with a beam of 58 feet and a draught of only 7 feet 6 inches. One hundred and ninety-two passengers are accommodated in cabins

183

A poster advertising passages on the Hamburg-South America Line for German emigrants to Brazil and Argentina.

In 1922 United States Lines were the first to introduce 'tourist third' traffic. This poster advertises the post-Second World War services of the S S *United States* and S S *America*.

and saloons decorated in the traditional river-boat style, but the radar equipment in the pilot house is a very modern addition. Operated from Cincinnati by Greene Line Steamers Inc., the *Delta Queen* makes about forty cruises each season on the Mississippi, Ohio, Tennessee and Cumberland Rivers, travelling about 30,000 miles visiting seventeen States and more than a hundred riverside towns. Dixieland bands and calliope music entertain the passengers, while the *Delta Queen* steams past historic river towns like Nashville, New Orleans, Louisville, St. Paul and St. Louis.

VIII THE DEVELOPMENT OF THE STEAMSHIP 1884–1914

The thirty years between 1884 and 1914 saw a tremendous development in the passenger steamers of the world, which can perhaps be compared with the remarkable changes in the design of fast sailing ships which took place in the period 1820 to 1860 and which were described in Chapter VI. In 1884 the Blue Riband of the Atlantic was held by the steamer *Oregon,* of 7,375 tons, with accommodation for 1,100 passengers. Propelled by a single propeller driven by three-cylinder compound engines of 13,575 h.p., the service speed of the *Oregon* was 18 knots, and her record Atlantic crossing in 1884 took 6 days, 10 hours, 10 minutes. Thirty years later the record was held by the *Mauritania,* of 31,938 tons, with accommodation for 2,165 passengers. The *Mauritania* with quadruple propellers driven by steam turbines developing 70,000 total shaft h.p. had a service speed of 25 knots and crossed the Atlantic in 1909 in 4 days, 17 hours, 21 minutes.

A number of factors brought about these great increases in size, and the improvements in accommodation, performance and speed of passenger vessels. Although, from the middle of the 19th century, steel had been used occasionally instead of iron for ships, it was not until the 1880's that this material was used extensively for ship construction and after 1890 was employed for nearly all new ships. Steel was more durable than iron and enabled the weight of a ship to be reduced by about 15 per cent without loss of strength. By 1890, twin-screw propellers, driven by improved reciprocating engines, had been generally adopted for the larger liners with better performances and higher speeds. In the reciprocating engine the pistons moved backwards and forwards, and it was necessary, at the end of each stroke, to bring the piston to a halt and then to start it moving in the opposite direction. The stresses and strains this produced limited the speed at which the engine could function efficiently, and a very great advance in the evolution of the marine steam engine took place in 1894 with the invention of a rotary engine, the steam turbine.

The development of the steam turbine and its application to marine propulsion was the work of Sir Charles Parsons. As a result of Parsons' experiments, the first turbine-driven vessel, the yacht *Turbinia,* was produced. This famous vessel was fitted with parallel flow turbines developing 2,000 shaft h.p. and attained a speed of 34.5 knots at a naval review at Spithead in 1897. This sensational performance, making the *Turbinia* the world's fastest ship at that time, proved to the officers of the British Admiralty that the steam turbine would be of great value for naval vessels in which high speed was particularly desirable, and the first turbine-driven destroyer, H.M.S. *Viper,* was ordered in 1898. The earliest passenger vessels to be fitted with steam turbines were the Clyde River steamers *King Edward* and *Queen Alexandra* built in 1901 and 1902 respectively. Steam turbines were fitted to new cross-Channel vessels built in 1902-3 and the first large liners to use this form of propulsion, and the first to be fitted with triple screws were the Allen Line steamers *Victorian* and *Virginian,* completed in 1905 for the Atlantic service.

The requirements for ships carrying passengers from Europe to South Africa differed from those of ships on the Atlantic service. There were fewer passengers for this route, the distance to be traversed was 6,000 miles compared with about half that distance for most Atlantic services, and for much of the voyage the temperature was much higher. The changes and advances in the design of ships for the South African trade were therefore somewhat different to those of passenger ships employed on the Atlantic routes, but in the thirty-year period ending in 1914, the time taken for the voyage was reduced from about thirty-five days to about sixteen. The British Castle Line, which amalgamated with the Union Line in 1900 to form the famous Union-Castle Line, started their steamship service to South Africa in 1872 with the *Iceland* of only 1,474 tons. Successive ships built for the line showed great improvements. For instance the *Kinfauns Castle,* of 3,560 tons, launched in 1879, was built of steel with a service speed of 12½ knots, and the *Norham Castle,* of 4,400 tons, launched in 1883, was some three knots faster. In 1894, quadruple-expansion engines were fitted to the *Tantallon Castle,* of 5,600 tons, giving a speed of 16 knots, and five years later the second *Kinfauns Castle*

moral Castle, built in 1910, was 570 feet long, with a breadth of 64 feet and of 13,360 tons. The quadruple-expansion engines of 12,500 h.p. drove twin screws giving a speed of 17 knots.

The accommodation in vessels with such a long voyage

A two-berth cabin aboard the *Omrah,* 1899. She had accommodation for 830 passengers and good cargo space.

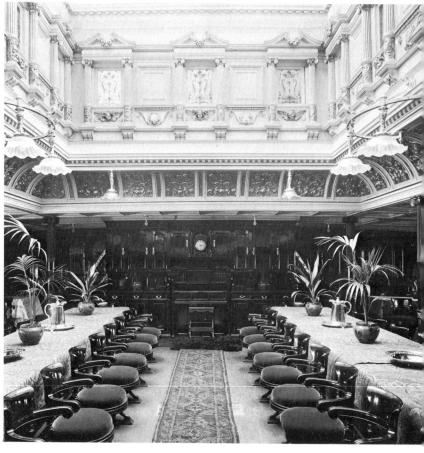

First-class saloon aboard the Orient Line's ship *Omrah,* built at Fairfield Yard, 1899. She was employed as a transport during the First World War, and was sunk by a U-boat in May 1918.

and the *Kildonan Castle,* the last mail steamers to be built for the Castle Line before the merger with the Union Line, were fitted with quadruple-expansion engines and twin screws, giving a service speed of 17 knots. Thus in twenty-seven years the steamers of this particular line increased in length from 250 feet to 515 feet, in tonnage from 1,474 to 9,692 tons and in speed from 10 knots to 17 knots.

The *Balmoral Castle* and her sister ship, the *Edinburgh Castle,* were the finest and largest ships built for the Union-Castle Line before the outbreak of war in 1914. The *Bal-*

through regions where the temperature conditions vary so enormously required special arrangements, and the passengers in the *Balmoral Castle,* as in all the later Union-Castle liners, were accomodated well above the water-line. There was therefore adequate natural ventilation, while fixed electric fans, together with a number of portable fans, fitted to suit the convenience of the passengers, ensured a free circulation of air. Steam-heated radiators were arranged throughout the ship on a system which enabled any one heater to be used at the will of passengers in any one cabin, without affecting the temperature of any other room.

The first-class accommodation started on the several decks about 100 feet from the bow, and extended for about 180 feet towards the stern. The public rooms were well forward, with a companion-way connecting the four decks. On the

The second-class quarters had for their accommodation several compartments abaft this, with companion-ways through four decks. The smoking-room was on the boat deck, the library on the promenade deck, and the dining-saloon on the main deck.

Life on board an ocean-going passenger liner, c. 1895. Some of the passenger are taking a brisk walk around the promenade deck while others sleep or read within the enclosure.

boat-deck there was a lounge and smoking-room; on the promenade deck a library, with a lounge for non-smokers around the balcony of a well giving light and ventilation to the dining-saloon on the next level—the upper deck. There were state-rooms on all these decks, as well as on the main deck.

The steerage passengers were right aft. The lounge, with piano, the library, and smoking-room were in a deck-house on the promenade deck aft, with large windows, ensuring effective ventilation, while the dining-saloon was on the level below—the upper deck.

The *Balmoral Castle* carried 319 first-class, 220 second-

187

A party of passengers watching a game of deck quoits aboard the S S *Circassia*, 1896.

class, and 268 steerage passengers. The first-class dining-room could seat 182 persons. Small buffets arranged between the tables assisted in giving a rapid service to the diners. The walls of the dining-room were panelled in mahogany and the furniture upholstered in light green and black striped material, with the company's monogram inter-woven. The first-class lounge had windows 6 feet deep by 2 feet wide, particularly large for the period. The adjoining smoking-room had a separate entrance from the open deck. This room (Ill. p. 199) was framed in oak, stained green and black and panelled with leather. The room was split up into bays suitable for card-playing, and each alcove was

The steel paddle-steamer *Tashmoo*, 1,200 tons. Built in 1900 at Detroit for A. A. Parker, the manager of the White Star Line. This type of vessel is still popular on rivers and lakes.

lighted from the sides with large opening windows and from above by dormer windows. The *Balmoral Castle* and the *Edinburgh Castle* served on the Southampton to Capetown route until the end of the 1930's.

A passage from London to Sydney, Australia, via the Suez Canal involved a voyage of about 12,000 miles and the Orient Line's *Omrah*, 8,130 tons, was an example of the type of twin-screw liner used on this route at the beginning of the 20th century. The *Omrah*, built at Glasgow in 1898, was 507 feet long, with accommodation for 160 first-class and 162 second-class passengers on the upper and spare deck, while 500 third-class passengers could be berthed on the lower deck. State-rooms were arranged for two, three or four persons (Ill. p. 186) and in some of the cabins the lower berths were fitted so as to draw out and make double berths. The first-class entrance was in the forward part of the ship, on the promenade deck, and led directly to the

entered from the dining-room without going out on to the promenade deck, a great advantage to passengers in rough weather. The *Omrah* was fitted with a refrigerating plant and electric light. While serving as a British troopship, the *Omrah* was torpedoed and sunk in May 1918.

A drawing that illustrates the number of passengers and the amount of provisions, water and cargo carried by a vessel of the Hamburg-America Line, *c.* 1900.

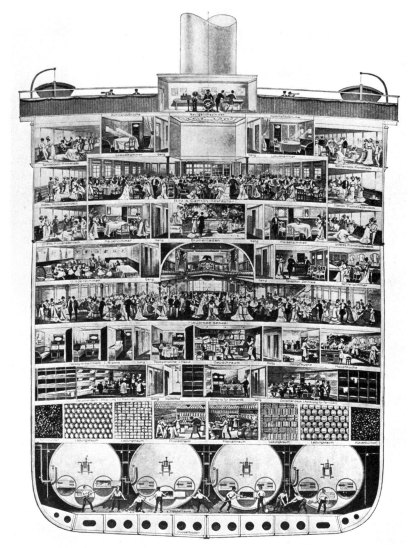

A pictorial representation of the midship section of the Hamburg-America Line's ship *Amerika.* She had accommodation for 420 first-class, 300 second-class, 300 third-class, and 2,300 steerage passengers.

dining-room (Ill. p. 186), a spacious room with light provided by a sky-light and well from the boat deck and by large square windows in the sides. The first-class smoking-room was situated aft of the saloon well and could be

The Lighting of Passenger Ships

The strict rules relating to the use of oil lamps and candles below decks in the early sailing-ships and emigrant ships

190

were very necessary because of the great danger of fire either from the lamp or candle or from a naked flame from it. In the first-class saloons, lamps were permitted, usually suspended from a single point or in gimbals, and thus more or less independent of the movement of the ship. Gas lighting upwards of three hundred lights, about thirty of which would be kept burning night and day. The gas was manufactured from oil in an apparatus consisting of a retort-stack, washer, condenser, scrubber, and gasholder. However, with gas installations in ships, considerable trouble

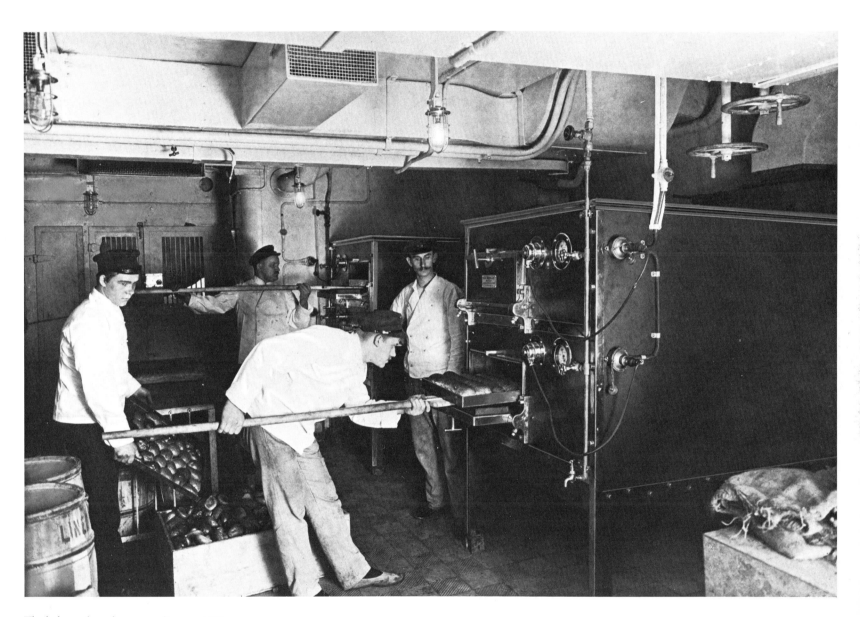

The bakery aboard an ocean liner, *c.* 1900.

for ships does not seem to have been a success. It was tried out in the Mersey ferry *Waterlily* in 1862 and fitted in the White Star Line transatlantic liners *Adriatic* in 1872 and *Celtic* in 1873. In the latter vessel it was intended to fit occurred through gas leaks in the pipes caused by the 'working' of the ship at sea. The first transatlantic liner to be fitted with electric lights was the Inman liner *City of Berlin* in 1879.

For the Australian service, the Orient liner *Chimborazo*, 3,847 tons, was fitted with an installation in 1880 which provided the current for seven incandescent lamps. Four of these lamps were in the main saloon and the remainder in the steerage. These lights must have been a great advantage to the emigrants. Indeed, in 1881, one eminent ship-owner was of the opinion that electric light was more useful in the emigrants' quarters than in any other part of the ship. A voyage in bad weather, when it was not possible to go on deck, among a thousand fellow-passengers crowded on two decks, could never be a cheerful experience but when in addition to the other discomforts, there was also gloom only just removed from darkness by the small and infrequent ports, the light from even a few electric lamps must have been most welcome. The Inman liner *City of Rome*, launched in June 1881, was provided with 100 Swan lamps in the saloon and 150 distributed in the drawing-rooms, smoke-rooms, and state-rooms, with ten in the upper and lower steerage. The *Servia*, the first Cunard liner to be fitted with electric light, had 98 incandescent lamps disposed in the following manner: 20 in the engine-room, 10 in the propeller-shaft tunnels, 50 in the grand saloon, 8 in the music-room, 6 in the ladies' boudoir, and 4 in the smoking-room. Twelve years later the Cunarder *Campania* was completely lighted by electricity. Forty miles of wire ran throughout the ship, with four sets of generating plant capable of supplying 1,350 16-candle-power incandescent lights — including eight large reflectors of eight lights each for working cargo — and in addition a powerful searchlight for facilitating the navigation of the ship in and out of ports.

The Advent of the Super-Liner

A new style of luxurious sea travel began in 1893 when the Cunard Line introduced the liner *Campania* into the North Atlantic service. This vessel of 12,950 tons was 620 feet long overall, with a breadth of 65 feet, and was the largest liner in service at that date. The *Campania* was magnificently appointed for the period and had been fitted up with the greatest possible luxury combined with comfort, strength, durability and perfect sanitary arrangements. It is interesting to note that there were coal-fire grates in all the principal

A sketch showing passengers arriving on board a vessel belonging to the Compagnie Générale Transatlantique, *c.* 1880–90.

The *Castelia*, launched 1874. Built by Thames Ironworks, Blackwall, for English ▶ Channel Steamship Co., she had two half-hulls each 290 feet long, separated by a gap of 26 feet and united by a superstructure with two paddle-wheels working in the space between. She was a failure and became an isolation hospital.

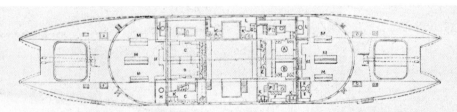

NUEVO BUQUE PARA LA TRAVESÍA DEL PASO DE CALAIS. — Plano de las disposiciones interiores.

Primera clase.

A B. Salon de las señoras. — **I E I K.** Camarotes reservados. — **M.** Gran salon. — **J.** Buffet. — **L.** Sala para los fumadores.

Segunda clase.

C D. Salon de las señoras. — **K.** Camarotes reservados. — **J.** Buffet. — **M.** Gran salon. **G.** Camarotes reservados.

Vista exterior.

193

Tahitian girls dancing a welcome to passengers from a liner belonging to the Messageries Maritimes Line.

rooms. There was accommodation for 600 first-class, 400 second-class, and 1,000 third-class passengers. The ship's complement consisted of 61 sailors, 195 engineers and firemen, and 159 stewards. The grand saloon was 100 feet long by 63 feet broad with seats at tables for 430 passengers. The grand mass of dark mahogany, richly carved, composing the walls; the delicate panelling of the ceiling in white and gold, with electric lights in the centre of each panel; the great crystal dome rising in the centre of

Natives coaling a ship. Built as *City of New York* in 1888 for the Thompson Line, she was transferred to the American Line in 1893 and renamed *New York*.

the room through the two decks above to a height of 33 feet; the splendid upholstery finished in dark russet velvet; and the graceful arches of ivory and gold with the frieze above them surmounted by the brilliant stained-glass colour of the dome; all these created, together, a most impressive effect.

The drawing-room, on the promenade deck, was a spacious and lofty room in the Renaissance style, with walls of satinwood and cedar, enriched with carved work. The fire-grate, built in and protected with asbestos, had a mantel-piece elaborately carved and surmounted by arched mirrors. The organ, grand piano and furniture were all in satinwood. The first-class smoking-room, in fumed oak, was fitted up in the Elizabethan style. It had a coach roof and a piazza arrangement along the sides with a table in each recess fitted round with settees covered in hogskin. The *Campania*'s cabin accommodation included single or double cabins with a sitting-room, the beginning of the 'suites' which were to become such a feature in later liners. The main engines, two three-stage expansion sets developing 31,000 h.p., were in separate engine-rooms, situated on either side of a centre-line bulkhead. In May 1893, the *Campania* made a record eastbound Atlantic crossing in 5 days, 17 hours, 27 minutes, and twelve months later a sister ship, the *Lucania*, reduced this time by 8 hours, 45 minutes. The *Lucania*'s fastest westbound passage of 5 days, 7 hours, 23 minutes also set up a record. The *Campania* and *Lucania* proved to be reliable and popular Atlantic steamers and the *Lucania*, the fastest of the pair, retained the Blue Riband until 1897. The *Campania* served as a seaplane carrier during the First World War and sank after a collision in the Firth of Forth in 1918, while the *Lucania* was badly damaged by fire at Liverpool in 1908, and was broken up in 1910.

In the mid-1890's the North German Lloyd Company started a programme for the building of six twin-screw Atlantic steamers. Of these vessels, two were to be 'express' liners and four for the regular passenger and freight service between Bremen and New York. The four regular steamers, the *Barbarossa*, *Bremen*, *Friedrich der Grosse*, and *Königin Louise*, were completed and put into service before the 'express' liners *Kaiser Wilhelm der Grosse* and *Kaiser Friedrich*. The four liners, known as the *Barbarossa* class, were each of about 10,500 tons and were 550 feet long overall with a breadth of 60 feet. With accommodation for about 2,000 passengers, the steamers were driven by quad-

Passengers aboard a ship held in quarantine off San Vicente, Cape Verde Islands, ▶ buying provisions from native traders in rowing boats.

ruple expansion engines of about 7,000 h.p., giving a speed of 14 knots. They presented an imposing aspect with their high superstructure, two funnels and two masts, and proved to be reliable steamers. The four vessels were employed on the Atlantic routes in the summer and ran from Bremen to Australia in the winter. The two 'express' liners were built with help of a subsidy from the German Government and the final acceptance of the vessels was subject to their being able to steam at a specified speed. The first of these vessels, the *Kaiser Wilhelm der Grosse*, of 14,350 tons, was built by A. G. Vulkan at Stettin and launched in May 1897. With an overall length of 648 feet and a breadth of 66 feet, the liner was the largest vessel in the world. On her maiden voyage to New York she reached a speed of 22.5 knots and thus also became the fastest liner in the world. The *Times* of September 28th 1897 reported that the *Kaiser Wilhelm der Grosse* on her maiden voyage across the Atlantic broke the record with a time of 5 days, 22 hours, 45 minutes. The passage from Bremen to Southampton and then on to New York took 6 days, 20 hours, with daily runs of 208, 531, 495, 512, 554, 564, and 186 miles. The second of the new North German Lloyd liners, the *Kaiser Friedrich*, of 12,480 tons, was slightly smaller than the *Kaiser Wilhelm der Grosse*, but was similar in accommodation and comfort, as the following report from the journal *The Steamship* of November 1897 shows:

'She has a double-bottom running from end to end, and is divided by 17 watertight bulkheads (of which 15 reach to the upper deck, and two to the main deck) into 18 watertight compartments, so that three adjoining compartments could be filled without the ship being endangered. The pumping arrangements in connection with this division by bulkheads are carried out with the greatest care, being so placed that each compartment can be pumped clear in a very short time by several pumps working simultaneously. Besides these extensive precautions the steamer had been provided with 22 lifeboats, which are on the awning deck ready for instant use in case of emergency by the well-drilled crew of the steamer. Provision has been made that in case of war the ship can be used as an auxiliary cruiser. Of deck structures, the ship has a forecastle 120 feet in length, and a

◄ Entrance to the music-saloon aboard the P & O S.S. *Maloja*, built in 1911 by Harland & Wolff of Belfast. She was sunk by a mine in 1916.

A portion of the first-class lounge aboard the *Winchester Castle*, built by Harland & ► Wolff of Belfast in 1930. She was 20,109 tons and carried 756 passengers. She belonged to the Union Castle Line and ran a mail service to South African ports.

midship erection which, together with the poop, extends to 444 feet. Upon the midship erection is a roomy deckhouse, 300 feet in length, which is covered by a deck the whole width of the ship, thus forming permanent awning for the first-class promenade deck. The arrangements for the accommodation of the passengers and crew are similar to those on board the *Kaiser Wilhelm der Grosse*. The seamen's quarters are forward; adjoining thereto are berths both on the main and lower deck for 750 steerage passengers. The whole midship portion of the ship is reserved for the first cabin, and the after part for the second cabin passengers. Nearly all the first-class sleeping cabins and most of the second class are in the deck structures above the upper deck, where the ports can be kept open in almost any weather. This arrangement of berthing ensures this most important advantage, that at night time and in foggy weather all the necessary openings in the bulkheads below deck can be kept closed without materially interfering with the free movements of the passengers. In the first class there are in all about 180 sleeping cabins, to hold together about 350 passengers. The greater number of these cabins consist of so-called Pullman rooms that have lately become so popular, and there are also a good number fitted up in princely style — whole suites consisting of sitting-room, sleeping-room, and bath and toilet rooms. The first-class dining-saloon is on the main deck amidships. For the accommoda-

The drawing-room aboard the Orient liner *Osterley*, 12,129 tons gross, built in 1909. The liner was used on the England-Australia service, via the Suez Canal.

tion of second-class passengers there are 111 cabins, and most of these will be fitted to contain each only two persons.

The second-class dining-saloon, with ante-room for ladies, and smoking-room for gentlemen, is on the main deck. The crew of this huge steamer will consist of 400 hands, 180 being for the engines alone, and the whole of the engine-room staff will be berthed in the immediate neighbourhood of the engine-rooms. Great care has been taken to ensure

breeze in any weather. The officers have comfortable quarters on the promenade deck.'

The performance of the *Kaiser Friedrich* proved disappointing as her average speed on the Atlantic crossings was only 20 knots, and, in 1899, in accordance with the building conditions, the vessel was returned to her builders F. Schichan of Danzig. She then sailed for a few voyages under charter to the Hamburg-American Line. In 1912 the *Kaiser Friedrich* was sold to a French firm and in 1916

The smoking-room of the *Balmoral Castle* of the Union Castle Line. This ship took their Royal Highnesses the Duke and Duchess of Connaught to Capetown in 1910, to open the first South African Parliament.

The smoking-room aboard the Orient liner *Orama*, built 1911. She was converted to an armed merchant cruiser at the beginning of the First World War.

the comfort of these men. The stokers and coal trimmers will have a mess-room to themselves, and the greater part of an awning deck has been set aside for their use. Here, after their hard labour below, they can enjoy the fresh sea

she was torpedoed and sunk by a submarine. The *Kaiser Wilhelm der Grosse* continued to sail for the North German Lloyd Company until the outbreak of war in 1914, when the ship was fitted out as a commerce raider and finally sunk by the gunfire of a British cruiser on August 27th 1914.

The Hamburg-America Company also entered into the competition for German domination of the North Atlantic passenger trade, with the *Deutschland*, of 16,500 tons, built by A. G. Vulkan of Stettin. On her maiden voyage in

5 days, 11 hours, 5 minutes, at an average speed of 23.5 knots. The North German Lloyd Company then ordered two more 'express' liners, so as to be able to run a weekly service between Germany and the United States. The first of the two vessels, the *Kronprinz Wilhelm,* of 15,000 tons,

The Ritz Carlton restaurant aboard the *Imperator,* 52,000 tons, built in 1912 for the Hamburg-America Line, purchased in 1921 by the Cunard Line and renamed *Berengaria.*

The first-class dining-saloon of the *Empress of Asia,* built in 1913, 16,900 tons, belonging ▶ to the Canadian Pacific Steamships Ltd. Operating between Yokohama and Vancouver, this ship was painted all white.

July 1900, the *Deutschland* made a record crossing in 5 days, 15 hours, 46 minutes, at an average speed of 22.42 knots and a year later completed an eastbound voyage in

was completed in 1901, and the second, the *Kaiser Wilhelm II,* of 20,000 tons, in 1903. Both vessels were capable of making Atlantic voyages at an average speed of more

than 23 knots and made record westbound crossings in 1902 and 1904 respectively. By 1903, the Germans with the *Kaiser Wilhelm der Grosse, Deutschland, Kronprinz Wilhelm,* and *Kaiser Wilhelm II* owned the fastest, largest and most luxurious liners on the Atlantic. The four liners, each with four funnels, arranged in pairs, were all elaborately equipped, and together could carry a total of 2,390 first-class passengers, providing the finest service for wealthy European and American travellers. The following descrip-

picked out with ribbed gold lines, while the ceiling for the most part is white; but the lights, instead of being on the woodwork covering the beams, as is usual, are placed on the panels, so that there is a greater variation in light and shade, of itself a pleasing feature. In the four corner alcoves the decoration is, perhaps, more elaborate. There are views of Rhine scenery, but it is characteristic of the times that all of these have a modern touch. The old-world spires and castles of Bacharach seem but the setting for signal-posts, telegraph

The third-class dining-saloon on the Orient Line ship *Orama*. In November 1914, when converted to an armed merchant cruiser, she chased and sunk the *Navarra*, but rescued the crew. Together with H.M.S. *Glasgow* and H.M.S. *Kent* she chased and cornered the German cruiser *Dresden* in March 1915, but the Germans blew up their ship to avoid capture.

tion of the *Kaiser Wilhelm II* appears in the journal *Engineering* of July 31st 1903:

'The main dining-saloon is panelled with silk tapestry

wires, and the modern railway paraphernalia. Capellen has its ship, tram, and railway, as well as its medieval castles. The embattled heights near Sanct Goar are in sharp contrast with the utilitarian barge and its great derricks. Even

Rolandseck is shown with the all-pervading motor-car in the forefront. Here and there throughout the saloon are small panels with Berlin views—historical, perhaps, more than artistic, in all cases. There is an immense glass cupboard above the sideboard, with hammered brass protection.

'The dome is entirely in white, except for the stained glass, which, representing in bold characters the Imperial Black Eagle, with a blue floral border, forms a ceiling at the level of the upper promenade deck. Both the upper deck and the main promenade deck are pierced by this light-shaft.

'At the level of the upper promenade deck, where the drawing-room is situated, there is an extension of the dome. It is in stained glass of delicate colours, representative of arts, crafts, agriculture, and mechanics. The ceiling of the drawing-room has paintings of horticulture in its more indolent moods; the walls are of tapestry of various shades of gold, with a deep frieze formed by aquatic paintings, the rivers of Germany affording the artist sufficient scope for his work. But, again, we have more than a suggestion of the modern desire of the German to subserve the beautiful and historical to the practical and material. The medieval jostles at all points with the mechanical, but no one can objet. The fact that a portrait by Ludwig Noster, of Berlin, of the Emperor William II in admiral's uniform dominates the whole is perhaps appropriate.

'The writing-room, at the forward end of the upper promenade decks, is in white, with rich red panellings, having paintings of birds of passage, not at all inappropriate in view of the flights of imagination of the average letter-writer when at sea. Even in the adjacent typewriting-room there are similar inspiring suggestions.

'The smokers' café on the sun-deck is divided up into about a dozen alcoves suitable for card-parties; the walls are decorated in gold and green, the upholstery being of the latter, as well as the stained-glass skylight.

'At the after-end of this café is a veranda, with the wireless telegraph-station adjoining.

'The smoking-room is, perhaps, the most successful of the public saloons in the ship. In the first place it is not square; the piercing of the deck at one end of the room for the boiler uptake, and at another part for a ventilating shaft, has resulted in an irregular form.

A passage way between the cabins on the Cunard liner *Saxonia*, 14,281 tons, built in 1900 by John Brown, Clydebank.

The galley aboard the White Star Line's ship *Adriatic*, 1907; built by Harland & Wolff, Belfast.

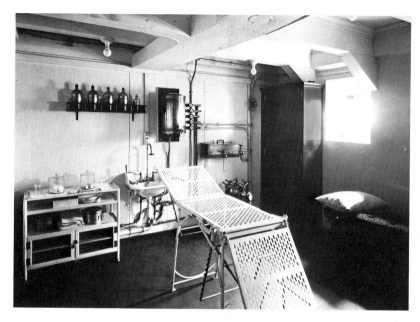

The operating theatre aboard the *Aquitania*. In 1916 she served as a hospital ship in the Mediterranean; she was laid up during 1917, but began carrying American troops to France the following March.

'At the widest part there is the main entrance, 11 feet high, and there are two large swing-doors with plate-glass, protected by hammered brasswork, with a lofty arched dome in stained glass. There is a marble fireplace opposite the door, with an electric heater, having in front a red glass with brass framing. There is an overmantel, in marble, of a draped figure lighting the World, and symbolic of Ger-

mania. The whole effect makes it difficult for anyone to conceive that he is on board ship. The ceiling is white, the walls are of rosewood, the moulding and panels being in stamped leather, which, with their gilding suggesting hammered brass, and the quaint allegorical designs, recall the styles of decoration of the Middle Ages. The upholstery is in olive-green leather, and the furniture of rosewood, the

The Hamburg-America Line's ship *Amerika*, built 1905 by Harland & Wolff, Belfast. A view of the barber's shop on the Roosevelt Deck.

The *Royal George* was built in 1910 for the Royal Line, but she was such an atrocious sea boat that she was nicknamed 'Rolling George.' A picture of a 'cabin de luxe.'

A first-class, two-berth cabin and state-room on board the *Empress of Asia,* built in 1913 for the Canadian Pacific Line.

A two-berth cabin aboard the *Saxonia.* Built in 1900 for the Cunard Line she was designed for the greatest comfort and had a splendid reputation for steadiness.

tops of the tables having a leather setting which is removable. There is throughout a feeling of the antique, which conduces well to comfort and restful peace. The cigar-lighters, by the way, are of a new type: a methylated spirit lighter being withdrawn from its reservoir, creates by friction an electric spark which lights the methylated spirit.

'There is a children's dining-saloon on the main promenade deck, close by the dome or light-well. It is in white, with panels painted in warm red tones, illustrative of the fairy tales of Hänsel and Gretel and other children's heroes.

'The Imperial suites of rooms include three rooms—a dining-room, drawing-room, and bedroom, with bath and toilet-room adjoining, the length being 40 feet, and the width, excluding passage-ways, over 10 feet.

'The cabins, *de luxe,* consist of a parlour and bedroom, with adjoining bath, and there are several special state-rooms, differing from ordinary cabins in location, size, and elegance of furniture, and having a private bathroom and toilet-room.

'The decoration of the corridors of the ship is a special

feature. Here, as throughout the ship, a bluish-green is the predominating tone, and there are frequent panels with paintings of German town life in the same shade. The gangways on the principal passenger decks have double swing-doors, the upper parts being of plate-glass and the lower of green leather, the whole protected by hammered brass-work. The main companion-way to the dining-room is painted sea-green.'

The larger British liners and the smaller 'intermediate' vessels were completely outclassed by the faster and more

The bridge of the Nelson Line ship *Highland Loch*, built by Cammell Laird & Co., Birkenhead, in 1911, (7,493 tons). She was later sold to the Jamaica Banana Producers Steamship Co. Ltd. and renamed *Jamaica Planter*. She was broken up at Glasgow in March 1935.

luxurious German 'express' liners with a consequent loss of national prestige and, perhaps more important, loss of passenger traffic. As an example, in 1903 the *Kaiser Wilhelm II* left New York on July 21st with 344 first-class passengers, while the Cunard *Etruria,* leaving on the 18th, the American Line *St. Paul* and the White Star *Majestic* both leaving on July 22nd — all well-known ships — together carried only 339 first-class passengers. From the returns of passengers embarking on various ships it is clear that the travelling public had a decided preference for the faster and

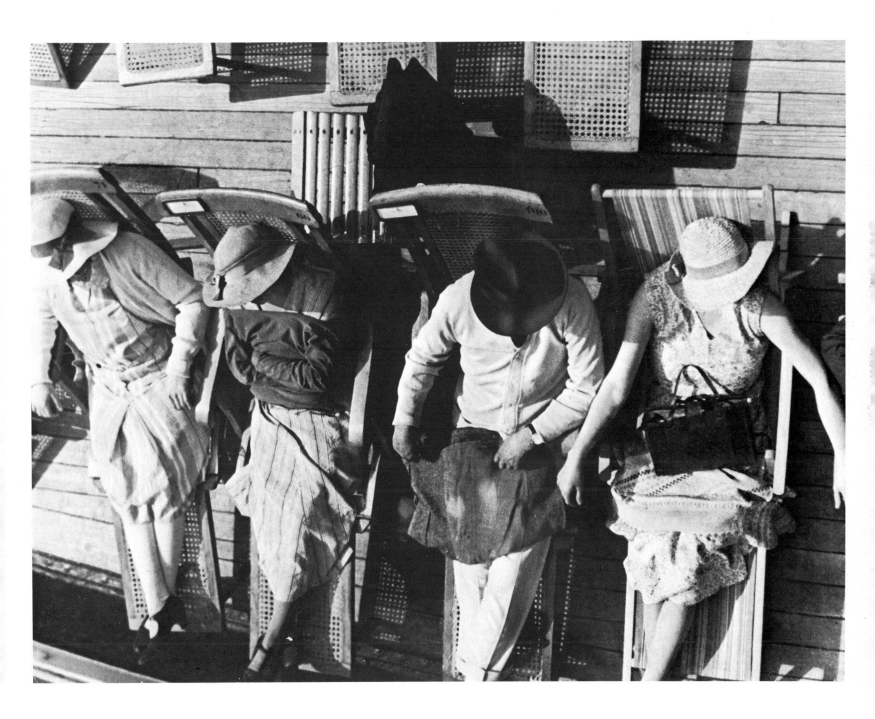

Passengers on one of the Hamburg-America Line's steamships taking an afternoon siesta on deck.

The Marconi room on the *Highland Piper*. Built in 1911 for the Nelson Line, she was later sold to Jamaica Direct Fruit Line and renamed *Jamaica Merchant*.

Swimming-pool aboard the *Mongolia*; built in 1903 as a large, fast freighter, but with good passenger accommodation, she changed hands many times.

more luxurious ships. As a result of these circumstances an agreement was arranged, in 1903, between the British Government and the Cunard Company by which two ships, the largest and fastest in the world, were to be built. The Cunard Company received a payment of £2,500,000 and an annual subsidy of £150,000 from the British Government, providing the new vessels could maintain a speed of 24½ knots in moderate weather, that the Cunard Company

The wreck of the excursion steamer *General Slocum* near Hell Gate on the East River, which divides New York from Long Island, June 1904. About 1,000 lives were lost.

remained a British firm, and the Government had certain rights to the vessels in the event of war.

As a result of this agreement, the *Mauritania* and her sister ship the *Lusitania* were built, the former by Swan, Hunter & Wigham Richardson at Wallsend-on-Tyne and the latter by John Brown & Company at Clydebank. The *Mauritania*, of 31,938 tons, was 790 feet long overall, with a breadth of 88 feet. There were seven principal decks. The lower, main, upper, and shelter decks were continuous for the whole length of the vessel. The promenade deck was 450 feet long, while the smaller boat deck was 60 feet above sea-level. Fifteen transverse watertight bulkheads extended upward to above the waterline. In all there were 175 separate watertight compartments and the 38 most important watertight doors were hydraulically operated and could be closed from the bridge. Additional protection was afforded by a cellular double bottom which extended above the bilge keels. The *Mauritania* and the *Lusitania*, the first Atlantic liners to be fitted with quadruple screws, were driven by Parsons steam turbines of 70,000 total shaft h.p. The installation consisted of two high-pressure turbines which drove the two outboard propeller shafts and two low-pressure turbines for the two inboard shafts. The bunkers carried more than 6,000 tons of coal and on a normal Atlantic crossing, the furnaces consumed about 1,000 tons of coal each 24 hours.

As built, the *Mauritania* could accommodate all 2,165 passengers as shown in the following table:

First class	One-berth rooms	Two-berth rooms	Three-berth rooms	Number of passengers
Boat deck state-rooms	3	26	—	55
Boat deck 'en suite'-rooms	—	4	—	8
Promenade deck state-rooms	6	64	16	182
Promenade deck 'en suite'-rooms	—	—	16	48
Promenade deck regal suites	8	—	—	8
Upper deck state-rooms	10	13	39	153
Main deck rooms	8	19	21	109
Shelter deck	(Children's room)			
Total	35	26	92	563

Second class	Two-berth rooms	Four-berth rooms	Number of passengers
Shelter deck	—	24	96
Upper deck	14	25	128
Main deck	20	50	240
Total	34	99	464

Third class	Two-berth rooms	Four-berth rooms	Six-berth rooms	Eight-berth rooms	Number of passengers
Main deck permanent rooms	13	118	10	4	590
Lower deck permanent rooms	—	18	6	—	108
Lower deck portable rooms	18	79	6	6	436
Lower deck open berths	—	—	—	—	4
Total	31	215	22	10	1138

On the boat deck were some of the finest *en suite* rooms and the first-class library, lounge, music-room, the grand entrance, and a veranda café. The promenade deck was almost entirely given up to cabin space, except at the stern where the second-class drawing-room and smoking-room were located. The dining-saloons for all the passengers were on the upper deck. Nine electric lifts were installed— two passenger, two baggage, two service and three food lifts. The first-class smoking-room, grand entrance and staircase were all decorated in sixteenth-century Italian style and panelled in walnut. The first-class dining-saloon and upper dining-saloon were designed as a double-tiered

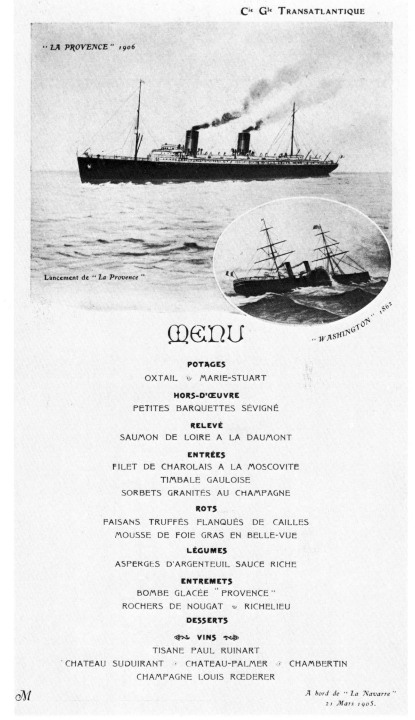

Cᶦᵉ Gᶦᵉ Transatlantique

"LA PROVENCE" 1906

Lancement de "La Provence"

"WASHINGTON" 1863

MENU

POTAGES
OXTAIL ⚜ MARIE-STUART

HORS-D'ŒUVRE
PETITES BARQUETTES SÉVIGNÉ

RELEVÉ
SAUMON DE LOIRE A LA DAUMONT

ENTRÉES
FILET DE CHAROLAIS A LA MOSCOVITE
TIMBALE GAULOISE
SORBETS GRANITÉS AU CHAMPAGNE

ROTS
FAISANS TRUFFÉS FLANQUÉS DE CAILLES
MOUSSE DE FOIE GRAS EN BELLE-VUE

LÉGUMES
ASPERGES D'ARGENTEUIL SAUCE RICHE

ENTREMETS
BOMBE GLACÉE "PROVENCE"
ROCHERS DE NOUGAT ⚜ RICHELIEU

DESSERTS

VINS
TISANE PAUL RUINART
CHATEAU SUDUIRANT ⚜ CHATEAU-PALMER ⚜ CHAMBERTIN
CHAMPAGNE LOUIS RŒDERER

A bord de "La Navarre"
21 Mars 1905.

Menu from the passenger liner *La Navarre*. She was built at Penhoët in 1892 for C.G.T. She served during the war as a patrol and troopship, and was broken up in 1925.

restaurant with an open well and could seat 470 persons. These rooms were decorated in a mid-sixteenth-century French style known as François Premier and were panelled in light oak very richly ornamented with elaborate carvings. The galleys, pantries, bakery, confectionery- and

209

knife-cleaning rooms were situated between the first- and second-class dining-room and extended for 130 feet, the full width of the ship. The main cooking range, heated by coal, was 24 feet long and 8 feet wide. In addition there were four large steam boilers, twelve steam ovens, and three electric this operation. The third-class galley, on the shelter deck, was 48 feet long by 28 feet wide and was fitted with a large cooking range, vegetable-cookers, and steam boilers. The galley was connected with the pantry below by an electric lift and staircase.

The *Titanic*, nearly 60,000 gross tonnage, built by Harland & Wolff, Belfast. She was sunk when she struck an iceberg on her maiden voyage on the night of April 14th–15th 1912. Eight hundred and twenty-five passengers and 673 crew lost their lives.

grills. The pantries were fitted with carving tables, electric egg-boilers, electric hot-plates, electric grids, and electric plate-washers. In the bakery there were numerous ovens and an electrically driven dough-mixer. The confectionery-room was provided with an ice-cream machine and a long marble-topped table. Four electrically driven knife-cleaning machines were provided in the room specially set apart for

The *Lusitania* was completed first and in October 1907 won the Blue Riband from the *Kaiser Wilhelm II* with an eastward crossing at an average speed of 23.66 knots and a westbound passage at an average speed of 23.99 knots. The *Mauritania* made her maiden voyage in November 1907 and completed the passage in 5 days, 5 hours, 10 minutes, at an average speed of 22.21 knots. During 1908 and 1909 the

R.M.S. "LUSITANIA"   SUNDAY, SEPTEMBER 13, 1914

Menu

Tortue Verte   Crême Chatrillon

Supreme de Sole—Palace

Mousse de Jambon—Alexandra

Sirloin & Ribs of Beef

Green Peas   Rice   Cauliflower á la Crême
Boiled, Mashed & Chateau Potatoes

Chapon—Chipolata
Salade de Saison

Pouding Saxone
Gâteau Mexicaine   Petits Fours
Bavarois au Chocolat

Ices

Dessert   Café

A menu from the Cunard Line R.M.S. *Lusitania*, built in 1907. She was one of Britain's fastest transatlantic liners at the time. She was torpedoed by the German submarine U20, off the south coast of Ireland on May 7th 1915 with the loss of 1,198 lives.

Originally one of the Hamburg-America Line's ships named *Vaterland*, this vessel was interned in New York on the outbreak of the First World War. When America entered the war she was renamed *Leviathan* and used as a trooper; after the war she entered service in the United States Lines. She was broken up in 1938.

speed of the two giant liners was gradually increased, until in September 1909 the *Mauritania* made a westbound passage in 4 days, 10 hours, 51 minutes, at an average speed of 26.06 knots.

The *Lusitania* was torpedoed and sunk by a German submarine on May 7th 1915, but the *Mauritania*, after service

The first-class saloon aboard the *Leviathan*. She was reconditioned after the 1914–8 war, but did not prove to be very successful, and in 1931 her tonnage was reduced.

The Cunard Line's giant *Aquitania* in dry-dock. Launched in 1913 by John Brown, ▶ Clydebank, and sold to the ship-breakers in February 1950. During her long career she steamed 3,000,000 miles and carried nearly 1,200,000 passengers.

A view of the underwater body of the *Aquitania* showing part of the rudder and two of the screw propellers. When the 1914–8 war broke out the Admiralty armed her as a cruiser, but collision damage delayed full conversion and she was paid off. In 1915 she transported troops to the Dardanelles.

as an armed cruiser and as a hospital ship, survived the war. In 1921-2 the liner underwent a major refit. The furnaces were converted from coal to oil burning, the passenger accommodation was modernized and the magnificent panelling and carvings in the public rooms, which had been protected during the war, were uncovered and renovated. Al-

though the *Mauritania* lost the Blue Riband to the *Bremen* in July 1929, this remarkable liner broke all her own previous records a month later with an Atlantic crossing at an average speed of 27.22 knots, and, in 1933, when twenty-seven years old, achieved the feat of steaming at an average speed of 32 knots for 112 miles. The *Mauritania*, truly the

The Palladian lounge aboard the *Aquitania*. Built as consort for *Lusitania* and *Mauritania* she fitted into a three-ship sailing schedule without difficulty. She carried 597 first-class, 614 second-class, and 2,052 third-class passengers. She was converted to oil fuel in the 1920's, and made regular 24 knot crossings.

Queen of the Atlantic, was finally broken up at Rosyth, Scotland, in 1935.

Following the success of the *Mauritania* and *Lusitania*, the British White Star Line ordered two new super-liners, the *Olympic* of 45,324 tons and a sister ship the *Titanic* (Ill. page 210). The *Olympic* sailed from Southampton on her maiden voyage in June 1911 and completed the passage to New York at an average speed of 20 knots. The *Titanic* left Southampton on her maiden voyage on April 10th 1912 under the command of Captain E. J. Smith, and five days later was at the bottom of the Atlantic. Carrying 1,316 passengers and a crew of 892, the *Titanic* made excellent time

This picture gives some idea of the elaborate decor of the first-class saloon aboard the Cunard liner *Aquitania*.

in calm but cold weather and the passengers and crew were said to have been very happy and contented in the comfortable liner. At about 11.40 p.m. on Sunday April 14th the *Titanic* struck a huge iceberg. Captain Smith soon realized that despite the safety measures, which included fifteen transverse watertight bulkheads and a double bottom, the 'unsinkable' liner was sinking. There was no panic on board when all passengers were ordered on deck and the sixteen lifeboats manned and lowered. After the women and children had got into the boats, men were allowed to occupy the vacant spaces, but only a third of the passengers and crew could be accommodated. It is not clear what happened to the four collapsible boats carried.

The *Titanic* was equipped with wireless and the operator remained at his post sending out distress signals. The steamship *Californian* was only about nine miles away, but the wireless operator was off duty and did not receive the calls for help. Seven ships answered the distress signals and steamed rapidly to the rescue. However, at 2.20 a.m., two and half hours after striking the iceberg, the *Titanic* stood vertically on end with her stern high in the air and then slowly disappeared beneath the water. The liner *Carpathia* arrived at the scene of the disaster soon after the *Titanic* sank, and rescued 703 people from the boats, but 1,505 passengers and crew perished in the bitterly cold sea in the worst disaster to a passenger ship in peace time.

A Court of Inquiry, with Lord Mersey as president, investigated the disaster and delivered its findings on July 30th 1912.

The main points of the judgment were:

The loss of the *Titanic* was due to collision with an iceberg brought about by the excessive speed at which the ship was being navigated.

Captain Smith kept at a high speed, because for many years it had been the practice of liners using the outward southern track when in the vicinity of ice at night in clear weather to keep the course, maintain the speed, and trust to a sharp lookout to enable them to avoid the danger. Lord Mersey accepted the evidence as to the practice and as to the immunity from casualties which was said to have accompanied it. But the event had proved the practice to be bad. Its root is probably to be found in competition and in the desire of the public for quick passages rather than in the judgment of navigators.

In the circumstances Lord Mersey was not able to blame Captain Smith, and it was to be hoped that the practice would now be abandoned for more prudent and wiser measures. What was a mistake in the case of the *Titanic* would without doubt be negligence in any similar case in the future.

The efficiency of the automatic arrangements for the closing of the watertight doors, which was questioned during the inquiry, had no important bearing on the question of hastening the sinking of the ship.

The *Titanic* was provided with twenty boats, giving accommodation for 1,178 persons. There had been no proper boat drill nor a boat muster.

The discipline during the lowering of the boats was good, but the organization should have been better, and if it had been, it was possible that more lives would have been saved.

Lord Mersey did not agree that any moral duty was imposed upon Mr. Bruce Ismay, because he was the managing director of the steamship company, to wait on board until the vessel foundered.

There was no unfair treatment of the third-class passengers.

Captain Rostron, of the *Carpathia,* 'did the very best that could be done'.

The S.S. *Californian* was not more than eight or ten miles away from the *Titanic.*

'When she first saw the rockets, the *Californian* could have pushed through the ice to the open water without any serious risk and so have come to the assistance of the *Titanic.*

'Had she done so, she might have saved many, if not all, the lives that were lost.'

The Court made a number of recommendations as to safety measures for passenger liners and as a result regulations came into force which required the provision of sufficient lifeboats to accommodate all the passengers and crew of a vessel.

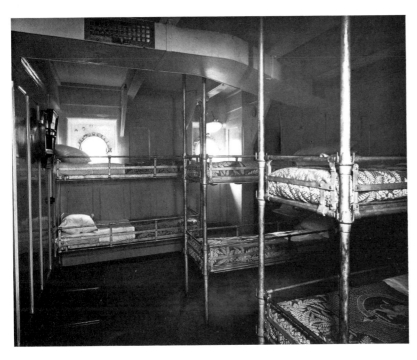

A third-class cabin on board the *Aquitania*. Notice the insignia of the Cunard Line on the bed-spreads.

The swimming-pool on board the *Aquitania*. She had completed three round voyages —the first commencing on May 13th 1914—when the First World War broke out.

IX BETWEEN THE WARS—
ATLANTIC LINERS AND CRUISE SHIPS

At the outbreak of the First World War in August 1914, the German Hamburg-American Line super-liners *Imperator*, 51,969 tons, and the *Vaterland*, 54,282 tons, had been added to their Atlantic services while their even larger *Bismarck*, 56,551 tons, launched in June 1914 had not been completed. The British Cunard Line's *Aquitania*, 45,647 tons, made her maiden transatlantic voyage in June 1914, and the *Britannic*, 48,158 tons (later sunk on war service) was being built for the White Star Line.

After the war the British liners *Mauritania*, *Aquitania* and *Olympic* (sister ship of the ill-fated *Titanic*) were available for the Atlantic services while the German liners *Imperator*, *Vaterland*, and the *Bismarck*, completed in 1922, were turned over to British and American authorities as compensation for wartime losses. The *Bismarck* became the White Star liner *Majestic* and served on the North Atlantic route between Southampton and New York until 1936; the *Imperator*, acquired by the Cunard Line, and renamed *Berengaria*, continued in the transatlantic service until 1938, while the *Vaterland* passed to the United States Line, and after an $8,000,000 refit became the *Leviathan*. Her first voyage as an American liner from New York to Cherbourg and Southampton was made in July 1923 and she continued in service until 1934. Thus for some ten years after the First World War the 'express' North Atlantic services were maintained by the Cunard Line's *Mauritania*, *Aquitania*, and *Berengaria*; by the White Star Line's *Olympic* and *Majestic* with a smaller liner, the *Homeric*, 34,356 tons, formerly the North German Lloyd liner *Columbus*, launched in 1913, while the *Leviathan* remained the lone American super-liner. As a result of legislation by the United States Government in 1924, severe limitations were applied to the number of immigrants entering the United States of America, and the

A decorative panel used in the first-class dining-room of the Messageries Maritimes motor-ship *Félix Roussel*, 16,774 tons, built in 1930.

prewar flow of more than a million immigrants in each year was reduced to about 160,000. One of the principal sources of revenue for passenger steamers was drastically reduced and the demand for very cheap steerage travel across the Atlantic curtailed. Consequently during this period con-

In the immediate postwar period an important alteration in marine propulsion systems was the change, almost universal for fast passenger liners, from coal to oil fuel. Filling a ship's bunkers with coal was a relatively slow and dirty process when automatic machinery was available, but was

In accordance with the traditions of the Messageries Maritimes Line, the decorations of the *Félix Roussel* were in the same style of art as that of some of the countries visited by the vessel. These panels are reproductions of a frieze at the temple of Angkor Vat.

siderable changes took place in the traditional class designations. Steerage was abolished, the best of the third class and some of the second class were combined to make 'tourist third cabin.' In the 1930's first class became 'cabin class' and second class 'tourist.'

much worse in more remote ports where hand bunkering was necessary (Ill. p. 194). Oil fuel could be pumped aboard quickly and efficiently while considerable saving on bunker space was possible, as one ton of oil provided the same work effort as 1.3 tons of coal. When the *Mauritania* was converted to oil-fired furnaces in 1922, 7,000 tons of coal in the bunkers was replaced by 5,350 tons of oil in the tanks, and it was possible to reduce the stokehold staff from 446 to 176 men.

Another innovation was the motor-ship. The first suc-

a small tanker built in 1904. The first Atlantic liner to be propelled by Diesel engines was the *Gripsholm*, built at Newcastle in 1925 for the Swedish-America Line's service between Gothenburg and New York.

The first large liner designed and built after the First

Grand staircase in the *Conte Grande*, 1928.

cessful application of the internal combustion principle for marine use was made in the late 1880's when a launch was fitted with a two-cylinder engine, in which petroleum or paraffin oil was used. The heavy-oil engine was introduced by Dr. Rudolf Diesel in 1893, and the first motor-ship was

World War was the French Line's *Ile-de-France*, 43,500 tons, launched in March 1926. This liner, propelled by quadruple propellers driven by steam-turbine engines, had a service speed of 24 knots. The decoration of the public rooms were in contemporary French design and created a sensation at the time. The *Ile-de-France* sailed on her maiden voyage from Le Havre to New York in June 1927, and with accommodation for 1,686 passengers, soon became a popular and successful liner.

The next major advance in the design of large passenger steamers came in 1929 when the North German Lloyd Line put into service the new liner *Bremen* (Ill. p. 225). Built at Bremen, and launched in August 1928, the *Bremen*, 51,656 tons, was 938 feet long with a breadth of 101 feet. The design of the liner incorporated a number of new features including a bulbous stem below the waterline, and streamlined superstructure and funnels. The *Bremen* could carry 732 first-class passengers, 593 tourist class, and 822 third class. The decoration of the public rooms were designed and carried out by leading German artists. The dining-room, decorated in ivory, gold and green, extended upward through three of the eleven decks and could seat 600 people. The walls of the special dining-room, known as the 'Porcelain Room,' were covered with tiles, with a relief of President Hindenburg as a central motif. Another special dining-room, known as the 'Hunt Room,' was decorated with tapestries. The first-class cabins were provided with hot and cold running water while the baths had both fresh water and salt water. Each cabin had a mahogany bedstead, fitted wardrobe, bedside table, and easy chairs. The swimming-pool had heated water and was fitted with a device

Ornate furnishings and decorations in the Italian liner *Conte Grande*, launched in 1927.

Passengers watch a movie in the first-class lounge of the *New York*. This transatlantic liner was built for the Hamburg-America Line in 1927.

which pumped water from the deep end to a water cascade at the shallow end. Frahm anti-rolling tanks were fitted to the *Bremen* and the liner was propelled by quadruple screws driven by four independent sets of single-reduction geared turbines with a total output of about 130,000 shaft h.p. A catapult was fitted to launch an aeroplane to expedite the mails and three days could be saved on the delivery of mails between New York and Berlin. On her maiden trip in July 1929, the *Bremen* crossed the Atlantic in 4 days, 17 hours, 42 minutes, at a mean speed of 27.83 knots and captured the Blue Riband which had been held by the *Mauritania* for twenty-two years. The *Europa*, a sister ship, but with several differences, including the shape and height of the funnels, went into service in March 1930 and crossed the

Tropical night in the South Atlantic. The *Cap Arcona*, 27,500 tons, was the Hamburg-South America Line's fastest passenger ship to South America in the 1930's.

Atlantic at an average speed of 27.91 knots, thus beating the *Bremen* by a small margin. Three years later the *Bremen* regained the record with a westbound passage at an average speed of 28.51 knots. Both liners were very successful, their low streamlined appearance and modern amenities attracted passengers and for some years the two liners together carried 12 per cent of the transatlantic traffic. The *Bremen* was bombed and set on fire during an air raid at Bremerhaven, during the Second World War, and was subsequently scrapped. The *Europa* survived the war and was taken over by the French Line. The liner was renamed *Liberté* and after an extensive refit sailed on her first voyage under French ownership in August 1950, finally being sold to shipbreakers in December 1961.

During the 1920's three Italian shipping companies were in competition for the passenger trade to America and in 1930 two of these companies — Navigazione Generale Italiana and Lloyd Sabaudo — each started to build a super-liner for the Atlantic service. To avoid unnecessary competition, the Italian Government decided that these two companies and the third company, the Cosulich Line, should amalgamate; thus in 1932, the now-famous Italia Line was established and the two new super-liners, the *Rex* and the *Conte di Savoia* (Ill. pp. 227, 232) were to sail under the same management. Both vessels were built in Italy, the *Rex* by the Società Anonima Ansaldo at Sestri, near Genoa, and the *Conte di Savoia* by Cantieri Riuniti dell'Adriatico at Trieste. The *Rex*, 51,075 tons, was launched in July 1931. With an

223

In this galley the food was cooked for the 680 passengers of the P & O liner *Viceroy of India*, launched in 1929.

overall length of 880 feet and breadth of 97 feet, the liner had eleven decks: the sun, sports, promenade, saloon and A to G decks. The hull was subdivided by fourteen watertight bulkheads and further protection was provided by longitudinal wing bulkheads which extended for about 260 feet amidships. Accommodation was available for 408 first-class, 358 special-class (a name adopted because of the prejudice by

Swimming-pool in the *Conte Grande*, 1928.

the public against second class), 410 tourist-class, and 866 third-class passengers. The propelling machinery consisted of four independent sets of Parsons turbines with a total output of 130,000 shaft h.p. and on trials a speed of 28.5 knots was attained. The *Conte di Savoia*, 48,502 tons, launched in October 1931 was 814.6 feet long overall, with a beam of 95.8 feet and had the same number of decks as the *Rex*. Three hundred and sixty first-class, 778 tourist-class, and 922 third-class passengers could be carried with a crew of 651. Both liners were luxuriously equipped, with the *Conte di Savoia* the more lavish of the two. An outstanding feature of this ship was the Grande Colonna Hall, 24 feet high with

Passengers keep fit in the gymnasium of the Union-Castle liner *Winchester Castle* in the 1930's.

a floor area of 5,918 square feet, which contained a central nave, reserved for dancing, with aisles on each side. The ceiling was decorated with a reproduction of a painting by Lucchesini of the battle of Lepanto. The large swimming-pool, which could be reached from the sun and sports decks, was part of the Lido which included a café and restaurant. The *Conte di Savoia* was the first large Atlantic liner to be fitted with a Sperry stabilizer device, which limited the roll of the ship, even in rough weather, to 3 degrees on either side of the vertical. It consisted of three gyroscopes each with a flywheel 13 feet in diameter and weighing over 100 tons. These flywheels were rotated at a normal speed of 8,000 revolutions per minute by an electric motor.

Over the years various methods of reducing the roll of a ship have been adopted; the fitting of bilge keels was a big step forward, while in the 1880's experiments were made with anti-rolling tanks in which water passed automatically from one tank to another and so retarded rolling. A more advanced method was invented in Germany by Dr. H. Frahm. Tanks of 'U' form, consisting of two vertical tanks joined at the bottom by a horizontal portion, were fitted thwartwise across the ship. The bottom tank was filled with water which was allowed to rise about half-way up the vertical tanks. As the ship rolled, water passed from one vertical tank to the other. The tops of the vertical tanks were connected by an air pipe fitted with a valve by which the movement of the water could be controlled. In 1910 the Frahm anti-rolling system was tried out in the Hamburg-America steamer

Ypiranga; later a number of liners—including the Cunard *Laconia* of 1912—were built with tanks forming part of their initial structure, and in 1928 the liners *Bremen* and *Europa* were built with a modified form of Frahm anti-rolling tanks.

The use of the gyroscope as an anti-rolling device was investigated in 1907 and developed into the Sperry system used in the *Conte di Savoia*. At the present time it is considered essential for a passenger liner to be fitted with stabilizers and the Denny-Brown system fitted to the Cunard liner *Queen Elizabeth II*, launched in 1967, has four folding fins fitted below the waterline. The angle of the fins can be controlled from the bridge.

The *Bremen*, built for the North German Lloyd Line and launched in August 1928. On her maiden voyage to New York in July 1929 the *Bremen* crossed the Atlantic in the record-breaking time of 4 days, 17 hours, 42 minutes.

To return to the *Rex* and *Conte di Savoia*, the two liners were put into a service between Naples and New York, and the *Rex*, the faster of the two vessels, captured the Blue Riband in 1933 with a record trip from Gibraltar to New York in 4 days, 13 hours, 58 minutes, at a mean speed of

Cruise Ships and Cruising

The idea of using a ship as a floating hotel for a voyage made for sightseeing or health reasons is by no means a recent innovation. In the 1840's the Peninsular and Orien-

The captain samples a new dish on the bridge of a Hamburg-America liner.

28.82 knots. The *Rex* was bombed and sunk by British aircraft in September 1944 and the sunken hull was broken up for scrap in 1947. The *Conte di Savoia*, also sunk by British aircraft in September 1943, was raised in 1945, but was not rebuilt and was broken up in 1950.

tal Steam Navigation Company—the P. & O. Line—were arranging sightseeing tours or cruises in the Mediterranean using their steamers, which made regular services from Gibraltar and Malta to Athens, Smyrna, Constantinople (Istanbul), Beirut, Jaffa, and Alexandria. Tourists using these steamers could travel from Alexandria to Cairo by river steamer and return, if they so wished, from Alexandria to Malta by a direct route. In an effort to publicize their cruises, the P. & O. Company gave the novelist William Makepeace Thackeray a free round trip in 1844. Thackeray to Jaffa and Alexandria. Thackeray made land excursions from Jaffa to Jerusalem, and from Cairo to the Pyramids, in organized parties.

The food served in these small steamers seems to have been particularly good for the period, probably because the

The *Conte di Savoia*, 48,500 tons, launched in October 1931 for the Italia Line. Her maiden voyage from Genoa to New York was in 1932 and in May 1933 she secured the Atlantic westbound record with a crossing from Gibraltar to the Ambrose Light at an average speed of 27.53 knots.

made the passage to Gibraltar via Vigo, Lisbon and Cadiz in the wooden paddle-steamer *Lady Mary Wood*, of 553 tons. The cruise was continued to Malta and Constantinople in the slightly larger steamer *Tagus*, while the *Iberia*, of 516 tons, was used for the voyage from Constantinople distances between ports of call were relatively short. A menu from a P. & O. Line Mediterranean steamer of the time includes: Mulligatawny soup, salt fish and egg sauce, roast haunch of mutton, boiled shoulder and onion sauce, boiled beef, roast fowl, pilau of fowl, ham, haricot mutton, and

227

Launch of the P & O liner *Stratheden* at the Barrow-in-Furness shipyard of Vickers-Armstrong Ltd. on June 10th 1937. This 23,700-ton liner was used on the service from Britain to Australia via Suez Canal and as a troopship in the Second World War.

A model of the Italian liner *Virgilio*. A motor-ship of 11,700 tons, the *Virgilio* was built at Baia, Italy, and completed in 1927. She served on the Navigazione Generale Italiana and Italia Line's services from Genoa to South America via the Panama Canal.

curry with rice. These dishes were served with French beans or cabbage, boiled or baked potatoes, and were followed by a choice of damson tart, currant tart, rice pudding or currant fritters. Writing after his return from the cruise Thackeray was lavish in his praise for what he called 'a delightful excursion' and recommended 'all persons who have the time and means' to make a similar journey.

In 1891, Albert Ballin, director-general of the Hamburg-America Line, arranged for steamers to sail to the Mediterranean and elsewhere as 'cruising yachts' and later some of the smaller Hamburg-America liners, not fully employed on the Atlantic routes during the winter months, were sent on

First-class single-berth cabin in the *Victoria*, 13,000 tons, a motor-ship built for the Lloyd Triestino Line in 1931.

The *Conte Biancamano*, 24,400 tons, built at Glasgow in 1925 for the Lloyd Sabaudo Line. The liner first served on the Genoa to New York service, but was transferred in 1932 to a service to South America.

pleasure cruises. For instance the Hamburg-America liner *Cleveland*, of 16,960 tons and built in 1907, normally employed on the Hamburg, Southampton, Cherbourg to New York service, sailed in January 1910 with 650 tourists on a cruise round the world. This cruise proved very successful and the liner was employed for cruising purposes during the winter months until the outbreak of war in 1914.

However, it was not until after the First World War that pleasure cruising in luxury liners became very popular with the public and during the 1920's and 1930's many of the famous steamship companies had fleets of liners devoted solely to pleasure cruising. In the 1930's the White Star Line operated the *Homeric*, *Doric*, *Laurentic*, *Olympic*, *Adriatic*, and *Britannic* as cruising ships. The *Homeric*, of 34,351 tons, reputed to be particularly steady in bad weather, was scheduled for no less than nine cruises, of fourteen days duration, between June and October 1933. The Orient Line's 20,000-ton steamers *Orford*, *Orontes*, and *Orama* were used for cruises on the Atlantic, Mediterranean, and in Scandinavian waters. The *Atlantis*, built in 1913 as the Pacific Steam Navigation Company's *Andes*, was acquired by the Royal Mail Line and refitted as a cruise ship

The Grande Colonna Hall in the *Conte di Savoia* took its name and style from the gallery of the seventeenth century Colonna Palace in Rome.

in 1930. A fourteen-day spring cruise to the Atlantic Islands in the *Atlantis* cost from 24 guineas in 1933. At the same time the Hamburg-South America Line operated a round voyage for tourists to Brazil in their famous liner *Cap Arcona* (Ill. p. 223), of 27,560 tons, at that time the largest and fastest ship sailing from Southampton to South America. It is not possible in the space available to mention all the fine passenger liners used for cruises between the wars, but the following description of the *Arandora Star*, known as the 'Queen of cruising liners,' provides some idea of the general conditions aboard a very luxurious cruise ship.

The *Arandora Star*, built by Cammell Laird & Company at Birkenhead for the Blue Star Line, was launched in 1929. The liner of 14,600 tons was 535 feet long overall, with a breadth of 68 feet, and was intended for the passenger and refrigerated-meat trade between London and South America. In 1929, the Blue Star Line had the *Arandora Star* converted to a first-class cruise liner with accommodation for about 375 passengers on the main, upper bridge and upper promenade decks. Suites of two or three rooms were available, in many cases with private bathrooms. There were no bunks, as every state-room was furnished with sprung beds, and kept cool with fans and punkah-louvre ventilation. There were four large public rooms on the promenade deck; a lounge and music room forward, a large smoking-room amidships, with an adjoining ballroom decorated in green and ivory, with a dancing area of about

cruising, the *Arandora Star* left Southampton on January 21st 1939 for what was to be her last winter cruise: Madeira, Leeward Islands, Windward Islands, Trinidad, Venezuela, Panama, Jamaica, Cayman Islands, Cuba, Bahamas, Florida, Puerto Rico, Barbados and the Canary Islands were all

This model represents the *Conte di Savoia*, the Italian luxury liner. The *Conte di Savoia* and the *Rex* were the largest and fastest vessels of the Italia Line in the 1930's.

1,500 square feet, and provision for concerts and cinema shows. Further aft on this deck was the garden lounge and verandah café. The fine Louis Quatorze dining-room on the upper deck was approximately 85 feet by 68 feet and could seat all the passengers at one sitting. Large clear deck space was available on the games deck and sun deck for recreation. The open-air swimming pool was tiled in blue and could be flood-lit for night bathing. After ten years of

visited before the liner returned to Southampton on March 16th 1939. The *Arandora Star* was torpedoed and sunk in the Atlantic by a German submarine in July 1940.

After the Second World War the popularity of cruising was revived and many famous ships were used regularly or occasionally for pleasure cruising. Even the great super-liners *Queen Mary* and *Queen Elizabeth* were used from time to time as cruise ships. To take advantage of the demand for this type of travel, passenger liners designed as combined passenger and cargo carriers were converted to carry only passengers. By the 1970's great changes had taken place in the development of the pleasure cruise business and four principal categories of cruises are available to holiday-makers.

fitted with stabilizers, air-conditioning and spacious public rooms including both restaurants and self-service cafeteria, these vessels are particularly suitable for the purpose. Thirdly, the 'flycruise,' a new conception of cruising, in which the passengers fly by charter plane to a suitable port

The *Conte Grande*, shown in this model, was built at Trieste and completed in 1928. The 25,660-ton liner was 652 feet long, with a beam of 78 feet, and had a service speed of 21 knots. She served on the Italia Line's routes to New York and to South America.

There is, firstly, the traditional cruise, sailing from a home port for a voyage of two or three weeks and then returning to the home port, that has remained popular. Some 150,000 passengers embark for this type of holiday from British ports every year. Secondly, the low cost, short duration or 'mini' cruise for four or five days, made outside the busy holiday season. The latest carferry ships of about 10,000 tons are frequently used for the cruises and, as they are usually

in the Mediterranean or Caribbean and then embark for a normal cruise. It is expected that more than half a million people will take advantage of this form of travel in 1973. Lastly, the 'cruise and stay' in which the passenger combines a stay at a shore hotel with a short cruise.

Some of the later cruise ships will be described in a later chapter, but to conclude this short account of cruise ships

233

and cruising it is interesting to return to the P & O Line and compare the cruising activities of this company in the 1840's and at the present day. In place of the tiny 500-ton wooden paddle-steamers like the *Lady Mary Wood* and *Iberia* carrying a few tourists on the regular services, the P & O Line now operates the largest cruising fleet in the world. The liners *Canberra*, 45,000 tons; *Oriana*, 42,000 tons; *Arcadia*, 30,000 tons; *Orsova*, 29,000 tons; *Himalaya*, *Orcades*, and *Oronsay*, all of 28,000 tons and the *Chusan*, 24,000 tons, were scheduled to make thirty-one cruises in 1972.

X THE *NORMANDIE* AND THE *QUEEN MARY:* RIVAL SUPER-LINERS ON THE ATLANTIC

Pivoting sidelights in which the angle of opening could be easily adjusted were fitted to some of the outboard state-rooms of the *Normandie*.

After the First World War techniques of ship-building and marine engineering developed sufficiently for the French Line and the Cunard Steamship Company to contemplate construction of passenger liners of a size and speed not previously considered possible. It was the ambition of each of these companies to maintain a regular weekly service at all times of the year between Southampton, Le Havre and New York with two ships instead of the three previously needed, an ambition which led to the construction of the two great super-liners of the 1930's: the *Normandie* and the *Queen Mary.*

The decision of the French Line to build the *Normandie* was followed by a series of experiments with models at the French Admiralty research station, and at Hamburg, to determine the hull form with the greatest stability and least resistance to water flow. The draught of the ship was limited by the available depth of water at Le Havre and New York, and this fact, coupled with the desired speed of about 30 knots, determined the final dimensions of the liner. The *Normandie* (Ill. p. 236) was built by the Chantier et Ateliers de Saint-Nazaire and launched in October 1932. The liner, of about 80,000 tons, had an overall length of 1,029 feet with a breadth of 119.3 feet, and had eleven decks: the sun, boat, promenade, upper and A to G decks. The hull was of unusual shape in relation to the waterline portion and also to the superstructure. The vessel was very full amidships and fine at the ends. The ship's side was flared forward, finishing as a clipper bow above water, but with a bulbous form at the forefoot (Ill. p. 238). The great height of the ship and the flare were designed to prevent waves breaking on the promenade deck in bad weather. This deck was turtle-backed and cleared of all obstructions. The double hull extended the full length of the ship and up the sides, and subdivision of the hull was effected by eleven transverse watertight bulkheads with hydraulically operated doors.

For propulsion, quadruple propellers were driven by four sets of Zoëlly impulse turbines each of 33,400 kw. output. Twenty-nine three-drum Penhoët water-tube boilers supplied steam at a pressure of 400 lb. per square inch at a

The *Normandie*, 79,300 tons, had an overall length of 1,029 feet and a breadth of 119.3 feet. First of the 1,000-foot liners, this handsome French Line vessel sailed on her maiden voyage from Le Havre to New York on May 29th 1935. The appearance of the *Normandie* was enhanced by the fine clipper bow with a whale-back forecastle and a breakwater, and by the streamlined funnels and upperworks.

temperature of 662 °F. The turbines ran at 2,430 r.p.m. and power was conveyed to four 40,000-h.p. motors, each of which was coupled to a propeller (Ill. p. 245). The ship attained a speed on trials of over 32 knots and, with a fuel

bunker capacity of 8,930 tons, the average consumption on a single Atlantic crossing was 5,000 tons of fuel oil.

There was accommodation for 1,972 passengers, 28 of *grand luxe* class in special suites, 30 in *de luxe* class, 790

Looking aft along the sun deck of the *Normandie*. Used as a games area the sun deck was a completely open deck as all ventilating gear, and other machinery normally found on deck was grouped below in special compartments.

first class, 16 intermediate, 654 tourist class, 139 mixed class, and 315 third class. The cabin accommodation varied in the degree of luxury provided, but only 126 of the cabins were inboard rooms. On the sun deck there were two *suites de grand luxe*, each of five rooms and, on the upper deck, two of six rooms each. Each *suite* consisted of two out-board bedrooms and two inboard bedrooms, a sitting-room, a dining-room with adjoining pantry, bathrooms, and toilets.

Each suite was named after a town in Normandy and the decoration was the work of eminent French architects. In the starboard upper deck *suite* one of the bedrooms had walls covered with blue lacquer and panels of etched glass, while the furniture was covered in Chinese sharkskin. In the drawing-room the walls were covered in parchment while the furniture was of Macassar wood. The *de luxe suites* were of two rooms each, also decorated individually. Some were modern, some period in decoration.

The first-class accommodation included 24 veranda suites, each for two or three people, as well as bedroom/state-rooms and sitting-room/state-rooms which could be grouped in pairs where necessary to give small *suites*. The furniture in all the *de luxe* and first-class bedrooms included full-length wardrobes, mirrors, chests of drawers, and chairs. The beds were all standard size with intersprung mattresses. A telephone and an electric clock were fitted in each cabin (Ill. p. 242). All had a private bath or shower and a water closet.

The public rooms achieved a spaciousness previously unknown on board ship due to the internal structural arrangements which allowed uninterrupted runs of up to 400 feet long. The general theme of the decorations was the history of Normandy since the 11th century. Passengers embarked on C deck into the main entrance hall, from whence stairs and electric lifts led to the other decks. The hall was two and a half decks high and was panelled in Algerian onyx with decorations in hammered glass. Huge gilded bronze doors led to the main dining-saloon. This room was 305 feet long, 46 feet wide, and its central portion extended through three decks. It was air-conditioned and seated 700 passengers at a sitting. The dining-saloon was panelled entirely in moulded glass tiles and hand-hammered strips of glass. It was lit by luminous glass panels fitted to the walls and ceiling, which gave the impression of fountains of light. Eight large bronze doors led to smaller dining-rooms. Large bas-reliefs in gilded plaster occupied a part of the end walls while a statue of *La Paix* was erected behind the commander's table.

The chapel on B deck (Ill. p. 243) was intended for both Catholic and Protestant services. The nave extended through two decks, and the walls were covered with Pyrenean marble. The decoration was the work of several artists and included a painted ceiling, side friezes and wooden

The handsome clipper bow of the *Normandie* was of bulbous form at the fore-foot below the water-line.

panels depicting the Path of the Holy Rood. The main lounge and smoking-room (Ill. p. 240) both had ceilings two decks high with large bronze-framed windows the full height of the rooms. The smoking-room was panelled entirely in Coromandel lacquer with gilt overlays, the panels depicting hunting scenes in the Egyptian style. Aft of the smoking-room a wide ornamental stairway led to the grill-room on the boat deck. At the top of this staircase stood a large lacquered statue of *La Normandie* (Ill. below), 7 feet, 8 inches tall and weighing 1,000 lb. Besides the smaller lounges, writing-room, grill-rooms, and bars, the passengers had a swimming-pool 75 feet by 18 feet of varied depth, a theatre whose stage was as large as that of several Parisian theatres, childrens' apartments comprising nursery, playroom (Ill. p. 242), dining-room and servants' quarters, and a winter garden.

The winter garden was at the forward end of the promenade deck. Lit by specially large windows constructed to withstand the full force of the seas which could strike this part of the ship, the winter garden was laid out with shrubs, plants, and turf. There were fountains and aquaria, and large cages of singing birds. On the aft wall was an arch of marble covered with a creeper. Beside the areas of enclosed promenade the first-class passengers had some 450 feet of the sun deck (Ill. p. 237) for a games area, as well as various other terraces, totalling in all some 46,000 square feet. The sun deck was unusual in that all ventilating gear and other pieces of machinery normally placed on deck were grouped below in special compartments, leaving a completely open deck space.

The sixteen 'intermediate cabins' were first-class cabins which were available for passengers travelling tourist class

The public rooms of the *Normandie* achieved a spaciousness previously unknown on board ship. This feature is well shown by the staircase in this illustration.

Statue of *La Normandie* at the head of the stairs leading to the grill-room on the promenade deck of the *Normandie*.

One of the large panels which decorated the first-class smoking-room in the *Normandie*. This panel entitled 'La Conquête du Cheval' was one of a series of panels depicting hunting scenes designed by M. Dunand.

who required better sleeping accommodation. The tourist-class passenger had the benefit of accommodation which on any other boat would have been of first-class standard. Their public rooms included a dining-saloon, lounge, writ-ing-room, snack-bar, smoking-room, gymnasium and swimming-pool, and a childrens' playroom. The total area of public rooms and deck space amounted to 29,600 square feet, about 45 square feet per passenger. Cabins were two-,

The theme of some decorations of the *Normandie* portrayed the history of Normandy since the time of William the Conqueror. This panel showed a Norman knight based on an illustration from the Bayeux Tapestry.

three-, or four-berth, with standard beds and Pullman-type upper berths. The 'mixed-class' cabins could be used for either tourist- or third-class passengers, as the need arose.

The third class catered for a smaller proportion of the passengers than was usual in North Atlantic liners of the time. However, they also enjoyed a similar degree of spaciousness, namely 45 square feet per passenger. They slept

The bedroom in one of the *Normandie*'s de luxe suites.

The children's playroom at the base of the forward funnel on the sun deck of the *Normandie*.

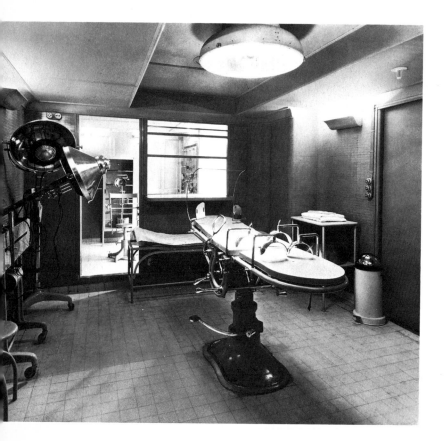

in two-, three-, or four-berth cabins and had their own dining-room, smoking-room, lounge, and bar.

The crew of the *Normandie* consisted of 66 officers, 120 deck crew, 187 engine- and boiler-room staff and 972 domestic staff who were able to supply services comparable to those of the best hotels ashore. The ship was equipped with four kitchens: the main kitchen preparing meals for most passengers and officers, the crew's kitchen, a small kitchen serving the grill-room, and a kosher kitchen. All cooking was done by means of electricity, with the exception of the grills, some of which were charcoal burning. The kitchen layout was similar to that of a large hotel, with various annexes; bakeries, larders, cold rooms, pantries, and sculleries. Service lifts and telephones communicated with the various dining-rooms. The several medical departments of the ship, staffed by three doctors and seven attendants, were laid out to conform to international regulations. There were 17 hospital beds for male passengers, 12 beds for women, 4 isolation beds for men and 3 for women,

The hospital on the *Normandie* included an operating-theatre and X-ray laboratory.

12 beds for the crew and 2 beds in the prophylactic hospital. Additionally there was one first-class isolation bed, a single bed observation room, two padded cells, and a mortuary. The surgical departments included an operating-theatre (Ill. p. 242), an X-ray laboratory, and an ambulance dressing-room. A small shop sold medical preparations to the passengers. Numerous other shops were provided on board where books, flowers, tobacco and other goods might be purchased. There was also a hairdressing service for the passengers. A printing service issued a daily bulletin of news from wireless broadcasts as well as shipboard events.

The Cunard Steamship Company considered the conception of an 80,000-ton liner in the late 1920's and devoted nearly four years to investigation of the best form of hull and engine design to provide not only a fast ship, but also one which would be comfortable even during the worst Atlantic storms. The final design was for a ship of 81,235 tons with an overall length of 1,019 feet, a breadth of 119 feet, and a cruising speed of about 30 knots. The keel of the *Queen Mary,* then known only as 'No. 534,' was laid down in August 1930 at the Clydebank yard of John Brown & Company. Due to the economic situation work on the vessel was suspended in December 1931 and not recommenced until April 1934, following the merger of the Cunard and White Star Companies, and a grant from the British Government. 'No. 534' was launched on September 26th 1934 and named *Queen Mary* by Her Majesty Queen Mary.

Like the *Normandie,* the *Queen Mary* was designed to carry a large number of passengers, with a high crew-to-passenger ratio, in conditions of great comfort, speed, and safety. There were twelve decks: the sports, sun, promenade, main, and A to H decks. The hull was divided by eighteen transverse watertight bulkheads fitted with hydraulically operated doors. A cellular double bottom formed

The chapel on the *Normandie*'s B deck had a nave which extended two decks high. Designed for both Roman Catholic and Protestant services, the chapel had an arched ceiling and the marble walls were relieved by fourteen panels depicting religious subjects.

243

Some of the oil-fired boilers which supplied steam to the Zoëlly impulse turbines of the *Normandie*, for a total maximum output of 160,000 shaft h.p. with synchronous electrical transmission.

an inner and outer skin running the full length of the ship. The upper part of her raked stem was constructed of rounded plates while the lower part was a steel casting. The cruiser stern carried an unbalanced streamlined rudder. The

Queen Mary's four propellers were driven by four independent sets of Parsons impulse-reaction turbines. Each set comprised four turbines grouped round a main gear wheel, each turbine driving a separate pinion which engaged with

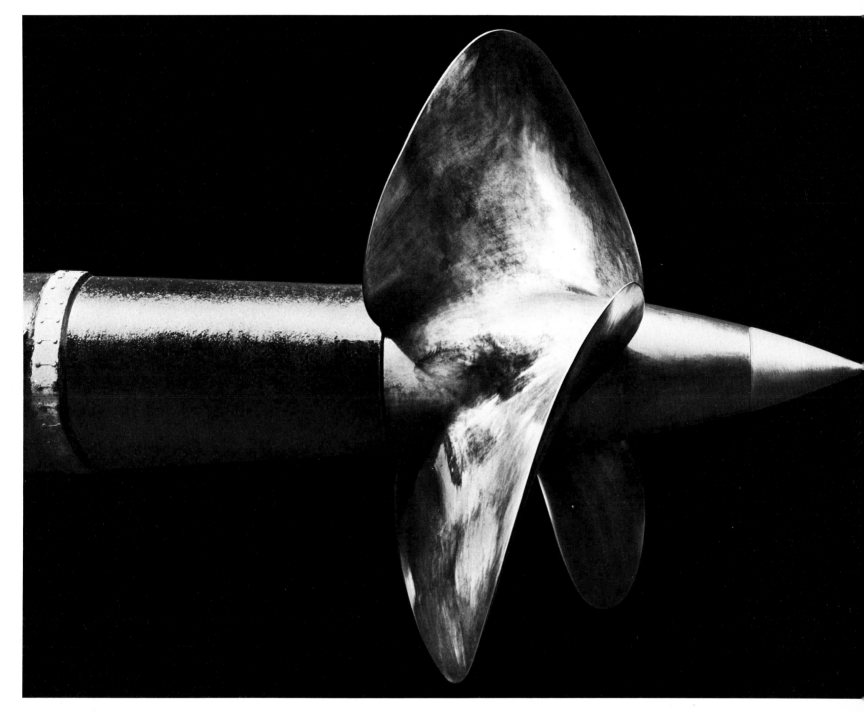

One of the quadruple three-bladed propellers first fitted to the *Normandie*. With these propellers the liner crossed the Atlantic on her maiden voyage at a record speed of 29.98 knots. In 1937 the *Normandie* was fitted with four-bladed propellers and established a new record crossing at an average speed of 30.58 knots.

the main gear wheel on the forward end of each propeller shaft. Steam for the turbines was generated by twenty-seven boilers in five boiler rooms, with a working pressure of 400 lb. per square inch at a temperature of 700 °F. Six thousand, three hundred tons of fuel were carried. On her trials, the *Queen Mary* is said to have attained a speed of nearly 33 knots.

To give internal service in this vast floating hotel three

boilers supplied steam to seven turbogenerators which constituted the ship's electrical power station (Ill. below). This power, nearly 10,000 KW per hour, lit and ventilated the ship and operated the lifts, galleys, cinema, telephone and wireless systems. In addition, the steering gear, deck machinery, anchoring and mooring equipment were all worked by electricity.

Seven hundred and seventy-six first-class or 'cabin'-class passengers, 784 tourist-class, and 579 third-class passengers could be carried in conditions of luxury never before found

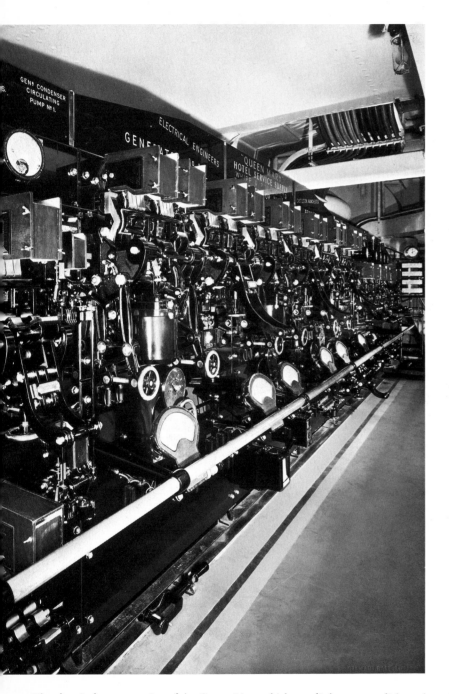

The electrical-power station of the *Queen Mary* which supplied current to light and ventilate the liner and to operate the lifts, galleys, cinema, telephone, and radio systems.

The *Queen Mary,* then known only as No. 534, under construction at John Brown & Company's shipyard at Clydebank.

246

The Cunard Line was founded by Samuel Cunard in 1839. First known as the British and North American Royal Mail Steam Packet Company, the name Cunard Line soon came into popular use and in 1878 became the official name.

Bronze grill-doors, surmounted by a painting in tapestry style, in the main dining-room of the *Queen Mary*.

on board ship for all classes. The *Queen Mary* had a vast air-conditioned dining-room extending through three decks and accommodating nearly 800 diners at one sitting. There were also two additional dining-rooms situated fore and aft on C deck and various private dining-rooms for smaller groups. Grill-rooms, lounges, bars (Ill. below), smoking-rooms, and children's playrooms were allocated to each class, and an area of deck space allotted to sports. These facilities included swimming-pools, gymnasia, and squash courts. The ship was well provided with shops and the

The cocktail bar in the observation lounge on the promenade deck of the *Queen Mary*.

services of hairdressers, a hospital, and a dog kennels. The *Queen Mary* was renowned for the beauty and elegance of the interior decoration of the ship. Thirty-three well-known artists, painters, sculptors and wood and metal workers applied their skills in a co-ordinated scheme throughout the public rooms. The large dining-room carried a decorative map of the North Atlantic, 24 feet by 15 feet, showing the course taken by the liner between England and New York, complete with a moving crystal model of the ship. Each of the fifty-four special state-rooms was also decorated with its own scheme. Great care was taken in selecting different varieties of fabrics and carpets, and large rectangular windows looking out to sea were provided, with special sliding shutters. In all rooms and cabins a variety of wood and vitreous panelling was employed to cover all expanses of metal, and even the use of metal fitments was avoided.

The *Queen Mary*'s crew, 1,101 officers and men, included 750 'hotel' staff, of whom 125 worked in the kitchens. The liner's kitchens, which occupied nearly an acre of space, had separate areas for cabin and tourist class. Separate kitchens served the third class, the grill-room, and the passengers taking kosher food. As in the *Normandie*, the cooking, mixing, vegetable-preparing machinery and washing up was all done by means of electric power. A vast amount of linen was carried; half a million pieces in all, of which at any time one third was on the ship and the other two-thirds being laundered in Southampton and New York.

When the ship docked all this linen had to be changed and sufficient food taken aboard to serve 50,000 meals on each voyage. The main hall of the ship, nicknamed 'Regent Street,' contained various shops where passengers could buy clothes, books, perfumes, and other goods. There was also a hairdresser, and staff were on duty at the gymnasium and swimming-pools. The medical service, which included a fully-equipped hospital, was staffed by a physician, a surgeon, and eight assistants and nurses.

Both the *Normandie* and the *Queen Mary* were designed with elaborate systems to prevent the outbreak or spreading of a fire, though with ample provision for rescuing the passengers and crew if the ship had to be abandoned. On the *Normandie* the superstructure above the main deck was divided into sections by fireproof bulkheads and doors so that each section could be completely isolated. Each section had independent safety arrangements and lighting and pumping systems. Outer cabins each had two portholes, designed to hinge outward and permit escape in case of disaster. All the wood panelling was asbestos-lined and a large proportion of the wood used was fireproofed, either by the interposition of a layer of asbestos or by the application of special coatings. Fifty-six lifeboats of various sizes were carried. These gave a total capacity of 3,582 people, 8 per cent in excess of the number which could be carried on the liner. The majority of these were motor-boats, but additional smaller self-lowering boats were carried in which the crew members who had launched the larger boats could be accommodated.

The *Queen Mary* was also constructed with fireproof partitions and screens throughout the ship in order to localize any outbreak of fire. All the wood employed in the ship's construction was fireproofed. An elaborate system of fire-mains, hoses and self-actuating extinguishers rendered unlikely any widespread outbreak of fire. In every enclosed space on board there was an instrument designed to record any marked increase in temperature and to transmit this automatically to the bridge. Special attention was paid to insulating the miles of electrical cable in the ship. The *Queen Mary* was the first liner in the world to carry only motor-driven lifeboats. These craft, twenty-four in all, were fitted with copper buoyancy chambers and carried 145 people each, giving a total capacity of 240 spaces over the total number of people aboard. All the boats carried standard emergency rations and two were equipped with wireless.

The *Normandie* left Le Havre in the early evening of May 29th 1935 on her maiden voyage to New York, and anchored at Cowes Roads about 11 p.m. to take on the passengers from England. All the accommodation was booked and hundreds of requests for places had been turned down. During the crossing the average speed was reduced to 22.76 knots on the run from Southampton to Bishop's Rock owing to fog, but afterwards the following speeds were recorded: first day, 29.76 knots; second day, 28.72 knots; third day, 29.92 knots; fourth day, 32 knots. The passage from Bishop's Rock to Ambrose Light was made in four days, three hours, two minutes, giving an average speed of 29.98 knots. The return eastbound crossing took four days, three hours, twenty-five minutes, the average speed being 30.35 knots. The *Normandie* had thus broken all the existing speed records with a good margin. During the first seven voyages she carried 15,282 passengers, including 7,558 eastbound and 7,724 westbound. These 15,282 passengers were made up of 6,056 first class, 5,828 tourist, and 3,398 third class.

The *Queen Mary* left Southampton on her maiden voyage on March 26th 1936, ten months after the *Normandie*, and later that year crossed the Atlantic westward in four days, twenty-seven minutes, and eastward in three days, twenty-three hours, fifty-seven minutes, with average speeds of 30.14 and 30.63 knots and gained the Blue Riband. The record was subsequently recaptured by the *Normandie* when she was refitted with four-bladed propellers, but passed back

Normandie was in New York harbour. Neither her owners nor the French Government made any attempt to use her for war service and she remained at her berth until the United States became a belligerent in 1941. She was then appropriated by the United States Maritime Commission which

A first-class state-room in the *Queen Mary*. From 1936 until the outbreak of war in 1939, first class was known as cabin class in the *Queen Mary*, but after the war the designation first class was reintroduced.

to the *Queen Mary* in 1938 with a crossing of three days, twenty hours, forty-two minutes, at 31.69 knots.

At the outbreak of the Second World War in 1939 the

handed her over to the Navy for conversion to a troopship. She was renamed U.S.S. *Lafayette,* and was refitted at New York with extra berths and messing accommodation, anti-aircraft guns and magazines, and more fresh water distilling apparatus. During the course of this refit fire broke out and the ship capsized and sank from the weight of water pumped aboard. After the disaster, which took place in February 1942, the decision was taken to raise the ship, and this was

lifted off the bottom and refloated. However the hull was in such a bad condition that the famous liner was eventually towed to Port Newark and broken up.

The *Queen Mary* was outward bound for New York at the outbreak of war. She was converted into a troopship

A decorative panel from the *Queen Mary*. Thirty-three well-known artists, painters, sculptors, and wood and metal workers applied their skills in a co-ordinated scheme throughout the liner.

eventually accomplished in October 1943, by dividing the ship with temporary cross-bulkheads and pumping the water out section by section. By this method the ship was

and steamed some half a million miles on war service. Afterwards she was restored to her previous condition and went back on the North Atlantic run in July 1947. Not many alterations were made, but some features that had proved popular on the *Queen Elizabeth* were added to the *Queen Mary*. Two garden lounges were added, a 200-seat cinema and an air-conditioned cocktail lounge. New and improved accommodation was provided for the crew, and an important aid to navigation — radar — was installed. Many of the other public rooms were carefully restored to their 1936 condition, with the original decorations refurbished.

The liner made her last voyage in 1967 when she left Southampton on October 31st bound for the Pacific Ocean and California. There she was converted into a floating 'Museum of the Sea.' This exhibition is designed to show the history of marine exploration, oceanography, marine sciences and the story of the *Queen Mary*. Visitors will be able to inspect the ship's bridge, pass through the captain's, crew's, and passengers' rooms, and see the engines.

R.M.S. "QUEEN MARY"   Monday, September 14, 1959

LUNCHEON

Juices: Grape Fruit   Pineapple   Sauerkraut

Sea Food Cocktail

Smoked Irish Salmon with Capers

HORS D'ŒUVRE
Cornet de Jambon en Gelée   Œufs, Rémoulade   Matjes Herrings
Antipasto   Salade Landaise   Asparagus, Vinaigrette
Tomato, Windsor   Filets d'Anchois   Salade Beaucaire
Boneless Sardines   Roll Mops   Herrings in Tomato
Saucisson: Cervelat, Salami, Liver, Lyon, d'Arles and Mortadella
Olives—Green, Ripe and Farcies
Salted Almonds and Peanuts

SOUPS
Consommé Brunoise   Potage Malakoff
Jellied Madrilène

FISH
Fried Scallops, Cole Slaw, Tartare Sauce
COLD: Crab Flake Salad, Mayonnaise

FARINACEOUS
Gnochis, Piémontaise

VEGETARIAN
Celery Fritters, Tomato Sauce

EGGS
Poached, Florentine   Sur le Plat, Lyonnaise
Omelettes (to order): Mexicaine and Limousine

ENTREES
Fried Chicken, Southern Style   Frankfurters with Sauerkraut
Navarin of Lamb, Jardinière

CONTINENTAL SPECIALITY
Entrecôte sauté, Chambord
Sirloin Steak seasoned and cooked in butter, served with Bordelaise Sauce and
garnish of Sliced Beef Marrow, Cépes Provençale, Parisienne Potatoes

GRILL (to order)
Escalope of Sweetbreads, Béarnaise   London Mixed Grill
Pork Chop, Apple Compote

AMERICAN SPECIALITY
Corned Round and Brisket of Beef
(Cabbage and Dumplings)

SUGGESTED MENU
—
Hors d'Œuvre, Variés
—
Consommé Brunoise
—
Pétoncles frits, Sauce Tartare
—
Côte de Porc grillée, Compote de Pommes
Haricots Verts   Pommes Sautées
—
Tarte aux Pommes à la Suisse
—
Fromage   Café

Passengers on Special Diet are especially
invited to make known their requirements
to the Head Waiter

VEGETABLES
Garden Peas   French Beans sautés
Young Carrots au Beurre   Buttered Vegetable Marrow
Stewed Tomatoes

POTATOES
Baked Idaho   Sautées   Creamed-Purée   French Fried

COLD BUFFET
Roast Ribs and Sirloin of Beef, Horseradish Cream
Boiled American Ham   Home-made Brawn   London Pressed Beef
Roast Turkey, Cranberry Jelly   Roast Lamb, Mint Sauce and Jelly
Terrine of Duckling   Rolled Ox Tongue   Jellied Veal

SALADS
Hearts of Lettuce   Baltimore   Sliced Tomato
Mixed Bowl   Française   Snowflake   Fresh Fruit

DRESSINGS
French   Chantilly   Figaro   Russian

SWEETS
Rusk Custard Pudding   Fresh Swiss Apple Pie
Pineapple Shortcake, Hawaiian   Deep Fresh Rhubarb Pie
Gâteaux : Boston Cream Pie   Caramel Layer Cake
Hot Lancashire Eccles Cakes
Compote of Apricots, Plums and Cherries—Whipped Cream

ICE CREAM
Vanilla   Peach   Burnt Almond   Nesselrode

CHEESES
Edam   Roquefort   St. Ivel   Gorgonzola   Port Salut
English Cheddar and Cheshire   Stilton   Cream
Old Blue Cheshire   Gruyère   Camembert   Pont l'Evêque

Fresh Rolls

FRESH FRUIT
Apples   Oranges   Tangerines   Pears   Grapes

Tea (Hot or Iced)   Coffee (Hot or Iced)

The *Queen Mary*'s kitchens occupied nearly an acre of space, with a staff of 125. Separate kitchens served the third class, the grill-room, and the passengers taking special food.

The Zim Israel Line's *Shalom*, 25,320 tons, was built in 1964 by Chantiers de l'At- ▶ lantique, St-Nazaire, France, and in 1967 was purchased by Hanseatic Schiffahrts-Gesellschaft. Renamed *Hanseatic*, the liner was renovated and is now employed by the Deutscher Atlantik Line as a transatlantic liner and a cruise ship.

XI THE MODERN PASSENGER SHIP

This chapter deals with a number of the renowned passenger ships which have gone into service since the end of the Second World War. It must be realized that the vessels described form only a very small proportion of the great shipbuilding programme that has taken place throughout the world during the last twenty-five years. The choice of vessels to be described and illustrated is arbitrary and it is hoped that readers will not be too disappointed if a particular favourite ship is not mentioned.

During the past twenty-five years scientific and technological advances have made possible tremendous improve-

ments in the design, construction, engines, accommodation, and catering facilities of a passenger ship. Welded construction and the use of aluminium or light alloy for upperworks and superstructure; the installation of efficient stabilizers and air-conditioning; the use of laminated plastics in the public rooms and cabins and of stainless steel in the galley; the provision of radar, improved radio communications and television; these not only give passengers a safer and more comfortable voyage, but also contribute to the efficiency of the ship and make possible competition with the aeroplane which now carries more than 80 per cent of transatlantic passenger traffic.

The *Bremen*, 32,336 tons, formerly the liner *Pasteur*, built in France in 1938, was purchased by the North German Lloyd Line in 1958. After an extensive refit the vessel was employed as an Atlantic liner and as a cruise ship operating from New York.

Germany

After the Second World War both the great German shipping companies, Hamburg-America and North German Lloyd, were stripped of nearly all their fleets, but from 1951 the lines were able to operate a joint cargo service, carrying a few passengers, to North and South America, the Far East,

and Australia. In 1954 the liner *Gripsholm*, built in 1925, was purchased by a German firm and, after an extensive refit, renamed *Berlin* and chartered to the North German Lloyd Line for the North Atlantic passenger service. A further advance was made in 1957 when the North German Lloyd Line purchased the French Line *Pasteur*, built at Saint-Nazaire in 1939. After a refit costing £6,000,000, the liner,

The *Hanseatic*, one of the world's most modern and elegant luxury liners with spacious and beautifully designed public rooms, ideally meets the requirements for a combined North Atlantic service with a capacity for 1,090 passengers, and cruises for 700 passengers.

renamed *Bremen* (Ill. p. 254), made her first voyage under German ownership, to New York in July 1959.

The luxury liner *Shalom*, 25,360 tons, built by Chantiers de l'Atlantique at Saint-Nazaire in 1964, was purchased from the Zim Israel Line by Hanseatic Schiffahrts Gesellschaft in 1967 and renamed *Hanseatic* (Ill. pp. 253, 256). The liner, 629 feet long with a breadth of 78 feet and a cruising speed of 21 knots, is employed on the North Atlantic service and as a cruise ship. Passenger capacity on ten decks is 1,090 for the Atlantic crossings and 700 when cruising. Every state-room is fitted with bath or shower and toilet, individually controlled air-conditioning, as well as radio and telephone in most cases. All cabins on the promenade deck and saloon deck have television sets. There are three

The Deutscher Atlantik Line's *Hamburg*, 23,500 tons, was built at Hamburg. She sailed on her maiden voyage to New York on March 30th 1969. With a cruising speed of 23 knots the liner is 644 feet long and accomodates 600 passengers.

swimming-pools and lido bars, a full-sized tennis court, two restaurants, and a theatre. The Alster Club, Hamburg Saloon and Atlantic Club on the saloon deck each have a dance floor and bar and together have seating for 640 passengers.

The first major passenger ship to be built in Germany since the Second World War, the *Hamburg* (Ill. above), was launched from the Hamburg yard of Howaldtswerke/Deutsche Werft AG on February 20th 1968. Intended principally for cruising, the *Hamburg*, 23,500 tons, was designed as a one-class hotel ship. The liner is 644 feet long overall, with a breadth of 90 feet, and is powered by two sets of turbines with an output of 11,000 shaft h.p., giving a service speed of 23 knots. The public rooms (Ill. p. 257) and cabins were all designed by Georg Manner of Munich and can accom-

The *Hamburg*'s Hanseatic saloon with dance floor and a bar.

The bar of the Alster Club on the promenade deck of the *Hamburg*.

modate 800 passengers when the liner is used for North Atlantic service and 652 when cruising. Public rooms occupy two decks and the location and style of these apartments cater for all tastes. The main ballroom known as the Hanseatic Saloon, extending across the fore end of the promenade deck, can seat 275 passengers round its large dance floor and full-size stage, and is adjoined by two clubs, the Alster and Helgoland, entirely different in atmosphere and seating 155 passengers. The ship's 290-seat theatre occupies the after end of this deck and extends into the deck below. Above, on the Lido deck, the Atlantic Club, with attractive circular bar and dance floor, provides a panoramic view ahead of the ship. A night-club on the same deck is well away from cabins so that late night revels do not disturb the sleep of other passengers. On the sun deck there is an outdoor swimming-pool, lido bar and a sports deck all well protected from the wind by glass screening.

The card-room also on the promenade deck of the *Hamburg*.

Dining-saloon on the Norddeutscher Lloyd Line's *Bremen*.

258

The Swedish motor-ship *Kungsholm*, 22,670 tons, built in 1957, was purchased by the North German Lloyd Line in 1965. Renamed *Europa*, the liner was used on the Bremerhaven to New York service and as a cruise ship.

Passengers can choose from three restaurants: the Hamburg seating 290, the Munich seating 190, and the Grill Room with 120 seats. Occupying three decks, the passenger cabins of the Hamburg are very standardized and consist of three types: 20 *de luxe*, 118 outside, and 111 inside cabins. Each apartment has two full-sized beds which convert into settees to make the cabin a sitting-room during the day, and has its own private bathroom or shower with all toilet facilities. Television with open or closed circuit depending on the vessel's location, dual-channel radio, telephone and individually controlled air-conditioning are all provided. The smallest cabin has an area of 135 feet.

Denny-Brown stabilizing fins are fitted to ensure that the *Hamburg* does not roll in rough weather, and the air-conditioning system can maintain reasonable temperatures in summer and winter. The *Hamburg* sailed on her inaugural cruise to West Africa and South America in April 1969.

259

France

The first large liners to be built in France after the war were the French Line's sister ships *Flandre*, 20,477 tons, and *Antilles*, 19,828 tons. The *Flandre* made her maiden voyage

Ile-de-France and the *Liberté*, formerly the North German liner *Europa* built in 1930.

In 1956, despite the threat of increasing competition from the air services, the French Line placed an order for a new super-liner, the *France* (Ill. p. 261), with Chantiers de l'At-

The motor-ship *Pasteur*, 18,000 tons, was completed in 1966 for the Compagnie des Messageries Maritimes, employed on a service from Le Havre to Portugal and South America.

from Le Havre to New York in July 1952 and the *Antilles* went into service a year later. At that time the other two French Line ships on the Atlantic service were the prewar

lantique. The first keel plate of the *France* was laid on October 7th 1957 on the shipway at Saint-Nazaire where twenty-eight years earlier the *Normandie* had been built. The new

260

liner with a length of 1,035 feet was six feet longer than the *Normandie*, but finer lines reduced the gross tonnage to 66,348 compared to the *Normandie*'s 86,496 tons. Welded prefabrication techniques were used extensively in the construction of the *France* and most of the superstructure was of aluminium; the clipper bow had a bulbous fore-foot and the cruiser stern carried a streamlined balanced rudder with electro-hydraulic control. The liner is propelled by quadruple screw propellers driven by four independent sets of single reduction geared turbines with a total output of

The French Line's super-liner *France*, 66,348 tons, launched on May 11th 1960, made her maiden voyage from Le Havre to New York in February 1962. The wings on the funnels are designed to keep the decks free from smoke.

261

160,000 shaft h.p., giving a service speed of 31 knots. Two sets of Denny-Brown stabilizers, with retractable aerofoil fins, were installed amidships. Both funnels were fitted with fins on each side near to the top to keep smoke away from the upper decks. The *France* has eleven decks fitted

three quarters of the crew are employed in hotel services, including 150 cooks who provide some 9,000 meals every day. The first-class dining-room can seat 410 and the very large and well fitted theatre/cinema can accommodate 664 people.

The motor-ship *Renaissance*, 11,724 tons, specially designed as a cruise ship, was built in 1966 by Chantiers de l'Atlantique, Saint-Nazaire.

entirely with non-combustible material and providing accommodation for 407 first-class and 1,637 tourist passengers with a crew of about 1,160 officers and men. About

The *France* made her first voyage from Le Havre to Southampton in February 1962. Although not originally designed for cruising, the *France*, like the other earlier super-liners still in service, has been forced by the fall in trans-atlantic seaborne passenger traffic to spend the winter months as a cruise ship.

New French liners were of course built for routes other than the North Atlantic. The *Pasteur*, 18,000 tons (Ill.

driven by diesel engines at a service speed of 20 knots. Fin stabilizers and full air-conditioning help to give the motor liner's 430 passengers a comfortable voyage. All first-class cabins have private toilet facilities, while the tourist class are accommodated in two- and four-berth cabins most of

The *Viet-nam,* 13,162 tons, built in 1952 for the Compagnie des Messageries Maritimes. Many of the first-class cabins had a private balcony while in the economy class there was a dormitory cabin for ten passengers. With a service speed of 16 knots the liner was employed on a route from Marseilles to Japan via Bombay and Hong Kong.

p. 260), was built in 1966 for the Messageries Maritimes service from Le Havre to Portugal and South America. With a length of 525 feet the liner is propelled by twin propellers

which have a separate toilet.

The importance of the cruise trade is emphasized by the construction of a specially designed cruise liner the *Renais-*

Three photographs taken during a cruise aboard the *Renaissance*. The liner specializes in cruises to the Spitzbergen Islands, the Baltic and the Norwegian fjords in summer. She then returns to the Mediterranean for her famous 'musical cruise', and winters in the Caribbean or South America.

sance (Ill. p. 262) for the Compagnie Française de Navigation. This vessel, of 11,724 tons, and built in 1966, is 435.5 feet long with a breadth of 69 feet. Fin stabilizers and air-conditioning are fitted. The cabins, sound-proofed for greater comfort, accommodate 440 one-class passengers, while special dormitories provide cheap sleeping room for 76 students. The *Renaissance* usually cruises in the Mediterranean, from Marseilles to Italy, Greece, and Israel.

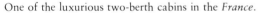
One of the luxurious two-berth cabins in the *France*.

The cinema and theatre in the *France* would seat 664 people.

Great Britain

The famous liner *Queen Elizabeth* (Ill. p. 269), nearly completed at the start of the war in 1939, sailed across the Atlantic to New York in March 1940 and then served as a troopship for the next six years. After undergoing a complete reconditioning, the *Queen Elizabeth* sailed on her first commercial voyage from Southampton to New York on October 16th 1946. The 83,673-ton liner, 1,031 feet long overall with a breadth of 118.6 feet, had a well-raked bow and a cruiser stern. There were 14 decks and accommodation for 822 first-class, 668 cabin-class, and 798 tourist-class passengers. The crew consisted of 1,296 officers and men. The *Queen Mary* made her first postwar crossing from Southampton to New York in July 1947 and the two great Cunard super-liners for some years maintained the weekly service between Southampton and New York which had been intended when the *Queen Mary* was built in the 1930's. Both liners were fitted with stabilizers and air-conditioning in the public rooms and were used as cruise ships during the winter season. The *Queen Elizabeth*'s first cruising season started in February 1962 with cruises from New York to Nassau, and she sailed for the last time

from Southampton in November 1968. The liner was bought by an American firm to use as a floating hotel and exhibition hall at Port Everglades, Florida. However in 1970, the *Queen Elizabeth* was bought by Mr. C. J. Tung to be made into the Seawise University in Hong Kong, but departure was delayed, and with engine trouble during the passage, the liner did not arrive at Hong Kong until July 1971. When work to equip the great ship as a floating university was nearly completed, fire broke out, and in January 1972, all that remained of the Queen of the Atlantic was a burnt-out and stranded wreck in Hong Kong harbour.

In 1961 the largest ship built in Great Britain since the *Queen Elizabeth* was the P & O Orient Line's *Canberra* (Ill. p. 266) built by Harland & Wolff at Belfast. The liner was launched on March 16th 1960 and on June 2nd 1961 sailed on her maiden voyage from Southampton to Australia, New Zealand, Honolulu, and the west coast of America. The *Canberra*, 45,270 tons, is 818 feet long overall with a breadth of 102 feet. The superstructure above the weather deck is made of aluminium and the use of this material has allowed an extra superstructure deck to be added and makes it possible for more passengers to be carried. Weight was also saved by the use of welded construction. The layout of the ship is unusual: the propelling machinery is at the stern thus allowing the centre of the ship to be used entirely for passenger accommodation and putting the sources of vibration as far aft as possible. The passenger capacity is 2,238 of which 548 are first-class and 1,690 tourist class. This num-

public rooms designed by Sir Hugh Casson, Mr. John Wright and Miss Barbara Ashley included an observation lounge and ballroom on the games deck, and a large writing-room, library, and private dining-room on the promenade deck. The first-class and tourist-class restaurants are on

The *Canberra*, 45,000 tons, built for the P & O Line by Harland & Wolff Ltd. at Belfast in 1961. The engines-aft design permits spacious passenger accommodation. In 1972 the *Canberra* has cruised in the Mediterranean and the West Indies.

ber could be varied as there are interchangeable cabins which accommodate two passengers as first-class or four as second-class. Groups of first-class cabins are arranged round courts so that each cabin has a view of the sea. The

E deck. A cinema to seat 332 is provided with projector equipment suitable for wide-vista viewing. Three swimming-pools are available, the first-class pool on the sun deck amidships and the tourist-class pools at the after end of the

On the sun deck of the *Canberra*, passengers enjoy water sports, deck games, or just laze in the sun.

The first-class games deck on the P & O liner *Chusan*.

The first-class library and writing-room in the P & O liner *Oriana*.

ship, one on the games deck and the other on B deck. To cater for the passengers and a crew of 960, the main galley, 150 feet long and 100 feet wide, is amidships between the two dining-rooms. The bakery, butcher's shop and the food-preparing room are on the deck below and are connected by lifts to the galley which is equipped with electrically-heated and steam-heated stainless-steel cooking apparatus. The equipment includes ovens, grills, hot-plates, ice-making machines, potato-peelers, dough-mixers, and dish-washing machines. The chef's staff of 194 includes 21 bakers and 11 butchers. Normally there are two sittings for the two main meals. The passenger on the *Canberra* enjoys freshly made bread every day, a tradition going back at least eighty years for luxury ships but rarely found in modern hotels. All the meals in the *Canberra* are prepared in the same galley but the first-class passenger gets a somewhat longer menu than the tourist class. The ship's radar, navigational and other electronic equipment includes a radar installation with the unit in which a cathode ray tube is photographed and the resultant film projected on a screen. Passengers can make a long-distance radio telephone call to anywhere in the world and the tiny 'wireless cabin' of the 1912's has become the 'radio office' with main and emergency radio transmitting and receiving equipment and a radio-telephone section. Television sets are installed in the public rooms and some cabins, and when the ship is out of range of television transmitters, the passengers are entertained by closed-circuit programmes. The *Canberra* has turbo-electric propelling machinery of 68,000 h.p. and a service speed of 27.5 knots. Between May 1972 and January 1973 the *Canberra* is scheduled to make six cruises, including voyages to Athens, the Canary Islands, and the West Indies.

Queen Elizabeth II: The Cunard liner *Queen Elizabeth II*, the latest addition to the list of super-liners, was originally intended to be an up-to-date version of the earlier *Queen Mary* and *Queen Elizabeth*. However, after a careful appraisal of the potential transatlantic passenger traffic the decision was taken to construct a dual-purpose liner specially designed for both the Atlantic crossings and for cruising. Full design studies were made to obtain the best form of underwater hull and an extensive test programme with models in watertanks was undertaken by John Brown & Company Ltd., who were to build the vessel, and at the

The main control room for the electricity supply on board the *Queen Elizabeth II*.

National Physical Laboratory at Feltham, Middlesex. After experiments with models in tanks with simulated waves, a bulbous-bowed hull form was adopted, with all-welded construction and aluminium superstructure to reduce top weight. The keel of the new liner was laid on July 25th ever provided in a liner. While serving on the North Atlantic route the *Queen Elizabeth II* carries 2,025 passengers in two classes, with a crew of about 900. When cruising, accommodation is limited to 1,400 one-class passengers. Many luxury suites are available and the majority of cabins

The Cunard liner *Queen Elizabeth*, 83,673 tons, built in 1940 by John Brown & Co. at Clydebank. Probably the best proportioned and most graceful of all the Atlantic liners. This magnificent vessel was withdrawn from service in 1968.

1965 at John Brown's yard at Clydebank, and on September 20th 1967 the new Cunarder was named and launched by Her Majesty Queen Elizabeth II. With a length of 963 feet and a breadth of 105 feet the *Queen Elizabeth II,* of 65,863 tons, is smaller than the earlier 'Queens,' but is reputed to have the highest standard of passenger accommodation have ports overlooking the sea. The principal public rooms are: the Double Room, the largest public room of any ship afloat and the world's only floating double-decker night-club, the 736 Club on the boat deck with a bar and gambling tables for dice, blackjack and roulette, the Queen's Room on the quarter deck, a garden lounge during the day and a

269

The twin funnels of the *Canberra*.

night-club by night and the theatre seating 513, also used as a cinema, conference room, and chapel. The Britannia Restaurant on the upper deck seats 790 passengers while the Columbia Restaurant and the Grill Room on the quarter deck can seat 470 and 100 passengers respectively. Glazed lounge promenades are provided on either side of the ship

The *Oriana* by night.

and at the stern there are terraced and sheltered decks. There are two outdoor and two indoor swimming-pools, with a gymnasium, sauna, and Turkish bath. The Cunard-

Marlborough London Gallery on the boat deck is the first permanent fine art gallery on an ocean liner and provides passengers with the opportunity of seeing specially selected examples of modern art. The two libraries have a total of more than 10,000 books, magazines and newspapers and there is room for 100 passengers to read and write in comfort. The cabins are larger than many hotel rooms and every cabin has fitted carpets, separate bathroom, six-

able to supervise operations from a control desk. Cooks preparing meat, fish, poultry and sauces work in units within the open area. From the kitchen, lifts operate to the store-rooms below, containing 12½ tons of beef, 200 lb. of caviar, 1 ton of lobsters, 10 tons of fresh fruit, 1½ tons

The P & O liner *Chusan*, 24,261 tons, built in 1950, was originally designed for services to the Far East, but is now also employed as a cruise ship. The *Chusan* was the first large British ship to be fitted with Denny-Brown stabilizers.

channel radio, and a telephone. Accommodation is designated first-class and tourist on the Atlantic service, but most of the public rooms and amenities are open to all passengers without restriction. All the restaurants and crew messrooms are served from a central open-plan kitchen with the chef

of duck, a mile of sausages, and more than 2,500 bottles of wine. *Queen Elizabeth II* is designed and equipped with safety standards far in excess of statutory requirements for passenger ships of the highest class. The ship is divided into fifteen compartments which can be made completely watertight by closing 58 watertight doors which can be controlled from the bridge. A safety control room amidships is manned at all times, and consoles with instruments and alarms give immediate warning of an emergency. The whole structure of the ship is incombustible and internal 110,000 shaft h.p. giving a service speed of 28.5 knots. On trials the ship attained a speed of 32.46 knots. Steam is supplied to the turbines by three boilers each with side-firing oil burners. Electricity for lighting, auxiliary machinery and equipment, including twenty-two lifts, is supplied

The *Oriana*, 42,000 tons, built for the P & O Line by Vickers Armstrong at Barrow in 1960 for their service from England to Australia, New Zealand, and California. The liner is now also used as a cruise ship.

areas are covered by an automatic sprinkler system. Life-boats and life-rafts are available to carry nearly 4,000 people although the total number of passengers and crew is under 3,000. The main propelling machinery consists of twin-screw geared steam turbines with an output of by three turbo-generators. *Queen Elizabeth II* is air-conditioned throughout and two sets of Denny-Brown swing-back fin stabilizers, controlled by a gyro system, have been fitted. Automatic, hand and auxiliary control of the rudder is available from the steering control unit in the wheelhouse.

The Cunard Line *Carmania*, 21,637 tons, formerly the *Saxonia*, built in 1954 by John Brown & Co. This liner was rebuilt in 1962–3 and converted to a cruise ship for operating from New York and Miami to the West Indies.

For passengers wishing to take their cars, space is available for 80 vehicles which can be driven on board over special ramps. The *Queen Elizabeth II* made her maiden voyage from Southampton to New York in May 1969 and completed the crossing from Le Havre Lightship to Ambrose Light in New York Bay in 4 days, 16 hours, 39 minutes. The liner had a great welcome when she arrived at New York harbour. About fifty small craft escorted her across the bay while tugs whistled, fire boats pumped jets of water high in the air, and crowds assembled on the Manhattan and Jersey shores.

Aristotle Onassis' private yacht *Christina*

Mr. Lindsay, the Mayor of New York at the time, proclaimed 'Queen Elizabeth II Day' and went aboard the liner from a coastguard cutter.

After some initial 'running-in' difficulties the *Queen Elizabeth II* has settled down to an ordered and prosperous condition as a transatlantic liner and as a cruise ship. However,

The outdoor swimming-pool on the boat deck of the cruise liner *Jason*.

even a stabilized super-liner with particularly good sea-keeping qualities has to give way occasionally to the power of an Atlantic gale. The day after the *Queen Elizabeth II* left New York on April 16th 1972 for Cherbourg and Southampton, an extremely severe gale started which was to last for four days. During the bad weather three members of the crew suffered broken bones and £2,500-worth of crockery and glass was smashed. Because of the delay caused by the storm, the *Queen Elizabeth II* did not call at Cherbourg and as the passengers landed at Southampton they were presented with a weather map showing the path of the storm and a certificate as follows:

The cruise liner *Jason*, 5,500 tons, built in Italy in 1967. One of the Epirotiki Line's fleet of passenger-carrying vessels, the *Jason* accommodates 350 passengers, all first class, and is fitted with stabilizers and air-conditioning.

Living-room aboard Aristotle Onassis' private yacht *Christina*.

Queen Elizabeth II

Storm Certificate

This is to record that on her North Atlantic voyage, leaving New York on the 16th April 1972, for Southampton, England, R.M.S. *Queen Elizabeth II*, of 65,863 gross tons, encountered exceptionally severe weather in position Latitude 42° 18′ North, Longitude 55° 52′ West.

During this storm, winds reached speeds in excess of 100 m.p.h. Combined with a heavy swell, waves were encountered of 50 feet in height.

This weather caused even the *Queen Elizabeth II*, with her exceptional size and sea-keeping qualities, to lie hove-to for 21½ hours between 17th and 19th April 1972, until the storm abated.

I commend all passengers in sharing this unique experience with great cheerfulness and calm.

Mortimer Hehir
Capitain

Between April and November 1972 the *Queen Elizabeth II* is scheduled to make twenty-four Atlantic crossings with fares ranging from £400 to £92 according to the class of accommodation and the season.

Swimming-pool aboard the *Christina*.

Italy

After the hiatus in the period immediately following the end of the Second World War, the Italia Line re-entered the North Atlantic passenger service with two new liners, both

over three years later met with disaster. At midnight on July 25th 1956, when steaming through dense fog some 200 miles from New York, she was struck amidships by the Swedish-America liner *Stockholm* 12,644 tons. The *Andrea Doria* was bound for New York from Genoa with

The Italia Line's *Leonardo da Vinci*, 33,500 tons, built at Genoa and launched at the end of 1958, sails from Naples, Palermo, and Genoa and makes calls in Spain and Portugal before crossing the Atlantic to Halifax and New York.

built at Genoa, the *Andrea Doria,* 29,000 tons, launched in 1951, and the *Cristoforo Colombo,* 29,100 tons, launched two years later. The *Andrea Doria* made her maiden voyage from Genoa to New York in January 1953 and just

1,706 passengers and crew, while the *Stockholm,* with about 750 passengers and crew, was on a passage from New York to Gothenburg.

One of the Italian liner's watertight compartments was

279

flooded and she at once took a heavy list which gradually increased until water was pouring in through some of her cabin portholes. Despite the gravity of the damage the *Andrea Doria* did not sink until about 10 a.m. on July 26th. The heavy list greatly impeded the launch of her life-boats

The swimming-pool of the Italian liner *Eugenico C.*

Huge chandeliers light the first-class ballroom of the *Raffaello*.

First-class swimming-pool and the latticed funnel of the *Raffaello*.

though some managed to get away and the *Stockholm*, though badly damaged, managed to take off 533 people before putting back to New York. Other ships contacted by radio were the French liner *Ile-de-France* which took off 760, the US transports *Cape Ann* and *Private William H. Thomas* which took off 129 and 156 respectively, and the US destroyer *Edward H. Allen* which took off 76. Forty-seven passengers and crew of the *Andrea Doria* were

as a replacement for the *Andrea Doria* and to alternate with the *Cristoforo Colombo*. Built by Ansaldo SA at Genoa for the Italia Line, the *Leonardo da Vinci* was 760 feet long overall, with a breadth of 91 feet. Passenger accommodation occupies nine of the eleven decks, and 1,326

The *Raffaello*, sister ship of the *Michelangelo*, was built at Trieste and launched in 1963. The streamlining of the hull and superstructure and the lattice work surrounding the funnels gives these Italian liners a most distinctive appearance.

lost and five of the crew of the *Stockholm*.

In June 1960 the new Italian liner *Leonardo da Vinci*, 33,500 tons (Ill. p. 279), entered the transatlantic service

passengers can be carried. The first-class quarters include two suites, two state-rooms, and 170 regular cabins, with some interchangeability among the classes. The total number of 524 cabins averages a little over two persons per cabin, and all the first-class state-rooms as well as the cabin-class state-rooms are equipped with private bathrooms. There are thirty public rooms with closed-circuit television in all the main lounges and infra-red ray heating plant in the first-class lido and round the swimming-pool. The twin-screw propellers are driven by steam turbines providing 60,000 shaft h.p. and a cruising speed of 23 knots. Below the water, the streamlined bow is of the bulbous type and there is a cruiser stern. A continuous double bottom contains

The *Guglielmo Marconi*, 27,900 tons, was built at Trieste for the Lloyd Triestino Line and was employed on their express service from Italy to Australia.

oil and water tanks, and the hull is divided into compartments by fourteen watertight bulkheads. Forward of the main machinery space are two holds and a garage for sixty cars, with refrigerating machinery and baggage rooms aft. Twin sets of Denny-Brown stabilizers are installed and the liner is fully air-conditioned for all weather conditions.

In 1965, when the 46,000-ton sister ships *Michelangelo* (Ill. below) and *Raffaello* (Ill. p. 281) joined the *Cristoforo Colombo* and the *Leonardo da Vinci* in the Italia Line, the four ships provided the most modern service between Europe

The *Michelangelo*, 46,000 tons, built for the Italia Line in 1964, is employed on the service from Naples and Genoa to New York and as a cruise ship in the Mediterranean and the Caribbean.

and North America. The *Raffaello*, built by Cantieri Riuniti dell'Adriatico at Trieste and launched on March 24th 1963, is 902 feet long and 102 feet in breadth. Outstanding features of the vessel are the accentuated streamlining of the hull and superstructure and the thin funnels (Ill. p. 280)

individual controls for the air-conditioning. Three hundred and thirty-five first-class, 550 cabin-class, and 688 tourist-class passengers can be accommodated. There are thirty public rooms including a large cinema seating 500 persons. The first-class ballroom (Ill. p. 280) on the promenade deck

The *Eugenio C*, 30,500 tons, built at Trieste in 1966 for the Costa Line, has a service speed of 27 knots. The liner sails from Genoa to South America and as a cruise ship.

surmounted by flat tops and surrounded by a lattice-work structure. The promenade decks are unusually wide and the 741 cabins are all equipped with toilet facilities and

is very large and finely proportioned saloon. The *Raffaello* and the *Michelangelo* are now employed on the Italy—North America service and on a series of cruises to the

Caribbean and the Mediterranean. The Atlantic crossings are made in seven days from Naples and eight from Genoa and Cannes at a mean speed of 26.5 knots.

The sister ships *Guglielmo Marconi* (Ill. p. 282) and *Galileo Galilei* were built at Trieste by Cantieri Riuniti dell'Adriatico for the Lloyd Triestino Line's express service from Italy to Australia. The ships were 709 feet long, of 27,906 tons, and made their maiden voyages to Australia in 1963, with a speed of 24 knots, thereby reducing the passage time from 31 to 22 days.

Specially designed for the Costa Line, the *Federico C*, 20,400 tons, was built at Genoa and sailed on her maiden voyage from that port to South America on March 22nd 1958.

The United States of America

The liners *America* and *United States* (Ill. p. 290) operated the postwar transatlantic service of the United States Line. The *America*, of 33,500 tons, was launched in August 1939 a refit entered the North Atlantic trade in November 1946 with a crossing from New York to Cobh in 4 days, 22 hours, 22 minutes, at an average speed of 24.5 knots. Since 1960 the liner has sailed as a two-class vessel with accommodation for 1,050 passengers. The 51,985-ton liner *United States*

Flagship of the Adriatica Line the *Ausonia*, 12,000 tons, was built in 1957 and carried 529 passengers on an express service from Trieste and Venice to the Lebanon and Egypt.

and sailed on her maiden voyage in August 1940 as a cruise ship to the West Indies. From June 1941 until February 1946 the liner was used as a troopship and after (Ill. p. 289), built by the Newport News Shipbuilding and Dry Dock Company, was the first great super-liner to be built in the United States of America and the fastest passenger liner in the world. The *United States* was floated out of the dry dock in which she had been built in June 1951. The liner was 990 feet long with a breadth of 101.5 feet and had watertight subdivisions of the hull on the same scale as that fitted to a warship. There were twelve decks and the on her maiden voyage on July 3rd 1952 from New York to Le Havre and Southampton. The liner covered the 2,982 nautical miles from the Ambrose Lightship to Bishop's Rock in the remarkable time of 3 days, 10 hours, 40 minutes, at an average speed of 35.59 knots, thus beating

The motor-ship *Sakura Maru*, 2,600 tons, built in 1962, was designed as a passenger ship and floating exhibition ship for Japanese goods. The vessel sailed from Yokohama to Honolulu, San Francisco, and South American ports.

height from the keel to the top of the superstructure was 122 feet. With a capacity for 888 first-class, 524 cabin-class, and 544 tourist-class passengers, the *United States* sailed all previous times for the voyage. The return voyage was made in 3 days, 12 hours, 12 minutes, and the *United States* acquired the Blue Riband of the Atlantic. During

The Norwegian motor-ship *Sagafjord*, 24,000 tons, was designed as a dual purpose ship for cruising and the transatlantic passenger service. The *Sagafjord* sailed on her maiden voyage from Oslo to New York in October 1965.

the first two years of service the liner carried 139,362 passengers and in 1960 the accommodation was altered to give a capacity of approximately 1,725 passengers in first class and tourist classes. The *United States* was of course fully air-conditioned with individual control in the cabins.

Nuclear Ships

Nuclear propulsion for ships was first developed for submarines and the United States submarine *Nautilus*, launched in 1954, was the world's first atomic ship. The earliest non-

The *United States*, 51,985 tons, the fastest liner in the world, sailed on her maiden voyage in July 1952 and crossed the Atlantic at a record average speed of 35.59 knots.

military nuclear powered vessel, the Russian ice-breaker *Lenin*, made her maiden voyage in 1959. The *Savannah*, 13,559 tons, the world's first atomic merchant ship, was built in the United States of America and launched in 1959. The *Otto Hahn,* built in Germany and launched in 1964, and the *Mutsu,* launched in Japan in 1969, are later examples of commercial nuclear ships. In these vessels the nuclear plant is a pressurized water reactor which supplies steam to drive turbines which transmit power to the propeller shafts. The main advantage of the nuclear plant over conventional oil-fired boilers for a ship is that the vessel can be operated for much longer periods without refuelling. In the *Savannah*, 17,000 lb. of enriched uranium fuel would suffice for 16,000 hours at full speed or three and a half years of normal services. However, the high cost of building nuclear-powered ships and the potential danger from radiation in the event of damage in a crowded harbour or port, would seem to make it unlikely that many nuclear cargo or passenger ships will be produced in the immediate future.

One of the state-rooms in the liner *United States*.

Hydrofoils

The constant demand for more speed for water transport has forced the designer to seek new ideas for vessels. The fric-

tional resistance and drag from water on a ship's hull is very much greater than that from air on land and air transport. Consequently, the tremendous increases in the speed of aeroplanes and land vehicles has not been achieved for ships. The maximum speed of an Atlantic liner of the 1970's is act like water skis or aeroplane wings and generate more lift as the speed of the vessel is increased. A vessel using this system was first used successfully in 1909 by Enrico Forlanini. Two years later Alexander Graham Bell purchased Forlanini's specifications and after further experiments with

The *America*, in the foreground, passes the *United States* in New York harbour. These two liners operated the post-war transatlantic passenger services of the United States Line.

little more than double that of a liner of the 1870's. It appears that it is only by lifting the hull out of the water that high speeds at sea can be attained with safety. One method of raising the hull of a vessel clear of the water, and so reducing drag by about 50 per cent, is by using foils which F.W. Baldwin built a hydrofoil which set up a world speed record of 61.5 knots in 1919.

Today hydrofoils range in size from about 12 feet to about 150 feet in length and are in use throughout the world. The two-seater fibreglass-hulled pleasure hydrofoil produced by Water Spyder Marine Ltd. in Canada is only 12 feet long and 7.4 feet wide with the foils extended, but is capable of speeds up to 40 miles per hour. The *PT 50* hydrofoil (Ill. p. 293) built by Supramar AG in Switzerland is 91.55 feet long with accommodation for 105 passengers on long operations and 140 for short services, and has a cruising speed of 34 knots. In 1969 the De Havilland Company of Canada produced the FHE 400 hydrofoil with an overall length of 150 feet and a cruising speed of 60 knots in calm water. Trials were undertaken with this vessel to establish

The motor-ship *Sardegna*, built in 1952 for the ferry service between Italy and North Africa. There was accommodation for 422 passengers and drive on/off facilities for cars.

the feasibility of a larger ocean-going hydrofoil capable of a speed of 50 knots in rough seas. Great attention has been given to the development of foilborne craft in Russia and more than a thousand hydrofoils are in use and carry three million passengers annually on the lakes and rivers of the Soviet Union. The first of the Russian large passenger hydrofoils, the *Sputnik*, carried 300 passengers between Gorki and Moscow in fourteen hours on a maiden voyage in November 1961. This craft is 157.1 feet long and has a cruising speed of 41 knots.

Motor-ship *Dragon*, 5,719 tons, a car and passenger ferry put into service in 1967 between Southampton and Le Havre. Built by the Ateliers et Chantiers de Nantes, the *Dragon* can carry 850 passengers and more than 250 cars.

Hovercraft

Another type of surface skimmer is a machine that rides on a cushion of air formed under the craft. In the 18th and 19th centuries various designs were produced with the purpose of electronics engineer, Sir Christopher Cockerell. After experiments with models and small boats Cockerell produced the first practical air-cushion vehicle and named it the Hovercraft. This first operational hovercraft, the SR. N1, was completed in June 1959 and after trials on the Solent made

Supramer PT 50 passenger hydrofoils operated by a Norwegian company on the service between Stavanger and Bergen.

reducing friction by interposing a layer of air between the bottom of a vessel and the surface of the water, but the final development of the theory was due to the work of a British the first crossing of the English Channel on July 25th 1959. The SR. N1, an experimental craft, was 31 feet long and 25 feet wide, with a speed of 25 knots. The British Hovercraft Corporation, formed in 1966, established the first-ever production line for hovercraft, and deals with a variety of uses of the air-cushion principle, but particularly with the development and production of amphibious hovercraft. Their SR.N4 Mountbatten Hovercrafts (Ill. below) operate long with a breadth of 78 feet and will carry 609 passengers, or 254 passengers and 30 cars. The maximum speed in calm water, with no wind, is 70 knots and the average service speed is 50–60 knots; the Channel crossing takes about 35 minutes.

A SR. N4 Mountbatten hovercraft operated by British Rail. 254 passengers and 30 cars can be carried across the English Channel from Dover to Boulogne by this hovercraft in about 35 minutes.

passenger and car-ferry services across the English Channel between Ramsgate and Calais, and between Dover and Boulogne. The SR.N4, the world's largest hovercraft, is 130 feet

The Future

Over the past seven hundred years conditions for sea travellers have improved each century. The 13th century voyager slept on a crowded lower deck of a small ship, which was at the mercy of the wind and weather; he existed on bad food cooked in a communal pot over an open hearth and had little hope of medical attention if struck down by fever or plague. His counterpart today travels in a floating hotel, sleeps in a bed in an air-conditioned cabin with hot and cold running water, toilets, and electric light. Television, radio and telephone are at his side. He has a choice from two or three restaurants and, from an extensive menu, can select food prepared in a kitchen equipped with stainless-steel fittings, electric ovens, and grills. A swimming-pool, cinema, chapel, bars and ballroom are available for his pleasure while the stabilized vessel moves through the water at 25 to 30 knots.

What more can be done to improve the sea traveller's lot? The pundits of the 19th century who stated the steam engine would not take the place of sails for long voyages and those of a hundred years later who said that the aeroplane would not take the place of the liner, prove how foolish it is to try and predict future events. It would seem that the increasing popularity of the cruising holiday—there were more than seventy cruise ships available to the British public in 1972—will ensure the continued construction of large luxury liners, but it is unlikely that any more transatlantic super-liners will be built. Developments in the North Atlantic service may take the form of large hovercraft carrying several hundred passengers and a number of cars from Europe to America in less than two days.

The hydraulically-operated stern doors of the car-ferry *Dragon* are designed to allow two-way traffic.

BIBLIOGRAPHY

ABELL, W. The Shipwright's Trade. Cambridge 1948.
AKERLUND, H. Nydamskeppen. Gothenburg 1963.
ALBION, R. G. Square-riggers on Schedule. Princeton 1938.
ANDERSON, R. AND R. C. The Sailing Ship. London 1926.
BAKER, W. A. The Development of Wooden Ship Construction. Quincy 1955.
     From Paddle-steamer to Nuclear Ship. London 1966
     (deutsche Ausgabe: Vom Raddampfer zum Atomschiff, Delius Klasing).
BARJOT, P., AND SAVANT, J. History of the World's Shipping. London 1965.
BEAVER, P. The Big Ship: Brünel's Great Eastern. London 1969.
BLANCKLEY, T. R. The Naval Expositer. London 1750.
BENSTEAD, C. R. Atlantic Ferry. London 1936.
BOWEN, F. C. A Century of Atlantic Travel, 1830–1930. Boston 1930.
BROGGER, A. W., AND SHETELIG, H. The Viking Ships. Oslo 1951.
BROOKS, F. W. The English Naval Forces, 1199–1272. London N. D.
CABLE, B. A Hundred Year History of the P. O. London 1937.
CCHATTERTON, E. K. The Old East Indiamen. London 1933.
CHAPELLE, H. I. The Baltimore Clipper. Salem 1930.
     The History of American Sailing Ships. New York 1935.
     The Pioneer Steamship Savannah. Washington 1961.
     The Search for Speed under Sail, 1700–1855. New York 1967.
CHAPMAN, F. H. Architectura Navalis Mercatoria. Stockholm 1768.
CHARNOCK, J. History of Marine Architecture. London 1800–02.
CLOWMES, G. S. L. Sailing Ships. London 1932.
COSGRAVE, J. O. Clipper Ship. New York 1963.
CROOME, A. Hover Craft. Leicester 1964.
DUGAN, J. The Great Iron Ship. New York 1953.
DUNN, L. Ships of the Union-Castle Line. Southampton 1954.
     Famous Liners of the Past, Belfast Built. London 1964.
ENTICK, J. A New Naval History. London 1757.
FAIRBURN, W. A. Merchant Sail. Maine 1957.
FARR, G. The Steamship Great Western. Bristol 1963.
     The Steamship Great Britain. Bristol 1965.
FALCONER, W. Universal Dictionary of the Marine. London 1769 and 1815.
FINCHAM, J. History of Naval Architecture. London 1851.
FLETCHER, R. A. Steamships and their Story. London 1910.
FRY, H. The History of North Atlantic Steam Navigation. London 1896.
FURTTENBACH, J. Architectura Navalis. Ulm 1629.
GIBBS, C. R. V. Passenger Liners of the Western Ocean. London 1952.
     British Passenger Liners of the Five Oceans. London 1963.
HARDY, A. C. History of Motorshipping. London 1955.
HEDDERWICK, P. Treatise on Marine Architecture. Edinburgh 1830.
HEYL, E. Early American Steamers. Buffalo 1953–67.
HOLMES, G. C. V. Ancient and Modern Ships. London 1910.
HUTCHINSON, W. Treatise on Naval Architecture. Liverpool 1794.
JOBÉ, J. editor, The Great Age of Sail. Lausanne 1967
     (deutsche Ausgabe: Der Segelschiffe große Zeit, Delius Klasing).
KVARNING, L.-A. Wasa. Stockholm 1968.
LANDSTROM, B. The Ship. London 1961.
LANE, C. D. American Paddle Steamboats. New York 1943.
LANE, F. C. Venetian Ships and Shipbuilding of the Renaissance. Baltimore 1934.
LE FLEMING, H. M. Ships of the Holland-America Line. London 1963.
LINDSAY, W. S. History of Merchant Shipping and Ancient Commerce. London 1876.
LUBBOCK, B. Barlows Journal, 1659–1703. London 1934.
     The China Clippers. Glasgow 1919.
     The Blackwall Frigates. Glasgow 1924.
     The Colonial Clippers. Glasgow 1924.
     The Last of the Windjammers. Glasgow 1927.
MEYERSTEIN, E. H. W. editor, Adventures by Sea of Edward Coxere. Oxford 1945.
MURRAY, A. The Theory and Practice of Shipbuilding. Edinburgh 1861.
     Shipbuilding in Iron and Wood. Edinburgh 1863.

NEWELL, G. R. Pacific Steamboats. Seattle 1958.
     Ocean Liners of the 20th Century. Seattle 1963.
NORWAY, A. H. The Post Office Packet Service, 1793–1815. London 1895.
OLSEN, O., AND CRUMLIN-PEDERSEN, O. The Skuldelev Ships. Copenhagen 1967
PARIS, E. Souvenirs de Marine. Paris 1882–1908.
PARKER, H., AND BOWEN, F. Mail and Passenger Steamships of the 19th Century. London 1928.
PARKINSON, C. N. editor, The Trade Winds. London 1948.
PHILLIPS, J. D. Salem and the Indies. Boston 1947.
POWELL, D. Bristol Privateers and Ships of War. Bristol 1930.
POTTER, D., AND FROST, J. Queen Elizabeth II. London 1969.
RALAMB, A. C. Skeps Sbyggerij eller Adelig Ofnings. Stockholm 1916.
ROWLAND, K. T. Steam at Sea. Newton Abbot 1970.
SMITH, E. W. Passenger Ships of the World. Boston 1963.
SPRATT, H. P. Outline History of Transatlantic Steam Navigation. London 1950.
     Merchant Steamers and Motorships. London 1949.
     Marine Engineering. London 1953.
     The Birth of the Steamboat. London 1958.
SPENCER, A. editor, Memoirs of William Hickey. London 1925.
STALKARTT, M. Naval Architecture. London 1781.
STEEL, D. Elements and Practice of Rigging and Seamanship. London 1794.
     Naval Architecture. London 1804.
STENTON, F. editor, The Bayeux Tapestry. London 1957.
STEVENS, J. R. Old Time Ships. Toronto 1949.
SUTHERLAND, W. Shipbuilding Unveiled. London 1717.
SVENSSON, F. Sails through the Centuries. New York 1965
     (deutsche Ausgabe: Segel durch Jahrhunderte, Delius Klasing).
TOUDOUZE, G. G. editor, Histoire de la Marine. Paris 1934.
TRE TRYCKARE. The Lore of Ships. Gothenburg 1963
     (deutsche Ausgabe: Seefahrt – Nautisches Lexikon in Bildern, Delius Klasing).
     The Viking. Gothenburg 1966.
TUTE, W. Atlantic Conquest. Toronto 1962.
TYLER, D. B. Steam conquers the Atlantic. New York 1939.
UNDERHILL, H. A. Masting and Rigging the Clipper Ship and Ocean Carrier. Glasgow 1946.
     Deepwater Sail. Glasgow 1952.
WILLIAMS, G. History of Liverpool Privateers and an Account of the Liverpool Slave Trade. London 1897.
WORKER, C. F. The World's Passenger Ships. London 1967.

PERIODICALS AND JOURNALS

Artizan, London 1843–1871.
American Neptune, Salem 1941 onwards.
Engineer, London 1856 onwards.
Engineering, London 1866 onwards.
Illustrated London News, London 1843 onwards.
Jane's Surface Skimmer Systems, London 1967 onwards.
Lloyds Register of Shipping, London 1760 onwards.
Mariner's Mirror, Cambridge 1911 onwards.
Motor Ship, London 1925 onwards.
Naval Architects, Institution of, Transactions, London 1860 onwards.
Neptunia, Paris 1947 onwards.
Shipbuilder and Marine Engine Builder, London 1919 onwards.
Shipbuilding and Shipping Record, London 1913 onwards.
Shipping and Transport, Liverpool 1934 onwards.
Steamship, Leith 1892–1916.
Times, London 1797 onwards.